ANTI-OPPRESSIVE SOCIAL WORK
THEORY AND PRACTICE

Other titles by Lena Dominelli:

Community Action and Organising Marginalised Groups
Women in Focus, Community Service Orders and Female Offenders
Love and Wages: The Impact of Imperialism, State Intervention and Women's Domestic Labour on Workers' Control in Algeria
Anti-racist Social Work, 2nd edn*
Feminist Social Work (co-author)
Women and Community Action
Women Across Continents: Feminist Comparative Social Policy
Gender, Sex Offenders and Probation Practice
Getting Advice in Urdu
International Directory of Schools of Social Work
Anti-racist Perspectives in Social Work (co-author)
Anti-racist Probation Practice (co-author)
Sociology for Social Work*
Community Approaches to Child Welfare: International Perspectives
Beyond Racial Divides: Ethnicities in Social Work (co-editor)
Social Work: Themes, Issues and Critical Debates, 2nd edn* (co-editor)
Critical Practice in Social Work* (co-editor)
Feminist Social Work Theory and Practice*

*Published by Palgrave Macmillan

Anti-Oppressive Social Work Theory and Practice

Lena Dominelli

Consultant editor: Jo Campling

palgrave
macmillan

First published 2002 by
PALGRAVE MACMILLAN
Houndmills, Basingstoke, Hampshire RG21 6XS and
175 Fifth Avenue, New York, N. Y. 10010
Companies and representatives throughout the world

PALGRAVE MACMILLAN is the global academic imprint of the Palgrave
Macmillan division of St. Martin's Press, LLC and of Palgrave Macmillan Ltd.
Macmillan® is a registered trademark in the United States, United Kingdom
and other countries. Palgrave is a registered trademark in the European
Union and other countries.

ISBN 0–333–77155–9 paperback

This book is printed on paper suitable for recycling and
made from fully managed and sustained forest sources.

A catalogue record for this book is available
from the British Library.

A catalogue record for this book is available
from the Library of Congress.

Editing and origination by Aardvark Editorial, Mendham, Suffolk

10   9   8   7   6   5   4   3   2   1
11   10   09   08   07   06   05   04   03   02

Printed and bound in Great Britain by
Creative Print & Design (Wales), Ebbw Vale

To those resisting oppression and social injustice, may better understanding mean that a brighter day will soon dawn for us all

Contents

List of diagrams   ix

Acknowledgements   x

Introduction   1
   Oppressive social relations: a concern for social workers   1
   The structure of the book   5

1 Introducing Anti-Oppressive Theories for Practice   7
   Introduction   7
   Retheorising oppression to understand its complexities   8
   The multidimensionality of context   23
   Social work as an oppressive caring profession   28
   Social work within an anti-oppressive framework   32
   Conclusions   35

2 Oppression, Social Divisions and Identity   37
   Introduction   37
   Identity as a central feature of oppression   40
   'Othering' processes as exclusionary   44
   Identity formation and exclusionary processes   47
   Identity in social work   51
   Conclusions   56

3 Anti-Oppressive Practice as a Legitimate Concern
   of Social Work   59
   Introduction   59
   Ethics in social work practice   62
   Human rights are a concern of anti-oppressive practice   69
   Legitimating anti-oppressive social work   71
   The backlash against anti-oppressive social work   77
   Conclusions   83

4   **Anti-Oppressive Practice in Action: Working with Individuals**   85
    Introduction   85
    Working with individuals in anti-oppressive ways   89
    Conclusions   107

5   **Anti-Oppressive Practice in Action: Group Interventions and Collective Action**   109
    Introduction   109
    Organising around identity   110
    Strengthening communities   127
    Managing poor people   133
    Conclusions   139

6   **Engaging in Organisational Change**   141
    Introduction   141
    Organisation(s) matter(s)   148
    Challenging the organisation   157
    Conclusions   159

7   **Beyond Postmodern Welfare: Establishing Unity between Content, Process and Outcomes**   161
    Introduction   161
    Postmodern insights   163
    The failings of postmodernism   168
    Conclusions   179

8   **Conclusions**   181

Bibliography   186

Index   199

List of diagrams

1.1   Contexts impacting upon the self   23
1.2   Multidimensionality of context   24

2.1   Controlling boundaries   44

3.1   Controlling racialised relations   80
3.2   Interconnected levels of interaction   81

8.1   Holistic intervention chart for anti-oppressive practice   184

Acknowledgements

A book is never simply the product of its author. Ideas germinate in chance encounters with others, in sustained conversations and in purposive research. It is, therefore, impossible to thank personally all those who have contributed to my forming the words contained within this volume. I want to record my heartfelt thanks and appreciation to all who have shared with me their views and life experiences. Also, I wish to thank the students whose critical questions have helped me to search for new answers to old concerns. They have kept my eye on the ball. Additionally, I wish to thank my parents whose wisdom and strength in overcoming the daily oppressions they experience have been a constant source of inspiration to me. And finally, I wish to thank David and Nicholas for their unending loving support and understanding.

LENA DOMINELLI

Introduction

Oppressive social relations: a concern for social workers

Eradicating oppression and asserting their right to self-expression in a world that they control has become a key concern of peoples[1] across the globe as they engage with one another to realise their hopes for a better tomorrow. Their demands for autonomy and empowerment, coupled with the creation of more egalitarian social relations amongst and between different populations, have challenged prevailing definitions of citizenship and participation within the nation-state, including its welfare component, and civil society (Dominelli, 2000). Together, these forces have had a major impact on the theories and practices of the caring professions, of which social work is one.

Consequently, the world of caring professionals in Western societies is in flux as *clients*[2] challenge the taken-for-granted assumption that scientific expertise qualifies practitioners to intervene in their lives whilst their own experiences and wishes count for little (Belenky et al., 1997). This state of affairs can be attributed to the growth of the 'new' social movements and the rise of a consumerism that has been linked to globalisation, for these have resulted in a questioning of traditional professional responses to the needs of a range of client groups – women, elders, black people, gay men, lesbian women, disabled people and people with mental health problems (Dominelli, 1999). The demands of people in these groups have exposed the unacceptability of many aspects of expert-led professional practice and have caused practitioners to rethink their traditional relationships with them, with the intention of revising the services they deliver to reflect more closely the aspirations

1

of their clients (Ahmed, 1990). The concepts of seamless services, user empowerment and anti-oppressive practice have been developed to provide guidelines that inform the responses of professionals attempting to take seriously user-led agendas (Craig and Mayo, 1995).

Additionally, their employers, in the form of politicians and civil servants running welfare states, have demanded greater accountability for the public resources expended in service provision. The employers' demands can also be attributed to worries about competitiveness engendered by a globalising world economy and the ascendancy of a New Right populism that requires value for money in public expend-itures alongside the demand that people look after themselves. Their proponents have engaged in discourses in which economics have become political ideology. Ironically, alongside these developments, practitioners and policymakers have mainstreamed the concerns of those seeking empowerment in their daily lives. In Britain, for example, the promotion of equal opportunities policies in the social domain, the ideas contained in the political philosophy of the 'Third Way' and the raft of policy initiatives that have emanated from its implementation have meant that at least the rhetoric associated with anti-oppressive practice is one familiar to all those working in the caring professions and the lay public alike.

The combined interaction of these forces in the welfare state has shaken the certainties that practitioners once had in their profession, whether this was in how they did their work, or in the nature of their career prospects. Former 'givens' are now being replaced by uncertain-ties and paralysing guilt for some, and opportunities for exercising real choices and developing new alternatives for others. At the same time, the ensuing developments have ruffled the complacency that both professionals and users have had about the previous consensus that has underpinned the welfare state and its assumed existence in perpetuity (Mishra, 1990). Indeed, in the more optimistic 1960s and 70s, coun-tries such as the United States were considered welfare laggards and conceptualised as anomalies with welfare systems that would in time converge around the ideal institutional model that was represented by Nordic states or, more specifically, the Swedish social democratic model of welfare (Wilensky and Lebeaux, 1965; Mishra, 1990). Today, in a reversal of its previous position, the United States is leading the choir in singing a different tune, as countries that formerly espoused publicly funded welfare regimes pursue market-driven, residual welfare state forms that compel individuals and families to look after themselves (Mishra, 1995; Teeple, 1995).

The neo-liberal mantras of targeting, means-tesι
services and demonised client groups have now become
day on the political agenda (Jones, 1993), regardless ι
government running the show is an allegedly leftwing one
for example, in the United States, the Clinton administrat.
Reaganite policies that culminated in the Personal Respoι   ..ιy and
Work Reconciliation Act 1996 (Zucchino, 1997). In Britain, Tony
Blair's New Labour government has adopted the former Tory proposals
of introducing part tuition fees for university students, imposing more
stringent workfare-type conditions on mothers of small children on
welfare, reducing lone-parent benefits and restructuring many parts of
the welfare state in accordance with market priorities (Kilkey, 2000). In
Germany, the Social Democratic government led by Gerhard Schroeder
has adopted a centrist path. The times, therefore, are not propitious
for either advancing the cause of client liberation or ensuring that
caring professionals commit themselves to an empowering practice that
prioritises the needs of clients over meeting economic and political
exigencies (Humphries, 1996).

A key worry of those espousing anti-oppressive practice is that neo-
liberal welfare policies will increase social exclusion, as a growing
weight of evidence reveals the growth in poverty and marginalisation
of those who survive at the edges of society, and exacerbate the varied
forms of oppression that characterise their lives (Cochrane, 1993). For
example, with regard to economic oppression, the world has seen a
widening gap between rich and poor. In 1960, the wealthiest 20 per
cent of the population globally disposed of 70 per cent of world
income. It rose to 86 per cent by 1994. During that same period, the
poorest 20 per cent saw their income share drop from 2.3 per cent to
1.1 per cent (Wichterich, 2000, p. 125). As poverty and hunger mount,
people's capacities to develop and interact with their world have
become dominated by the struggle for basic survival and they have had
to work harder to get those who are better off to listen to them and
prioritise their concerns.

This task becomes immeasurably harder in a world that has made
profits rather than people its key obsession. With the loss of the
consensus upon which social democracy was predicated, we have a
new economic ideology guiding the planet into increasingly dangerous
terrain. Instead of a paternalistic capitalism, we are being overwhelmed
by a predatory capitalism which greedily ingests those who do not
subscribe to its tenets and then spews them out as worthless garbage.
Its caricatures of poor people encourage others to demonise, despise

and fear them, and greed replaces respect for other peoples and the planet that we all share.

Social workers have a responsibility to challenge this grotesque image of poor people and, besides bringing to public notice the strengths of those who battle to transcend social exclusion, to work to empower those who are engulfed by the weight of circumstances in which they are embedded. Promoting social justice and human development in an unequal world provides the *raison d'être* of social work practice, and is a key way of discharging society's contract in assisting vulnerable people in its midst. Finding ways of countering oppression by understanding its dynamics and developing empowering forms of practice is the major preoccupation of this book.

Oppression, of course, is not solely the condition of the dominated. There are many forms of oppression and even rich and powerful people may experience their own particular ones, for example the tyranny of the workplace, leading empty spiritual lives. But these are different from those that affect people who are excluded from participation in the fundamental social, political and economic institutions within which their lives are located. So, their concerns will not be considered directly within these pages.

This book is aimed at assisting practitioners to achieve the goal of providing more relevant services to clients whose life experiences have been shaped by the forces of oppression. That is, it focuses on those who are excluded from realising their creative potential as a result of the disadvantaging contexts that they contend with daily. It seeks to go beyond the additive approach to oppression whereby each social division, be it class, 'race', gender, age, disability or sexual orientation, is considered separately from the others while the effects of each different form are 'added on' to the one initially under consideration. At the same time, it asks social workers to understand that being oppressed is only one aspect of a reality that both they and their clients are embedded within. In other words, the people that they are working with may be playing key roles in oppressing others. And, moreover, they as social workers may be oppressed themselves whilst both oppressing and attempting to empower people at the same time. In taking this more complex theoretical position, this book attempts to go beyond the formulations of oppression implied by authors such as Thompson (1993) in his well-known PCS (personal, cultural and structural) model, where a focus primarily on discrimination, I would argue, emphasises only one element in the web of oppressive social relations.

Moreover, the additive approach to the complexities of oppression casts the resolution of conflict in both intellectual and practical terrains, in competitive terms resulting in a winner and a loser. This approach tends to be unhelpful in that it usually produces an unstable outcome whirling around an ever-extending spiral of conflict in which the losers seek to become the winners while those in the ascendancy attempt to (re)entrench their position. Moreover, additive approaches rank oppressions in a hierarchy that prioritises one form over another. I intend to transcend the problematics of a competitive approach to resolving the contradictions that surround various forms of oppression in social work practice by developing a holistic framework that enables users to play a greater role in the design and delivery of the services they require and professionals to respond more appropriately to the agendas that they set.

The structure of the book

This book has as a major aim the linking of theories of oppression to the realities and dilemmas of practice in order to suggest ways of improving services for clients through anti-oppressive approaches to practice. In Chapter 1, I embark on considering the types of theories and understandings that would enable us to develop an anti-oppressive framework for practice that goes beyond the additive approach. This draws upon some of the insights that have been developed in the 'classical' literature that focuses on oppression from the point of view of a particular social division. I examine the social, political and economic contexts in which social work has had to carve out its status as a profession. But I also conceptualise the world as interdependent, for in interpersonal relations the behaviour of one individual affects others, and what happens in one country impacts upon another. Handling the subsequent implications requires reformulating national welfare considerations within a global concern for others. The ideas of solidarity, reciprocity and mutuality are posited as ways of securing a globalised citizenship that transcends the divisions between low-income and high-income countries. I continue arguing for anti-oppressive practice as a legitimate part of social work in Chapter 2. This requires me to address the ethical and moral issues that arise when social work becomes a political entity. In Chapter 3, I focus on identity as a crucial issue for the development of an empowering social work practice.

Demonstrating the use of anti-oppressive practice in work with individuals forms the backbone of Chapter 4. Exploring the operation of anti-oppressive practice in action within group and community settings becomes the basic preoccupation of Chapter 5. In Chapter 6, I highlight the importance of engaging in organisational changes that can sustain the development of anti-oppressive practice across time and space. Chapter 7 argues for a universal, citizenship-driven welfare state that transcends the limitations of the fragmented welfare provisions that characterise market-driven approaches to welfare, although the latter are more in keeping with the postmodernist world favoured by politicians in the industrialised societies. I conclude the book in Chapter 8 with guidelines for practice and affirm the arguments for a globalised citizenship in which the interdependencies between and within individuals and countries provide the basis for welfare states that are rooted in social solidarity, reciprocity and mutuality.

Notes

(1) Language is a tool that we use to communicate. But, our choice of words also reveals the ideologies that underpin our views of the world and the power relations inherent within these. I use the plural version of 'people', which is itself a plural noun, to indicate that I wish to draw attention to the diversities that exist within this category.

(2) 'Client' is a contested term. It is currently being replaced in the United Kingdom by the phrase 'service users', which I think is equally problematic. In this book, I retain the word 'client' as it is understood more clearly worldwide, although I occasionally refer to 'users' to avoid constant repetition of the word 'client' when one use of it follows another in close proximity. I intend both terms to mean simply the person or persons that approach professional social workers for services or assistance.

Chapter 1

Introducing Anti-Oppressive Theories for Practice

Introduction

Popular understandings of 'oppression' tally with dictionary definitions of the word as 'the exercise of power in a tyrannical manner; the cruel treatment of subjects, inferiors; the imposition of unjust burdens' (*The Shorter Oxford English Dictionary*, Vol II, 1967, p. 1376). These definitions depict a binary division between peoples: those who oppress and those who are oppressed. And, they focus largely on the interpersonal interaction between these two groups. Useful as these insights into oppression are, they are inadequate for painting a full picture of oppression: how it works; how it is experienced; how it is reproduced; and how it might be resisted and eradicated.

In this chapter, I intend to examine the concept of oppression, identify the limitations of thinking about it in dichotomous terms and move into retheorising oppression in ways that enable me to reconceptualise anti-oppressive practice so that it moves further in empowering directions. I do this by considering the interactivity of the dynamics of oppression within a framework that reveals that although there are many different kinds of oppression, some elements of the *processes* of oppression with regards to one social division are similar to those found in the others, whilst some are distinct. I conceptualise oppression as existing in a continuum that extends from oppression to anti-oppression to non-oppression. This spectrum can be conceived as one that underpins the survival strategies of oppressed peoples in responses that run from various forms of accommodation, or coming to terms with a subjugated status, to resistance to oppression and moving on to create egalitarian relations that celebrate and accept 'difference' within an ethical framework that validates equality and social justice. My starting point is that unless they understand oppression and the dynamics that (re)produce it, social workers can oppress disadvantaged residents directly and indirectly when assisting their (re)integration into the broader society or helping them to assume more control over their own lives.

Retheorising oppression to understand its complexities

Humans are complex beings who make strategic choices about their interactions with others. When forming oppressive relationships, people engage in strategic decisions that exclude certain groups or individuals from formally and legitimately accessing power and resources. In a society that aims to be egalitarian and promote democratic relations between individuals and groups, the collective failure to live up to these aspirations requires urgent attention.

Oppression involves relations of domination that divide people into dominant or superior groups and subordinate or inferior ones. These relations of domination consist of the systematic devaluing of the attributes and contributions of those deemed inferior, and their exclusion from the social resources available to those in the dominant group. In creating oppressive relationships, those in the dominant group seek to deny agency in those whom they deem inferior. Furthermore, the ruling group defines the lesser position of those at the bottom of the social pile as one of a passivity that has little scope for change. They draw on mechanisms of normalisation that promote dominant values and priorities to impose a range of social control systems aimed at curtailing the activities of subordinate groups within the grounds that the dominant group designates as legitimate. Thus, oppressive relations are about limiting the range of options that subordinated individuals and groups can readily exercise. As these relations are conducted as *interactions* between people, how these expectations are realised in practice can vary considerably from those posited. Those in oppressed groups do not engage in social relations *solely* on the terms set by those in dominant positions. They also act in ways that reflect their own interests and endeavours at either accepting or resisting their oppression in the process of asserting these. The dynamics of oppression provide the context in which oppressed individuals and groups exercise agency and attempt to shape their world as they envisage it. These dynamics involve processes of oppression that are shared across a range of social divisions, for example 'race', gender, class, age, disability and sexual orientation.

Conceptualising oppression simply as cruel or unjust treatment entailing the enforcement of *power over* others, focuses the exercise of power in social relationships primarily on the interpersonal level. Defining the issue in these unidimensional terms leaves out the multiplicity of the structural elements of power that are located in the institutional and cultural domains. Yet, these are crucial in the processes of reproducing inegalitarian relations because they embed oppression in the everyday practices and routines of life so that they do not have to be consciously thought about.

Oppression takes place in the social arena in the form of interactions between people. Consequently, oppression is socially constructed through people's actions with and behaviours towards others. Its interactive nature means that oppressive relations are not deterministic forces with preordained outcomes. They have to be constantly reproduced in everyday life encounters and routines for them to endure. Thus, resistance to oppression can always take place. Moreover, resistance can occur at both personal and structural levels and can be undertaken both by individuals and through groups.

Oppression is a comprehensive experience that touches all aspects of a person's life and affects both public and private spheres (Balbo, 1987). The dynamics of oppression are evident in every aspect of the human condition, and are especially evident in its psychological, social, economic and political fields. Oppressive dynamics are manifest in both individual and collective domains. Oppression has to be thought about as multidimensional and fluid. But the bottom line is that oppressive relations target people's sense of self, that is, who they are. Oppressors attack identity – its formation and reformation – at its core, by depicting a socially constructed status as natural and immutable and, crucial to an oppressive framing of it, as inferior to that held by them. The unalterability of identity posed in negative terms is central to an oppressive framing of people's sense of who they are individually and collectively. Although identity involves a complex set of relations, any aspect of it can be socially constructed and presented in fixed oppressive terms. The way that concepts are framed, discussed and understood will shape how people act and react to them because these influence how they think and behave and identify what actions they believe it will be possible for them to take.

Strategic responses to oppression

Identity is constituted through interactions between people. These occur at both individual and collective levels and involve negotiations around their perceptions of each other, their status and position in the social world, their access to psychological, social, economic and physical resources, and their own personal attributes and aspirations. People enter a particular interaction in ways that seek to take account of what each brings to that situation prior to their interaction. In this, they do not negotiate with each other as purely autonomous beings without a social context, but as contextualised beings who carry with them as an integral part of their being ontological realities such as skills, knowledge, values and social resources which they use in the hopes of influencing and changing their world. In other words, there is some recognition that human interactions are embedded in contexts that have been framed by others, within particular legal, social, cultural, political and economic parameters. There is no blank page on which they write, but complex webs of relationships or networks at both the personal and structural levels in and through which people negotiate with each other. However, at any one point in time, individuals will emphasise some aspects of their identity and situation over others, according to what they wish to achieve. In this sense, there is a rationality to the choices that are made – a rationality that attempts to link ends and means. As people seek to realise their goals, they utilise the networks that they are embedded within to negotiate with others to achieve change at macro-, meso- and/or micro-levels, depending on what their objectives are.

As identity is configured in and through social relations, oppressive relations also have a role in identity formation. However, these are not played out as a one-way track in which the path has been predetermined by those in the dominant group. Those in subordinate groups are also implicated in their creation. They may have accepted the dominant group's definition of who they are, or they may have rejected it and seek to establish their own alternative formulations.

People whose lives are embedded within oppressive relationships engage in their reproduction in and through their interactions with others. Central to these interactions are their responses to how others frame their situations and how they frame or want to frame it themselves. The (re)actions of people who have been oppressed revolve around three possible courses of action: acceptance, accommodation and rejection. Any one individual or group may use any one of these in a tactical manner to secure a particular end and may move from one to the other in no particular order.

If people's strategic responses to their oppression involve an uncritical approach to their position, they embrace existing patterns of social relations as a matter of course and do not believe that there are other options open to them. They internalise dominant norms and values to adopt what I call an *acceptance* mode response to their situation. Those assuming acceptance strategies are unlikely to perceive their particular circumstances as other than those within which they are located. These coincide with the definition of their position that is advocated by those endorsing the status quo. An alternative vision lies beyond the realms of the possible unless it is opened up for them through their interactions with others. Although acceptance responses depict people's embeddedness in a position as defined by those holding hegemonic power over them, people are not mere pawns in someone else's games. Having accepted life as it is, there is little inducement for them to want to change their ways. This is not a fixed stance, but a rational one arrived at through life experiences. Should these and their understandings of them change, their position vis-à-vis those who oppress them may also alter. Thus, the other options of accommodation and resistance are potentially open to those who are in acceptance mode.

Those who use *accommodationist* solutions to the structural difficulties they encounter have internalised the dominant norms and values to a lesser extent than those pursuing acceptance strategies. For this group and individuals within it, realising their interests involves balancing a mild critique of the system with obtaining the best compromises from those who endorse it or hold power over them. Although they may experience some discordancy with the prevailing social order or certain of its features, they opt to maximise whatever opportunities are available to them. Individuals utilising accommodationist responses may engage in limited reforms of the system in pursuit of specific goals. This is likely to happen when legitimate expectations are blocked and they view this as an unwarranted infringement upon their ability to operate effectively within the system. They may become accepting of the system if it works consistently in their favour, or they may switch to rejectionist mode if their ambitions are continually thwarted.

Those who resist the internalisation of dominant norms *reject* the current arrangements because they find these oppressive. That is, their critique of the system is so fundamental that they seek to undermine existing social arrangements and devise alternatives to them. Working in resistance mode, they entertain a vision of a more just social order and attempt to organise their existence so as to optimise their chances of realising it. Consequently, they often embark on attempts aimed at implementing their vision. Their ability to achieve this objective is likely to be patchy and their outcomes can range from success to failure, depending on the constellation of people, factors and events present at the time. Resistance may occur at both individual and collective levels. And, it may take a variety of forms ranging from subtle acts of subversion in everyday life to direct, and at times, violent action at the societal level. Their ultimate goal is to transform the existing social order. The use of violence advocated by some within this group is often contested by those who otherwise share a particular alternative view of society and can lead to conflicts or splits within the group. The division of the American civil rights movement into those who supported Martin Luther King in non-violent approaches to eliminating racial discrimination and those who advocated violence as indicated by the adherents of black power movement exemplify such rifts.

Each of these positions flows from the life experiences of individuals and groups who are oppressed. The strategies they use to respond to their predicament are not easily separable one from the other and do not follow one another sequentially in linear fashion. They can co-exist alongside each other and overlap. Moreover, one individual may utilise all of these strategies in any given set of circumstances, developing a sophisticated blend of options depending on the 'allocative and authoritative resources' at his or her disposal and the responses of those interacting with them, who bring with them their own sets of 'allocative and authoritative resources' (Giddens, 1994).

Oppressive relations are countered through anti-oppressive initiatives that are intended to eradicate the injustices that these reproduce in the routines of everyday life in both the private and public domains.

Anti-oppressive measures aim to deconstruct and demystify oppressive relations – stepping stones on the road to creating non-oppressive ones. Becoming engaged in rejecting oppression involves a process of con-scientisation (Freire, 1972, 1974), that is, of becoming aware of how oppression works and is reproduced in and through daily interactions (Essed, 1991). The ultimate goal of anti-oppressive initiatives is the creation of non-oppressive relations rooted in equality. Because these relations constitute and are constituted by social interactions, the definition of equality occurs within them and is subject to constant redefinition as different people contribute to its (re)definition. Equality is likely to be constantly contested and can be undermined as well as reinforced. Therefore, the goal of moving from oppression to anti-oppression is neither easy nor predetermined.

In conceptualising the issue in this interactive, non-linear fashion, my views of the reproduction of oppressive relations and people's attempts to free themselves from these differ from those espoused by Cross (1978) who posits discrete stages of progression, at least with regards to the development of a racial consciousness that can counter racial oppression. Referring to black people, his model presupposes a linear movement from a position of non-consciousness to consciousness around racialised identities, although there is no guarantee that a person will proceed through all the stages outlined. How progress through each stage occurs is not detailed by him. Furthermore, Cross (1978) disregards the interactive nature of black people's relationship with the dominant group, and the importance of other social divisions including gender in the experience of racialised discrimination and oppression. In my view, these are serious shortcomings in this model. Moreover, whatever the responses of oppressed individuals or groups, they are not passive recipients when they challenge hegemonic positions, even if it is from within an accommodationist mode.

People who are oppressed in one aspect of their lives may be oppres-sive in other elements of it. That is, they may be simultaneously oppressed by others and oppressing of others. Those who oppress others or are in a position of dominance over others, whether in a particular domain or more generally, also have a range of strategies open to them. I characterise these as *demarcationist, incorporationist* and *egalitarian*, depending on how those concerned exercise power in directing the use of social resources and whether they value differ-ence. These three positions can also co-exist and overlap with each other. Moreover, an individual may hold more than one of them simultan-eously, or different ones at alternate points in time, depending on the goals he or she intends to realise through his or her interactions. Except for egalitarian strategies, these responses are exclusionary, for the dominant group publicly defines 'difference' in ways that privilege their particular attributes and methods of doing things at the expense of those they consider inferior.

People following the *demarcationist* option have a hierarchical view of the world and are the most exclusionary, that is, they orient their actions to keeping power and resources in their own hands by seeking to augment the power they hold over others. They are primarily concerned with maintaining their privileged position and vest their energies in sustaining the status quo, usually by opposing any move to change it. In keeping with their exclusionist tactics, they will not allow into their group those whom they classify as inferior. They see rigid demarcations between those whom they exclude from their forms of social organisation and those they do not. They label those they exclude 'them' or 'other' and juxtapose 'them' to 'us', that is, those they include within their hierarchical ordering of social relations. The 'other' is posited as their opposite – 'an enemy within' – to be kept within tightly constraining boundaries. Apartheid is at the extreme end of demarcationist strategies that seek to maintain a privileged racialised status for the dominant group. Wiping out their opponent, at least from within their world, is part of their plan.

The *incorporationist* strategy covers the option of collaboration with the 'other'. The terms of incorporation or assimilation into the dominant group continue to endorse the privileging of the dominant group, but those who are 'othered' can permeate its ranks provided they know their place and maintain a respectful distance. Those using incorporationist strategies can also adopt a reformist stance in their interactions with oppressed individuals or groups. Although their ultimate objective is to retain the prevailing social order, they may endorse piecemeal change which does not threaten the overall social structure. Those supporting incorporationist solutions can engage in social reforms aimed at improving what they deem a basically sound system. The dominant group may try to initiate low-level change through the selective inclusion of people drawn from the ranks of the 'other'. That is, those in the dominant group will attract people outside their ranks who they feel they can trust to be true to their values and traditions by incorporating them into the 'us' category as 'honorary' members.

But, the status of being honorary is a precarious one in that the dominant group can withdraw it from the subordinated person (or group) at any point that he or she fails to live up to his or her part of the bargain. Thus, an honorary status is a privilege that lasts only as long as the behaviour of the person who is designated as 'inferior' pleases the dominant group. The dominant group's capacity to act in an arbitrary manner that dispossesses him or her of the privileges accrued through this position can engender uncertainty and fear amongst those so elevated. This response secures a certain amount of compliance, for those who have been accepted into this role are aware of their vulnerability and know that the opportunities extended to them can be withdrawn at the pleasure of those in the dominant group regardless of their wishes or aspirations. Moreover, the reasons for the withdrawal of this status may not be divulged.

Then there are those in the dominant group who reject the current social order because they consider it unjust and unfair – the *egalitarianists*. They seek to change the system into something that is more egalitarian and inclusionary of 'difference' on equal terms. Inclusionary elements are evident to a slight extent in incorporationist strategies. It is mainly the terms on which recognition occurs that are different. Incorporationists seek to set the terms; egalitarianists engage in mutual discussions with those who wish to present their own and seek to reach an agreed compromise that respects the concerns of both.

The fluidity of these positions makes the simple dichotomy of oppressor and oppressed inadequate in describing the range of behaviours exhibited by either the dominant group or those that it seeks to subordinate. Moreover, the multiplicity of dimensions around which identity is formed means that people acting as either individuals or members of a group can be both oppressors and oppressed at the same time. It depends on which social division is being considered and where and how they are located within any oppressive relationship. This complexity constitutes a further reason for my considering inadequate the model for defining oppressed persons advocated by Cross (1978).

I would apply similar criticisms to models that draw on Cross's work in their attempt to define the stages that oppressed people undergo in reaching liberation. The possibility that a person may be oppressed by others around a particular attribute, whilst at the same time oppressing others on another basis, is neglected by these models. This shortcoming is also exemplified by Robinson (1995, 1998) whose model draws upon a unidimensional definition of personality. In these texts, one is cast as either an 'oppressor' or 'oppressed', thereby ignoring the whole person and his or her complex engagement in both oppressive and oppressing social relations. This does not mean that individuals or groups will not choose to emphasise or work upon one social division to the exclusion of others when prioritising where they will place their energies and setting targets for change, as black women have done with regards to gender (see Bryant et al., 1985).

The potential for the same individual or a group of people to be both oppressing and oppressed can be illustrated in the following inter-action between women. A black middle-class woman, privileged along the class dimension, may oppress a black working-class woman on the basis of class or other social division, such as age, religious or faith adherence (Shah, 2001). Similarly, a white middle-class woman, who enjoys racial privileging but is oppressed on the basis of gender, can oppress a black middle-class woman with regards to 'race' (Ware, 1992), thereby racialising the latter's experience of gender and class. Although the white woman racialises the condition of the black woman, she may be totally unaware of the racialised privileging of her own experience, and relate to the black woman only as an equally oppressed sister, and thus negate a large swathe of her experience.

Moreover, people exercise agency in their relationships with one another within specific social contexts in which each person uses various kinds of power to engage in a series of negotiations aimed at obtaining his or her wishes. That is, people enter into arrangements to meet objectives that they define as relevant to them. They negotiate with others in the course of their realisation. The extent to which they can achieve their aims depends on a number of factors, which include their social situation and the 'allocative and authoritative resources' that they carry with them as a result of earlier negotiations or agreements reached by either themselves or others to whom they might be linked in various ways.

Oppressive power relations

As feminists have indicated, power is created and recreated through negotiations between and amongst people (French, 1985). Thus, power cannot be considered as a zero-sum entity in the way postulated by Parsons (1957). Instead, it is a force that arises from a combination of different factors and can be endlessly extended and recreated through interpersonal interactions that are embedded within particular social institutions (Foucault, 1980). The terrain within which power is exercised is contested (Clegg, 1989; Dominelli and Gollins, 1997), that is, no one individual or group has a monopoly over its forms and so cannot dictate the outcomes of a particular interaction as if it were predetermined. So-called 'powerless' people also exercise power and there are situations in which 'powerful' people are 'powerless' (Dominelli, 1986). Power can be used to achieve both positive and negative ends. Feminists conceptualise power as a capacity for exercising agency within specific contexts that may feature disparities in the resources and practical advantages that are available to each party. It exists in three major forms: *power over, power to* and *power of* (French, 1985).

Power over is the expression of relations of dominance. Foucault (1988) adds that each participant to an interaction is engaged in a game of convincing the other that they are both mutually engaged in the production of truth and that such actions can reinforce the discourses of the everyday that privilege the dominant group. The enactment of *power over* relations requires the use of their 'allocative and authoritative resources' to define social relationships in ways that favour the group that is deemed superior. The dominant group exercises power in zero-sum ways to normalise its particular view of the world, thereby defining who is included and who is excluded from the group considered 'normal'. This process naturalises its position and casts the others, that is, those excluded, as abnormal or 'different'. Here, an aspect of the 'othering' process involves treating 'difference' as deviant or pathological and, therefore, undesirable. If the dominant group's definition of normality is accepted, it becomes the yardstick whereby everyone is measured. That is, their norms become universalised and taken as the natural way of ordering daily practices or conceptualising events. Those who then have alternative views to propose can only do so in opposition to those of the dominant group and are likely to be considered deviant and dangerous, thereby confirming their being deemed unnatural and undesirable beings by those who disagree with them. *Power over* relations are conducted within a presumption that those who are being dominated are passive victims of other peoples' actions. That is, they are denied recognition of their capacities as social actors and the opportunity to demonstrate agency wherever possible. Those so defined do not necessarily accept their definition as such and may embark on a range of actions aimed at breaking down this casting of their behaviour.

Power to relations indicate people's potential to take action to achieve certain ends, that is, enact transformative power. It can be brought to bear against *power over* interactions. This can occur when those who are oppressed exercise agency consistent with resisting their oppression.

Then *power to* interactions appear in the form of challenges to oppressive situations. The *power to* do things can be enacted either by individuals or groups. Moreover, without vigilance, activities rooted in *power to* dynamics can lead to the exercise of *power over* others. This occurs when one dominant individual or group is replaced by another and treats those who are subordinated as passive victims required to comply with their demands. Feminist analyses of power have also suggested that to realise the *power to* take action, subordinated groups such as women can come together in groups to enact *power of* relationships.

Power of relationships draw on collective strengths that are constituted when individuals come together for specific purposes. *Power of* initiatives often involve collaboration or collective action amongst members of similar identity groups to achieve a common objective (Cleaver, 1971). Aimed at individual and/or group empowerment, their activities can reproduce *power over* relations if they are aimed at subjecting others to their control or seeking to deny others their capacity to act (Foucault, 1980). Because power is interactive and multidimensional, no one individual or group is either completely powerful or powerless (Dominelli, 1986; Dominelli and Gollins, 1997).

'Othering' is an important aspect of the processes of oppression. 'Othering' involves constructing an individual or group as the 'other', that is, as someone who is excluded from the normal hierarchies of power and labelled inferior or pathological. In 'othering', the normative yardsticks of the ruling group are used to reach decisions that label 'others' as inferior and legitimate the exercise of *power over* them. Thus, 'othering' processes are exclusionary ones aimed at reproducing relations of dominance. These create a 'them–us' division which privileges those who are considered 'us' and deemed to 'belong' to a particular social order as a taken-for-granted aspect of their lives. Meanwhile, those cast in the 'them' category are outsiders who are not valued as human beings on the same basis as those in the 'us' group. 'Othering' can occur on a range of different attributes and involve a range of binary divisions so that a person can be 'othered' on multiple levels. 'Othering' is socially constructed through social interactions within the biological, social, political and/or economic domains.

Body images and oppressive relations

'Othering' draws on attributes of identity as socially constructed statements of who each person is on both the individual and collective planes. A person's identity is formed through social interaction with others on a number of different domains simultaneously. Authors such as Trew (1999) argue that identity is rooted in the body. The body is taken as a signifier of our commonalities because everyone is endowed with one. I am inclined to disagree with this view, for although we each may have a body, its meanings are different for each individual, depending on the attribute that is being (de)emphasised, the person's social status and whether or not he or she feels comfortable with how bodies have been socially defined. An individual's reaction to his or her body depends to a certain degree on how it is socially constructed by both him or herself and others (Wendell, 1996).

Moreover, the imaging of the body has varied over time. Each society has its own icons of what constitutes the body beautiful or its reverse and these images are impacted upon by a range of social divisions. They are particularly gendered and racialised. And they are associated with specific images of well-being (able-bodiedness) and age. In other words, the fact that our bodies are socially constructed means that 'the body' is experienced differently by different groups of people and individuals.

Additionally, there are further reasons why a monolithic construction of the body that roots our similarities in its physical and social elements does not appeal to me. Some of these have greater applicability in non-European cultures. For example, the mind–body duality at this historical conjuncture is more relevant to individuals of European origins than to other peoples (Bruyere, 2001; John-Baptiste, 2001). The emphasis placed on spirituality and the capacities of the emotional and intellectual realms by indigenous people in both Western countries and other parts of the world, particularly New Zealand and Australia, challenge this binary division. Although the spiritual domain may be thought of as resting within the body, it involves more than the body or any particular part of it (Adelson, 2000). Moreover, spirituality engages with both physical and non-physical dimensions of being. Thus, it resides both within and outside the body, thereby reflecting the impact of social as well as biological processes in its formation.

An individual's feelings about his or her body may be related to a considerable extent to the degree that their particular physique reflects the 'idealised' body of their society and culture. In the Western world, the ideal body is likely to be cast in terms of being young, white, blond-haired, blue-eyed and athletic for men and young, white, blond-haired, blue-eyed, slim and sexy for women. Both these images of bodies are also sexualised in accordance with heterosexual norms, and they are taken as being without physical or mental flaws. The object-ification of the body in hegemonic discourses results in some body shapes, conditions, sizes and colours being more valued than others. In other words, a hierarchy of body worth is established, and in this contest of worth, the bodies of old, disabled, black, lesbian women are valued least.

Focusing on the body does not enable us to identify the basis of our commonalities even if each person were to agree that feeding, housing and clothing his or her body was a shared objective. Each person has different ideas about how to achieve this goal, and it would be difficult to achieve a global consensus around acceptable types of food, shelter and clothing. Meeting these bodily requirements occurs within highly contested terrains. These are reflected in and impacted upon by religious injunctions, cultural arrangements, political organisations, social orders and economic relations. Furthermore, each of these fields is itself highly contested.

However, within a context of inegalitarian social relations, success in finding commonalities within the varying positions that people adopt depends on a number of factors. These include the range of 'allocative and authoritative resources' that individuals bring into the interaction alongside any unintended consequences and the purposes for which they seek to unite with each other across differences. These are likely to affect the value accorded to any particular body attribute and contribute to shaping the outcome in any interaction or negotiation. Thus, disabled people might come together as a group to challenge disablist conceptions of their existence (Oliver, 1990).

At other times, disabled people will organise themselves differently for the purposes of highlighting another aspect of the injustice some of them experience, for example when disabled women come together to highlight their specific experiences of oppression as disabled women (Morris, 1991; Wendall, 1996). Their critique is aimed at both disabled men who treat women as part of a homogeneous category of disabled people and the broader society that also ignores their specific claims to equality. The same point can be made with regards to any other social division and its intersection with others. By ignoring this diversity, the richness of peoples' experiences can be depicted as a narrow frag-mented one. This fragmentation is transcended by individuals coming together as a specific group organising in specific ways to achieve particular goals.

The diversity that is evident in definitions of human needs across time and space means that attempts to universalise these at high levels of abstraction fail to address this complexity. For example, Maslow's (1970) hierarchy of needs ignores their contentious nature and posits a universality that does not reflect the realities of many people's lives, particularly how those needs are neglected or suppressed because they are living in conditions of dire poverty. Nor does it acknowledge the ordering of need on other than the psycho-physical terrain. Thus, the impact of social attributes such as gender or 'race' in their ordering is neglected. An illustration of this is how women in a number of societies reserve the best food for their husbands, or in situations of scarcity feed their children before themselves.

Additionally, Maslow's typology does not recognise the possibility of manufacturing need through the marketing of particular goods and services and the advertising of specific commodities. Indeed, the commodification of need and identity under modern capitalist social relations is aimed more at creating needs that people do not know exist for the purposes of making a profit (Ritzer, 2000) rather than meeting basic needs, for example the Nike shoes advert that appropriates Michael Jordan's athletic prowess and suggests that an individual purchaser could acquire the same through the act of buying the trainers. As a result of its focus on meeting manufactured needs, consumerism has grown, with little regard for the failure of the capitalist system to meet the needs of large proportions of the world's population to have sufficient food to eat or clean water to drink (UNDP, 1998), and in blatant disregard of the physical environment which is being exploited for the appropriation of resources which will yield substantial profits (Wichterich, 2000) to a limited number of people. At the same time, identity has been commodified and brought to market.

The quest for universals that apply to all people is longstanding. But what are the commonalities that we can all share? And how can these commonalities, if desired, be constructed so that they do not homogenise the needs of all those who wish to participate in the real- isation of such an ambition? These are difficult questions to answer because there is little in the social arena that is not subject to constant negotiation and renegotiation. Moreover, I do not believe that there is one overriding attribute that can unite everyone. I think it is more fruitful to consider those values that enable us to interact with each other on the basis of equality and the possibilities of forming alliances around discrete matters covering specifically agreed goals.

Forming alliances for practical purposes immediately pitches us into the political arena where power relations are crucial in influencing the outcomes of our interactions. Into this sphere, we take our 'allocative and authoritative resources' including our knowledges, social positions, social status, social roles, cultural traditions, political clout and economic resources. With these, we create particular discourses which will assist us in achieving our objectives, or not as the case may be. As these involve institutional practices that generate social identity, they also constitute the self (Foucault, 1988).

The context within which people interact becomes important because this provides the site through which the 'allocative and authoritative resources' that are passed on to each individual through social arrangements that transcend generations, time and space are accessed. This context is also multi-layered. Although centred around and surrounding the individual, it includes:

● the personal level;

● the institutional domain that encompasses familial relations, schools, the welfare state, social policies and legislation;

● religious or faith affiliation;

● the spiritual realm;

● the cultural sphere;

● the local community;

● the national domain;

● the economy – local, national and global;

● and the physical environment.

Anti-oppressive practitioners seek to address this complexity by situating the person in the contexts of their social and physical environments even when their interventions involve actions primarily at the local individual or family level. Social workers, like other members of society, negotiate identity in both their personal lives and their working relations and need to consider the impact of both these dimensions in their work with clients.

Diagram 1.1 depicts the different layers of context that impact upon the individual client and the practitioner when they work together. Although the context is an all encompassing one, the individual may be aware of the impact of only some of it, or may choose to deliberately focus on only a few of its dimensions, that is, those that seem most relevant in particular circumstances.

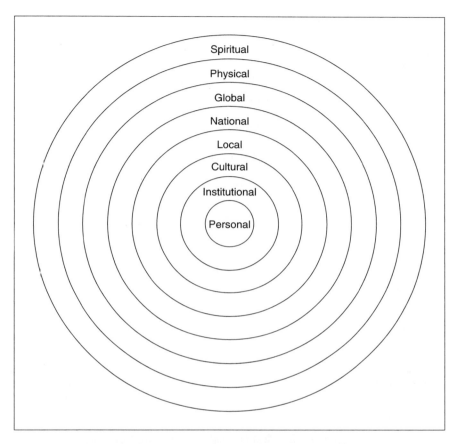

Diagram 1.1 Contexts impacting upon the self

The multidimensionality of context

Theorising oppression and understanding the contexts under which it occurs are important for social workers who seek to deal with the individual in his or her situation – a feature that distinguishes social work from other caring professions (Younghusband, 1978; Dominelli, 1997c). But if practitioners and social work educators are to avoid creating cardboard people to fit particular stereotypes, they have to engage with the complexities of both their own contexts and those of the individual or groups with whom they are working.

Diagram 1.2 indicates some of the multidimensionality of the context that has to be addressed in social work interventions that aim to strengthen individual or group capacities for self-empowerment. It begins

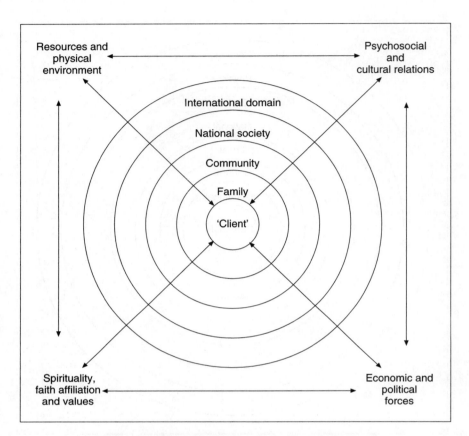

Diagram 1.2 Multidimensionality of context

with the individual (client or self) in the centre because identity is experienced at the personal level even when located within the setting of a particular group, and it is also the site in which most social workers begin their work. Unlike traditional practice which abstracts the individual from his or her social context, this model embeds the individual within it and acknowledges the processes of interaction involved in forming social relations with others. The practitioner is likewise situated. Neither exists in a freely suspended vacuum from which practice emanates to be carried out by an expert professional upon a seemingly passive client lacking in knowledge about his or her own affairs.

Having a commitment to placing the individual and the practitioner in his or her social context makes the work that is done highly political, for it involves power relations and negotiated realities. The exercise of power entails a series of negotiations around the intricacies of their positions and each side's use of agency in the hopes of achieving their specific objectives. Thus, empowerment cannot be 'done' for or to a client by a practitioner (Oliver, 1990). What a professional can do, however, is to facilitate the negotiation of different contexts or provide an environment in which self-empowerment can flourish (Dominelli and Gollins, 1997).

Placing the individual in his or her social context requires knowledge of the networks within which the person is located. These stem outward from the centred self to the family in its diverse forms to other institutions that impact on their lives, including the cultural terrain that they inhabit, the nation-state in which they reside and the global economy that shapes their locality's potential for development (Castles et al., 1996). Understanding the interaction between all these levels enables practitioners to see the contingencies that shape clients' lives and strengthen their capacities to relate to them in ways that recognise their ability to make decisions for themselves.

Respecting clients' rights to make decisions requires social workers to treat them as capable, relatively autonomous individuals. And, rather than pathologising clients for their plight, focusing on their strengths without undermining their responsibility for the choices they make. In recognising clients' capacity for agency, practitioners have to be prepared to respond to the agendas that clients have set. This perspective has been made particularly evident in the activities of the disability movement (Oliver, 1990), through which disabled people have demanded the right to speak for themselves, decide what they want to do and take action for and on their own behalf. In their schema, practitioners are expected to serve client-defined needs, not dictate to them what should be done. However, in taking a client-centred approach, the practitioner has to prepare him or herself for potential tension between what the user may want to do and what the practitioner can or is permitted to do by the constraints within which they operate. In other words, social workers cannot act or lead clients to believe that they can intervene without being held accountable by their employers, the legislative framework within which they operate and the broader society that authorises their interventions. Disagreements about allowable actions may subsequently become a source of conflict between a practitioner and a client, or the practitioner and his or her employer.

Thus, responding to clients' agendas can place practitioners in awkward positions that give rise to a range of moral and ethical dilemmas that may be difficult to resolve. Not only can they be acting against many of the principles upon which their socialisation into the profession has been based, for example their belief in professional knowledge and expertise, their desire to maintain a detached and distant professional pose vis-à-vis their clients, and their accountability to their employers and the public at large, but they also have to make a leap of faith and jump into unknown territory which is riddled with risk-taking alternatives that may leave them jobless and purposeless. Thus, their commitment to changing their practice to accord with client-led parameters cannot be assumed. They may respond by rejecting, incorporating or embracing these within their existing practice.

Change is easier if the directions that professionals and users wish to follow coincide. For example, claimant demands for respect and dignity in their treatment were incorporated into the modern welfare state developed in Britain after the Second World War. At that time, the welfare state was beginning to execute its social democratic modernising project in the form of developing publicly funded welfare provisions for the whole of its population, and made little formal differentiation amongst its citizenry. This era of welfare state building was marked by a move away from residual state forms with highly stigmatised access, to universalism and equal access for all. However, this form of universalism treated each subject or citizen as identical and normalised provisions according to white men's needs (Williams, 1989). Nonetheless, the context of universalism has facilitated professionals' willingness and ability to incorporate claimants' wishes for respect and dignity into their usual routines. However, within the current historical period of the welfare state, responding to user-led demands for control and emancipation may place social workers in a difficult position vis-à-vis employers who endorse a neo-liberal modernising project.

Community workers in the Community Development Projects in Britain, for example, experienced the closure of their programmes when they supported local demands for corporate accountability from multinational employers and economic and political autonomy at the level of community (Remfry, 1979; Dominelli, 1990). Now that welfare provision has moved into a highly differentiated 'targeting' mode, social workers who endeavour to support user-led agendas for universal needs-led provisions are unlikely to be popular with policymakers and local politicians. Appreciating the risks that accompany professionals working to empower excluded individuals and communities is a skill that contemporary social workers should not be without.

Under neo-liberalism, Victorian-like residual forms in the restructuring of welfare provisions are becoming dominant. This regime makes welfare resources available only for those groups that have been specifically targeted as needing them. In the process, the notion of 'deserving' and 'undeserving' clients is being resurrected in popular discourses, this time within tightly defined boundaries aimed at reducing the numbers of people covered by a helping remit. This is the reverse of the universalism which, at least in theory, applied to everyone in equal measure under the social democratic consensus over welfare (Clarke and Newman, 1997).

In this context, liberalism as the philosophy that has underpinned social work's altruistic base in working with vulnerable groups has been undermined. It is no longer fashionable to argue for making good the shortcomings of society with respect to those who are casualties of the system. Indeed, there is little recognition of the system producing any people in this position. Anyone who fails to make it in today's society is held personally culpable (Culpitt, 1992). The spread of the notion of choice and its association with alternative lifestyles has facilitated the redefinition of vulnerability away from being caused by structural failings in the social order to the personal inadequacies of individuals and families who fail to conform to the status quo. Dominant discourses are conducted in terms of people doing things for themselves without help from the state. Indeed, state help is deplored and deprecated as second rate. Even the civil servants formally in charge of the welfare state have been castigated for their 'nannying' propensities. These are bemoaned for encouraging dependencies on all levels and are branded undesirable in a world in which individual (or family) self-sufficiency is applauded.

Social work becomes oppressive by focusing on issues of control that seek to justify bureaucratic aims rather than enhancing human well-being. For those relating to gender, (white) women social workers end up imposing on (white) women clients the prevailing definitions of femininity whether or not this is how they actually lead their lives or what they want. Thus, practice exemplifies forms of social control that constrain women within dominant discourses of inequality. This occurs because agencies have not made arrangements for many of the caring tasks that women undertake without pay inside the home to be socially valued and done for payment by both women and men outside the home. And, service providers ration resources in ways that exclude particular groups on the basis of assumptions that bear little relationship to their realities, as happens, for example, when black people are denied elder care because the extended family is expected to 'look after its own' (Patel, 1990; Ahmad, 1993), or when ignoring the impact of various kinds of abuse against older people because old age is revered

(Biggs et al., 1995). Configuring discourses around need in this manner is also racist, classist, ageist and disablist.

Social work as an oppressive caring profession

Social work has been implicated in oppressive processes by fostering relations of dominance that are consistent with supporting the status quo. These have to do with social work's position as a unifying force within the nation-state (Lorenz, 1994). As part of the state's project of modernity, helping professionals have aimed at promoting cohesion by uniting diverse peoples into a homogeneous whole around a set of somewhat arbitrary definitions about who was included and who was excluded. Social work, therefore, reflected a nation's aspirations in realising citizenship entitlements amongst vulnerable groups. However, its task has been a contradictory one. It has had to help those who are the casualties of a deeply divisive and inegalitarian social order inextricably bound up with the processes of industrialisation within liberal capitalist societies, while simultaneously curtailing demands for resources within politically acceptable limits.

Politicians have been afraid that without restraints upon their entitlements, individuals within disadvantaged social groupings would abuse available resources and refuse to lead a 'moral, industrious life' (Bauman, 1992). Their fears have become enshrined in social workers' responsibility to separate claimants into 'deserving' and 'undeserving' ones by applying their discretionary powers to release resources to benefit the former while denying them to the latter. To impose their professional authority over those whom they consider recalcitrant individuals, social workers offer persuasion and ultimately coercive measures or sanctions legitimated through legislation, such as taking children away from their parents and putting them into institutions.

Social work's remit as a caring profession has revolved around ambiguities (Parton, 1998) about who would or would not be helped and under what conditions. Its mandate has involved both inclusionary and exclusionary dimensions, making social workers a part of society's social control arrangements at the same time as encouraging them to respond to those in need. The requirement for social workers to be either coercive or helpful depends on the assessment made of individuals and their circumstances and the conditions of eligibility in force at the time. These constraints have had particular implications for practitioners and restrained their capacity to act as fully autonomous professionals. It has also ensured that despite being part of the welfare state, the personal social services have not been framed as a universal benefit such as education and health which, in theory, are available to all, free at the point of need. Rather, these have been constructed as residual services under the auspices of a marginalised profession charged with integrating into broader society the most deserving of those in disadvantaged groups. Social work has traditionally concerned itself primarily with providing people with a 'hand-up, not a hand-out'.

This refrain has echoed through the ages in British social work and is evident even now in the political aspirations of New Labour, as represented by its 'New Deal' (Blair, 1999) and reflected in its blueprint for reforming the welfare state (Jordan, 2000). This has made workfare and individual willingness to join the ranks of the employed – even while there is a dearth of well-paid and meaningful work to draw them out of poverty – the vehicle for identifying the new 'deserving' poor. The personal advisor it has introduced to plan an individual's re-entry into society is a social worker by another name. Moreover, the piece-meal restructuring of the social work profession by this and other means has resulted in the bypassing of a public debate about the role and purpose of social work in contemporary society.

However, the injunction to apply both care and control in practice has constrained the development of social work as a profession committed to altruistic ideals concerned solely with 'helping people', and embedded it instead in an ideology of conditional universalism that has been assimilationist in its project because it has *presumed* that everyone is equal, when the daily experiences of many individuals and groups have exposed this *assumption* as a lie.

The assumption of sameness at one level is a legalistic device that has enabled ruling elites to unite diverse peoples within a nationalist project encompassed within the territorial boundaries of a particular nation-state. The creation of a consensus around formal equality before the law and access to citizenship rights embedded within the welfare state of which social work is part becomes possible because, in principle, the prevailing discourse claims that no one is excluded from its remit. However, this unity is a presumed one and, from the very beginning, access to the body politic has been highly differentiated (Williams, 1989).

The hegemonic view of citizenship has been familialist and normalising. When analysed, the 'typical citizen' was exposed as a white, middle-class male (Dale and Foster, 1986; Pascall, 1986;

Dominelli, 1991b). In Britain, women and black people were initially denied access to the welfare state in their own right and were left out as specific groups with their own particular claims (Williams, 1989). Women's eligibility for welfare resources on an independent basis was curtailed by an assumed dependency on their fathers or husbands who were expected to provide for them through the 'family wage'. Racist prejudices and practices excluded black people from being considered full and equal partners in the national enterprise. Key to their relegation was the dominant white group's belief that black people did not belong in the same country as them. Black people were considered temporary residents whose claims to welfare services could be legitimately ignored (Gordon and Newnham, 1985; Dominelli, 1988, 1991a). At its more extreme, black people were also considered abusers of welfare resources rather than contributors to their development by paying taxes and undertaking waged labour within them.

The struggle for full equality of access to the welfare state is ongoing. In the current neo-liberal conjuncture of limiting state responsibilities in providing care, the idea is that someone other than an unrelated (as in blood ties) citizen is responsible for providing it for those excluded from its remit. The notion of social interdependence and the expression of social solidarities through welfare provisions available to all at the point of need have been downplayed in favour of family-based self-sufficiency and independence. This independence is defined as abstaining from requiring publicly financed welfare provisions. As a corollary, dependency within the family has been intensified, particularly for young people who are expected to be supported by their parents for increasingly lengthy periods of time as a result of policy changes in the social security system, housing benefits and educational system. Similar assumptions are evident in the community care legislation with regards to caring for older people (Hughes, 1995). In these discourses, women are usually assumed to be providing free care within the framework of dependent familial relations in which heterosexual marriage is a key institution. Both positions ignore adult women's needs for time for themselves and the right to develop their own skills and talents through waged careers if this is what they wish. Sponsored immigrants have also been subjected to depending on extended families for meeting their welfare needs as part of their conditions of entry into Western countries such as Britain, Canada and the United States (see Gordon and Newnham, 1985).

At the same time, other groups have also been cast as 'undeserving'. Unmarried couples and same gender couples have constantly had to fight for the right to declare their partners as beneficiaries for the purposes of insurance, pensions and other social security benefits and have them publicly accepted as such. Their struggles for recognition have resulted in some recent gains. However, their successes have been placed within the dominant discourses, that is, asking for the same rights as those enjoyed by married heterosexual couples, and access to these resources has been conceded on the same grounds of assumed dependency as those accorded to spouses in heterosexual arrangements.

Success in these terms is problematic. In projecting their demands within familialist arrangements, unmarried and same sex couples are lending heterosexual institutions a new lease of life and strengthening their legitimacy. Rooting their definition of the problem and its solution within hegemonic discourses also carries with it the danger of undermining some of the struggles for equality that women within heterosexual unions have undertaken, for example the goal of disaggregating resources within the 'family' unit. As feminists such as Pahl (1985) have demonstrated, familialist relations disguise an unequal distribution of power and resources within intimate heterosexual married relationships, and they cover up the inadequacy of the 'family wage' in catering for the needs of all its members. Moreover, in aggregating responsibilities and finances within the 'family' unit, familialist discourses reinforce social policy assumptions about the 'familial' basis of dependency on a number of matters ranging from social security benefits to taxation (Dominelli, 1991b). These arguments, therefore, also weaken social claims for support and solidarity from and amongst people who do not know each other – a positive demand that at least had been endorsed earlier through the social democratic consensus.

Traditionalist discourses are also problematic with regards to children's rights (Franklin and Franklin, 1996) for the familialist arrangements which disadvantage them are shaped in terms that are adultist, that is, these empower adults and privilege their views over those of children (Dominelli, 1989, 1999). Additionally, familialist approaches discourage discussions about social solidarities that cut across familial bonds, such as those signified by the broader community taking responsibility for the well-being of each dependent member within its borders – an argument with particular relevance to children. Ironically, the profession of social work has been created in part to recognise these obligations. Such considerations have underpinned the universalist aspirations of the welfare state and are evident in social work's preoccupation with socially vulnerable people.

Social work's professional marginality is linked to its remit as a caring profession dominated by women and its dependency for fiscal resources on the state (Dominelli, 1997c). The subjugation of social work's remit to economic exigencies and political interventions is a function of its position as a dependent profession within the welfare state. The recent redrafting of the welfare contract is more in keeping with familialist obligations that are being reinforced through the restructuring of the welfare state to accommodate the demands of globalisation (Clarke and Newman, 1997; Dominelli, 1999). This orientation has produced a shift in professional emphasis away from relationship-building and the recognition that people work with each other to promote change, to a bureau-technocratic arrangement based on narrowly defined criteria of eligibility. As a result, a new set of controls has been placed upon practitioners and the nature of professional social work has been redefined.

At the same time, the directions that those in charge of the state are setting for practice are being challenged by the demands of user groups for more participatory forms of social work intervention and recognition of their rights to emancipation. These have exacerbated the tensions between professional workers endorsing the status quo and articulate user groups and professionals questioning it. Although highly marginalised endeavours, users' claims to more relevant services have also led to more creative responses being developed by practitioners concerned with reducing the gap between themselves and their clients, for example social work-supported projects involving disabled people and those with mental health problems that are controlled by the users (Barnes and Maple, 1992). In other words, their joint efforts have demonstrated that it is possible for social workers to form alliances with clients that are able to foster user-led agendas in service formation and delivery (Bishop, 1994).

Social work within an anti-oppressive framework

What will a social work practice that is carried out within an anti-oppressive framework look like? Existing literature makes it clear that it will be client-centred and empowering (Dalrymple and Burke, 1995). On its own, the approach that Dalrymple and Burke (1995) articulate will be insufficient, for its strength of addressing how the interpersonal dynamics between the social workers and their clients can be reshaped by legal process treats the worker–client relationship as a primary one that is independent of its complex social context. Moreover, Dalrymple and Burke (1995) ignore working relations and the importance of employers not oppressing their employees. The agencies they work within have to be committed to addressing the structural components of oppression rooted in institutional practices and cultural norms alongside the interpersonal ones. The working environment has to be an anti-oppressive one throughout. Employers have to treat their employees, the social workers, in anti-oppressive ways. The absence of these two dimensions will make it difficult for practitioners to practice in an anti-oppressive manner. Thus, the extent to which anti-oppressive practice can survive and flourish within organisations that are not committed to its precepts at the personal, institutional and cultural levels remains a crucial issue. This concern goes beyond formal legality in the context of a less than egalitarian society.

Another question is whether anti-oppressive social work can flourish if only their employing agency subscribes to it. Expansive growth is highly unlikely if only one organisation engages in it, for enhancing anti-oppressive practice within a change-oriented agenda would require anti-oppressive principles of practice to permeate the entire social order. The bleakness of the current situation makes its realisation in welfare relationships and social services provisions improbable in the short term. Thus, the question becomes one of what can be achieved in societies in transition between the nation-building emphasis of the post-war period and a more international and global consensus. And how can social work as a profession transform itself to fit the globalising agendas on terms that are consistent with clients' aspirations for full and empowered lives in their own communities?

As part of the welfare state, social work is a small profession within a large state bureaucracy. However, the inclusion of private, voluntary and household sectors contributes to making it a larger grouping overall. These sectors are interlinked in that they are highly dependent on the welfare state for funding, whether this is in the form of funds through contractual agreements, grants, or the provision of services which individuals can access. Professional social work is also intricately linked with more informal types of social work that can be found in some voluntary agencies and household arrangements. In these, caring is provided as a 'labour of love' (Graham, 1983) and can become yet another burden borne by women (Finch and Groves, 1983). The classification of social work as 'women's work' also provides a basis for devaluing it as a *professional* activity (Dominelli, 1997c).

Social work's position as a dependent entity within the welfare state has caused social workers who question existing service arrangements and delivery to critique or work in and against the state to secure change within it (London-Edinburgh Weekend Return Group, 1979). The contradictory demands make their position a precarious one. Challenging current arrangements needs considerable collective organisation to progress anti-oppressive practice. Furthering anti-oppressive practice also requires social workers to form alliances with and carry with them other professionals, professional groupings, community groups, user groups and politicians.

Engaging in these activities means that social workers will have to undertake a number of consciousness-raising exercises at all levels of society as part of their normal routines. Although not all social workers have to be individually involved in such organisational initiatives, a substantial number of them will be. Consciousness-raising efforts should be rooted in local communities (however these may be defined). Here, as part of their consciousness-raising work, practitioners can collect data to demonstrate the high price that large numbers of people are paying for the various forms of social exclusion that keep them trapped within run-down, crime-ridden estates with only their own resources to draw upon. Once obtained, social workers can utilise this information to indicate both the nature of the problems and assist in the process of formulating the solutions required to meet the needs of the people living in these locations. The relevant plans of action can be devised by the local populace using practitioners as enablers of the processes of information-gathering and presentation, helping them to reconstruct it in ways that make their story clear to those living outside these areas.

On the interpersonal level, social workers have to alter the way they conceptualise their relationships with clients and move away from privileging their own expert knowledges while devaluing those of the people with whom they work. They have to use information and communication skills to demystify the basis of their powers and engage in power-sharing endeavours that respond to the whole person, and pay attention to the processes in and through which they intervene in people's lives.

Consciousness-raising is a task to be undertaken at a both the personal and societal levels. It has an educational dimension of providing information about what is actually happening in communities in which people are either unaware of what is going on or from which they are distanced socially and geographically. But education alone is not enough, for the bottom line is that the existing social relations are unjust and these have to be transformed to give every single person on this earth a valued place within it. Change is necessary to ensure that no one has to worry about how they are to access social resources to meet basic needs and promote more egalitarian power relations in social interactions between individuals and groups.

Additionally, change efforts have to promote institutional and organisational change. Unfair legislation has to be repealed, unjust policies and practices have to be exposed, and non-oppressive alternatives put in their place. Furthermore, cultural changes fostering egalitarianism have to be advanced. Achieving this goal means countering the values and belief systems that legitimate unjust action and replacing these with those that are rooted in democratic values and consistent with respecting the dignity of those different from oneself and promoting egalitarian relations between peoples. As custodians of society's commitment to helping its vulnerable members, undertaking activities aimed at realising the rights of disadvantaged people is an essential part of a social worker's remit. This, in my view, makes practitioner involvement in empowering processes a normal part of their duties. And, by engaging in these activities, social workers are working with the political nature of their work directly.

The growing connections between the local and the global mean that social workers have to promote egalitarianism at the global and international level alongside the local and national ones. That is, the social work profession has to become centrally involved in international organisations aimed at redistributing social resources more equitably across the world and enforcing the realisation of human rights, particularly for women and children who constitute the most numerous of the oppressed groups (Wichterich, 2000). Moreover, in recognising the multiple sources of oppression and the possibility of people being both oppressed and oppressing, social workers will have to ensure that they address both issues. For example, when focusing on inegalitarian gender relations, social workers have to support oppressed men in initiatives aimed at ending their oppression within a patriarchal, capitalist social order alongside their abuse and exploitation of others.

Conclusions

Identity, that is, who people are, both from their own personal point of view and how they are perceived by others, is an important aspect of interpersonal relationships. Identity issues are relevant for and apply to both practitioners and clients. Consequently, social workers have to accept that they are part of the social work relationship and not working outside it in a detached and neutral manner. Who they and their clients are is as important as what they are trying to do with their clients because identity relations impact on the work that practitioners and service users do with each other. Identity is an important dimension in anti-oppressive practice because it counters those oppressive dynamics that decry attributes that make up an individual's sense of identity or self.

Anti-oppressive practice is not a panacea for all the inegalitarian social relations that are reproduced in and through social work interventions. However, its tenets can be used to identify unjust practices in social work and provide a framework within which more egalitarian forms of client-centred practice can become the norm. Social workers engage in interactive processes that can be either oppressive or anti-oppressive or both. How the interaction pans out in any particular intervention depends on both the social worker and the service user and how one negotiates with the other. The practitioner begins from a position of relative strength, for he or she brings considerable power and resources into the equation as a result of his or her statutory and professional remits. The client, unless he or she is part of a group collectively negotiating to enhance their rights vis-à-vis professionals, occupies a position of relative weakness, for his or her capacities are rooted in his or her personal knowledge, skills and charisma – attributes which the practitioner also holds. Nonetheless, within their particular constraints, the client and practitioner negotiate with one another to achieve specific objectives. They may or may not converge, depending on the outcome of their negotiations.

Anti-oppressive practice addresses the whole person and enables a practitioner to relate to his or her client's social context in a way that takes account of the 'allocative and authoritative resources' that both the practitioner and the client bring to the relationship. Thus, anti-oppressive practice takes on board personal, institutional, cultural and economic issues and examines how these impinge on individuals' behaviour and opportunities to develop their full potential as persons living within collective entities.

Chapter 2

Oppression, Social Divisions and Identity

Introduction

Identity has been a major arena in which oppressive relationships have been elaborated. This is because identity is intricately bound up with people's sense of who they are and who others are in relation to themselves. Connected to this is what they look like. Identity formation uses difference to mark one individual or group off from another. These differences can emanate from a number of sources including the physical, psychological and sociological terrains. However, identity differentiation picks up on these differences to distinguish one person or group from the others in an evaluative sense which usually sets one in a binary opposition to another. This allows one trait to be identified as superior or more desirable than another. Thus, differences become politicised by being used to differentiate between people on the basis of a superior–inferior polarity, creating borderlands that can be policed by those on both sides of the binary divide that is established between them.

The politicisation of difference creates both symbolic representations which privilege the attribute of one individual or group at the expense of the others and creates various sets of binary oppositions which are exclusive. That is, a 'them–us' division between people is created. If an individual or group does not have the characteristics specified as desirable, they become socially excluded and subjected to marginalisation. In other words, people are configured as 'insiders', that is, those who belong to the 'insiders' group or have the features defined as 'dominant', mainstream or normal and those who are 'outsiders', that is, those who do not belong because they lack the 'superior' characteristics that the dominant group has elevated to that station. Thus, they become configured as marginalised, deviant or abnormal. Configuring discourses about identity from their own vantage point, and being able to ensure that others participate in the reproduction of their definition, has enabled a dominant group in society to benefit socially at the expense of those whom they have defined as inferior. Such discourses also privilege the voice of the ruling elite at the expense of those with lower status in the prevailing social hierarchy.

These dynamics underpin the social construction of oppression. Oppressive relationships encompass identity formation through power relations that draw on the categorisation of the world in dichotomous terms, whereby one person or group of people is defined as superior or dominant and the other(s) as inferior or subordinate according to the values ascribed to particular attributes and social positions. Relations of domination also shape the social context that must be negotiated by an individual as she or he establishes an identity within the collective organisations including the family into which she or he is born. People involved in the 'new social movements' have questioned these arrangements by challenging the derogatory labels ascribed to certain attributes and social divisions. For example, the women's liberation movement has rejected the subordinate status of women vis-à-vis men, black people have done so in relation to white people, and gay men and lesbian women have questioned the privileging of heterosexuality (Laird, 1994).

Similar claims have been made by people with disabilities, older people and people with mental ill health amongst others. Each of these groups aims to mobilise around a particular social division to demand equality of treatment and the right to define themselves in their own terms. The struggles to achieve these objectives have been termed 'identity politics'. In the course of affirming their own positive self-definition, these groups seek to undermine the universalist and essentialist bases of the claims made by the dominant group that has sought to disempower them and define them and their social status or place in society in immutable and derogatory terms. They have also sought to highlight the structural basis of these inequalities and the interactive nature of social divisions as these intersect with and contribute to the experience of the others.

Thus, identity becomes a site of struggle or a field of contestation within the 'new social movements' and between them and the broader society as those involved in them seek to establish their own grounds for defining who and what they are. Negotiations over one's place in society are usually conducted along two axes of response: one being accommodation or acceptance; the other is resistance or rejection. Moreover, these categorisations divide people in any given situation into those who are included and those who are excluded. Exclusion draws upon and perpetuates 'othering' processes which confirm unequal social relations.

Anti-oppressive practice is aimed at creating new, non-oppressive social relations. As a result of this agenda, anti-oppressive practice is integrally involved in the process of contesting identities. It considers two aspects of identity as central to understanding how to deal with peoples' abilities to interact with others in egalitarian terms. These are: people's sense of themselves, that is, who they think they are; and what others think of them, or who others think they are. In challenging established 'truths' about identity, anti-oppressive practice seeks to subvert the stability of universalised biological representations of social divisions to both validate diversity and enhance solidarity based on celebrating difference amongst peoples. Thus, identity is conceptualised as a fluid and constantly changing terrain which can be fixed in a temporary sense to achieve particular purposes – what Nancy Hartsock (1987) defines as 'strategic essentialism' or Sandra Harding (1993) calls 'strong objectivity'.

I prefer to call this characteristic *tactical fixedness* because this term suggests its temporal nature – a temporary (that is, of limited duration) arrangement for a specific purpose. In it, people agree to treat a particular attribute as symbolically defining them to achieve a particular goal. With regards to anti-oppressive practice, this would be in relation to securing liberation from a particular type of oppression. And, as identity is multiple, it can develop along a number of different dimensions in which each social division intersects and interacts with the others. Therefore, I question the claim that people exist in parallel universes of oppression that have little to do with each other. They participate in what I call *intersecting universes of oppression* through social interactions with one another.

In this chapter, I explore how oppression constructs particular kinds of identities that are consistent with keeping people in their place. I also consider how people challenge these constructions of themselves to establish new identities more in keeping with their own visions of who they are or should be.

Identity as a central feature of oppression

In a dichotomous view of the world, identity, that is, what one is, becomes juxtaposed against what one is not. Moreover, in this schema, identity is considered fixed and unchanging (see Jenkins, 1996). Theorists who endorse the dichotomous tradition argue that the undesirable traits in one's personality are projected onto those they reject, or call the 'Other' (Rutherford, 1992). This version of identity is inadequate even though it underpins popularly endorsed conceptions of it because it ignores the multiple fluidities in people's sense of who they are. Postmodernists have argued that the embodied individual who shapes aspects of identity into a coherent narrative that stands as his or her life story (Flax, 1990; Benhabib, 1992) is a more apt representation of the process of identity definition. At least this representation reflects the transient construction of identities, and in theory can cope with its multiple dimensions.

Identity formation involves an interaction with others to arrive at a statement of who each person is, both individually and collectively. The identity of the individual, whether as subject or object of other people's definitions, is enacted through the social relations in which they both engage. As identity formation involves individuals in relationship with others to form their identity, the individual is a social creation. She or he does not operate in a vacuum. The social context in which he or she lives and works is a crucial factor that he or she brings with him or her to the negotiations that take place within any interaction or encounter with others.

Within this social context, the individual's 'allocative and authoritative resources' are located. Some of these are contributed through the social position that the individual occupies. Thus, if the individual is a member of a dominant group, there are a number of social resources that accompany him or her to the negotiating table. For those in the dominant group, these include their sense of belonging to the society in question, being entitled to participate in its affairs and having the right to exercise choice in what they wish to do. Those in subordinate groups arrive at the negotiating table with little more than their personal skills including charismatic powers. Their exclusion from the dominant social order means that they have to constantly establish their right to engage in discussions about their place in society rather than simply taking it for granted.

It is in and through this interaction with others that identities are created, negotiated, recreated and renegotiated. Because identity formation is an interactive process, identity is fluid and changing, with those involved in these social relations emphasising different elements at different points in time. Identity is composed of many different elements. How these dimensions are configured and their relationship to one another alters over time and according to different situations and contexts. Identity should, therefore, be conceptualised as multiple and fluid. In other words, an individual's identity contains a number of different and changing aspects that are constitutive of the self, even when certain elements of it maintain stability by being reproduced continuously through his or her interactions with others.

Identity formation also encompasses a process of separating or differentiating oneself from another or others. Consequently, identity formation involves exclusion as an integral dimension of its development. That is, the formation of one's identity relies on creating and maintaining differences. This focus on difference at various levels distinguishes the uniqueness of one individual from another. Differentiation would not be problematic except that it has been traditionally carried out within a context of ascribing values to differences and the valuing of some more highly than others. The valuation of difference in mutually exclusive terms is what endorses negative assessments of people and contributes to oppressive relations in which some people are cast outside the category of humanity altogether. The devaluing of difference is central to power relations of inequality and underpins the dynamics of oppression and the derogatory treatment of excluded persons. In being constituted as inhuman or subhuman by the privileged group, those from the oppressed or allegedly inferior group can experience violence perpetrated against them. And they are placed in the position of having to accept, accommodate or reject this definition of their status and role in the social order.

At the same time as individuating people from one another, identity formation has collective dimensions. That is, a number of its features are shared with others. For instance, a single parent mother is an individual in her own right and belongs to a social entity that has been configured in particular ways which are both of her making and not of her making (Coll et al., 1998). Her identity as a single parent woman will have been created through interactions with others. These will construct her parenthood in particular ways which may or may not reflect her own views about herself as a parent. She may also feel that this characterisation does not represent her position as a unique individual who has more to offer the world than her parental status. So, she will resist some of these constructions or aspects of them as applied to her and amplify others, if she thinks they are relevant.

Policing the boundaries of identity formation

Dominant discourses have configured single parent women in negative terms and have been evident in the polemical debates against lone mothers. In Britain, one of their latest variants was initiated by Peter Lilley in the mid-1980s. These discourses have been crucial to painting single parent women as feminists for wanting to be independent of men, but also as abusers of welfare resources by becoming pregnant and bearing children in order to jump housing queues and become dependent on the charity of others through the benefit system instead of going out to (waged) work. At the same time, this representation of lone mothers has reconfigured them as workers rather than mothers.

This construction of their situation has drawn on New Right ideological antipathy to feminism and women who have used the welfare state to secure their independence from men (see Gilder, 1981) and on the expressed desire of many lone mothers to work if childcare provisions would enable them to do so. Eventually, legislative changes to benefits have required lone parent women to find work rather than stay home and look after their children (Millar, 1999). Such changes have allowed these women to participate more fully in paid employment, but particularly at the lower paid, less secure end where their ability to rise out of poverty through paid work cannot be assured. Targeting these social policy changes on poor women suggests that the right to be a self-defining mother (or parent) has been limited to those who have enough money and resources to keep them away from the neo-liberal welfare state. In other words, the state provides regulatory codes through social policies and legislation that are formulated to govern poor women's behaviour, especially those surrounding their sexuality and parenting capacities. Consequently, inequalities between women as mothers have been exacerbated rather than eased.

The household, civil society and the state form key sites in which and through which the boundaries between public and private lives are constituted and patrolled. Together, these draw the lines that regulate individual behaviour. Moreover, these borders are used to identify and confer legitimacy on some types of activities and disallow others. State or public regulation of private life interacts with personal forms of governance undertaken by individuals within the contexts of the household they live in, the communities that they belong to, and the organisations in which they participate. Individuals usually behave in ways consistent with the value system, religious beliefs and cultural traditions in which they are embedded. The communities (which can be based on interests, geography or identity) to which the person belongs also provide codes of conduct which will impact on his or her behaviour and may form further sites from which his or her conduct can be called to account. Holding people accountable for their action requires a policing of the boundaries between what is and what is not permitted by the different codes of conduct guiding individuals, groups and institutions amongst which the individual locates him or herself.

At the same time, the individual him or herself may have either accepted these boundaries and made them their own by internalising them, or rejected them and sought to form their own codes of conduct which will guide their behaviour. Exercising self-discipline forms an important part of the private policing of the boundaries. Any action that is taken involves negotiations about the borders between these two at both the conscious and unconscious level. Diagram 2.1 demonstrates the interaction between the key institutions which police the boundaries between the public and private domains. It highlights the more formalistic codes that emanate from state organisations. Whilst there are overlaps between some aspects of policing, the borders are discrete, in that they are the prerogative of one or other domain. Nonetheless, those who influence each of these spheres use resources – which are given or refused – to either maintain, control or empower people in what they (want to) do.

Besides being involved in policing behaviour, state policies also structure the material conditions under which poor women can exercise a modicum of choice in what they do. Although policymakers play an active role in setting these constraints upon women, women respond to them in a variety of ways, not all of which endorse politicians' expectations of them. For example, women continue to

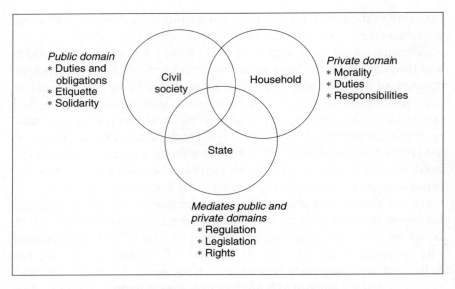

Diagram 2.1 Controlling boundaries

consider having children as single mothers, making it a positive choice (Kilkey, 2000; Strega et al., 2000). They also draw upon the support and resources of other women to create their own living spaces and supplement state benefits. Networking has been a major method that women use to extend the resources at their disposal (Stack, 1975). Women also have more than the one role of being mothers. These other roles interact with their parenting activities and may contribute to their subverting the state's intentions vis-à-vis their behaviour as mothers, particularly when 'role conflict' is experienced (Merton, 1957).

'Othering' processes as exclusionary

Exclusion is rooted in 'othering' processes which draw on a primary 'them–us' dyad. This dyad uses difference to establish divisions between those who belong to the desirable or included categories and those who belong to the undeserving or excluded ones. The principles of exclusion and inclusion can apply to any number of social divisions. 'Race', gender, sexual orientation, age, disability, mental health and class are key ones. This is not an exhaustive list, and any number of these divisions can be present within a particular individual or group.

Each one of these is configured around a binary division or dualism of inequality in which part of the dyad is characterised as superior and the other as inferior. For example, white is portrayed as superior to black in racist constructions of the 'race' dyad, women as inferior to men in a sexist gender dyad, heterosexuality as superior to homosexuality in a homophobic sexual orientation dyad and so on. In short, one part of each division is considered superior and is privileged vis-à-vis the other, which is deemed inferior. These valuations are enacted in the power relations that structure each social encounter that occurs between members of the dominant and subordinate group and amongst those in the same group.

The dynamics of a dualism rooted in inequality are essential to the 'othering' processes, whereby people ascribed a subordinate status are configured and constrained when engaging in social relations aimed at making them feel different from and inferior to those occupying the dominant positions. The tenacity of these dynamics reflects the dominant person or group's power to define their own social standing and that of others vis-à-vis them. In other words, the 'othering' process involves a competitive comparison between people and categorises one of them as insider(s), that is, those who are included, and the other(s) as outsider(s), that is, those that are excluded through the exercise of power and the definitional criteria for inclusion and exclusion. The 'insiders' constitute the privileged group, the outsiders, the disadvantaged or excluded one.

The process of 'othering' also dehumanises people, that is, it denies their personhood, and, in putting them beyond the circle of inclusion, it turns them into 'outsiders' against whom violence and other atrocities can be committed (Memmi, 1965). Additionally, 'othering' turns their needs into commodities which are subjected to controlled access favouring the dominant individual or group. 'Othering' ensures that people objectively are and feel excluded from key elements of social life. It also provides a means whereby inegalitarian relations between people are configured and maintained at both the individual and the collective level. Oriented around specific attributes, 'othering' is a dynamic process which encompasses all social divisions. 'Othering' is also experienced subjectively by oppressed people regardless of the basis of their oppression. The dynamics of oppression feature as one of the shared commonalities amongst people who experience different forms of oppression. However, the actual experience of 'othering' processes is different for each individual as these vary according to the specific social divisions and contexts that apply in his or her particular case. The 'othering' process is multidimensional so that any given individual can be 'othered' simultaneously on a number of different counts, as happens, for example, if one is a woman who is an old, disabled, black lesbian. The dynamics of 'othering' in her case will emanate from the social divisions of 'race', gender, disability and sexual orientation, each of which contribute to her being an oppressed person through a complex interaction in which she both (re)configures herself and is (re)configured by other people as she interacts with them.

Because identity is multidimensional, an individual person or group of people can be oppressed on some aspects of their identity whilst at the same time oppressing others along different ones. For instance, a black middle-class woman employing a white working-class man as a gardener on low pay may feel oppressed by him on the basis of 'race' and gender, but may be oppressing him on the basis of class. A white working-class woman might share the feeling of being oppressed as a woman with a black working-class woman whilst simultaneously oppressing her on the basis of 'race'. Being identified as an oppressor can cause feelings of paralysis and guilt, especially where it is difficult for the individual concerned to individually extricate him or herself from a privileged status. This becomes an uncomfortable position for privileged people to occupy. Furthermore, oppressors who retain their privileged status have difficulty demonstrating empathy with those who are oppressed, although they might sympathise with them at an intellectual level. And, they cannot occupy the insider–outsider role with regards to the particular social division(s) in which they are privileged.

The experience of being both oppressed and oppressive provides individuals with insights into the world of those who oppress others and gives rise to a multiplicity of being which enables an oppressed person to feel that she or he is an insider–outsider who straddles both the world of the oppressor and that of the oppressed. In this position, the individual who is oppressed along one or more social division can empathise with those who are oppressed and his or her capacity to oppress others enables him or her to understand their oppressor. In addition, people who occupy the insider–outsider role can reject their exclusion from the major social origins of power and resources and demand inclusion into mainstream society. Their resistance to being 'othered' is what makes their involvement in the development of anti-oppressive practice possible.

Anti-oppressive practice, because it does not focus on only one aspect of identity to the exclusion of others, enables its proponents to address the multiple forms of oppression encountered by an individual. However, each of these has to be highlighted as a specific social division that needs to be addressed. Hence, anti-oppressive practice emphasises holism as the way forward and rejects the hierarchies of oppression and dualism integral to 'othering' processes.

Identity formation and exclusionary processes

Exclusionary processes and oppressive dynamics are linked to identity formation in all its complexities. An oppressed person's sense of who he or she is affects his or her reaction to his or her situation, insofar as he or she seeks to establish control over his or her circumstances and (re)define his or her identity on his or her own terms. An individual's attempts to do so draw on their personal perceptions, their group positioning in a social hierarchy and the 'naming' of their status by others, including the dominant group. Their responses range from various forms of accommodation to rejection. The connection between identity formation and oppressive or exclusionary processes is crucial to people's responses to oppression. Those who take the accommo-dationist route to dealing with oppression may or may not accept the dominant definition of their position, but they are determined to seek ways of making the most of their lot within the constraints within which they are embedded. Their approach is consistent with playing a lesser role in the activities of the society in which they live. They operate within the interstices of the power of the possible by pushing at boundaries that frame actions within limits that do not challenge prevailing norms or leave them exposed and vulnerable. Thus, they remain largely excluded from mainstream society, but, at the end of the day, they can accept their position within it.

Those who take a rejectionist way out of their predicament seek to carve out a space that they define as theirs. It too focuses on identity, or their sense of who they are. This can result in an attempt to reclaim a previous identity, parts of which belong to either a real or mytholo-gised past. Or, they may seek to define a completely new and different identity. In practice, a combination of the two is likely to prevail, in that the past is trawled for role models that can be used in the present to challenge existing definitions of identity as promulgated by the dominant social group and create new ways of defining oneself in the future on the basis of one's own definition of reality. Cleaver (1971) portrays one such struggle with regards to the African-American civil rights movement.

Gay men, lesbian women, older women and disabled people are currently engaged in struggles for their identities as fully accepted members of society. In this, they often look for continuities between their present position and that occupied by similarly oppressed individuals and groups in the past for inspiration and role models. Lesbian women, for example, have gone back to Sappho in ancient Greece for inspiration in celebrating their identities today. They have challenged their exclusion in relation to sexual orientation which has drawn on their being defined as deviant against the heterosexual yardstick of normalised sexuality.

The idealised perfect body plays a normalising role in relation to disability (Wendell, 1996). Disabled people have argued against this image for it has been used by non-disabled people to organise social relations and physical resources in ways that prevent their full participation in society. This is particularly relevant to disabled people's claim that the social construction of disability is responsible for turning their impairments into disabling ones instead of treating these as factors that need to be taken on board in facilitating their getting on with their lives (Oliver, 1990).

Permeable boundaries in the identity creation processes

In traditional cultural discourses identity has been presented as static and fixed (Modood et al., 1994), and its relevance depicted in unitary or universalistic terms. The possibility of altering one's culture is held to be extremely limited. The lack of permeable boundaries in its representation has enabled those invoking this rigidity to more easily reproduce processes of exclusion. In addition, this approach makes little allowance for overlaps between one cultural category and another. Each individual adherent of a specific culture is expected to be socialised into its prescribed precepts and accept them in an unquestioning manner. Their acceptance of these becomes the basis for inclusion into those around whom acculturated boundaries are drawn. Those who fall outside these boundaries are defined as deviant. The universalised image of a particular culture also provides the basis for assimilationist processes. Only those who can be readily assimilated into the dominant culture can be included in its remit and acquire the benefits that inclusion endorses. Assimilation into the dominant group constitutes the basis of citizenship under a patriarchal capitalist nation-state. Current challenges to this definition of citizenship are occurring on the basis of being included notwithstanding 'difference'.

Monolithic views of culture have been challenged extensively by postmodern theorists who argue cogently for a fluid, constantly changing and multiple identity (Modood et al., 1994; Modood and Werbner, 1997). Celebrating 'hybridity', as a complex identity that is acquired through a combination of factors that emanate from a number of different sources, has become a hallmark of their thinking (Modood et al., 1994; Modood and Werbner, 1997). Hyphenated identities such as British-Asian and African-American are becoming more popular than totalising categories such as Black British or Black Americans (Modood, 1988). These labels represent more than identity. They also signify positions in the struggles to legitimate self-definition. For example, African-Americans called themselves Black Americans during the civil rights movement when skin colour was used as a symbol for establishing unity, in a context in which skin colour was the prime discourse around which racism was centred (Cleaver, 1971). Now, ethnicity and the cultural arena have come to occupy the same space (Barker, 1981). So 'hyphenated-Americans' seek to establish common bonds that express both the celebration of their ethnic differences and their unity against racist practices today. Thus, identity is socially created and can be used to promote political purposes such as the affirmation of counter identities when resisting negative stereotypes imposed by others.

Crucial to celebrating 'hybridity' is decentring or deconstructing the dominant categories of identity to diminish their hegemonic potential. Although this has proved difficult, some movement has been made in deconstructing dominant discourses relating to 'whiteness' (Roediger, 1990; Frankenberg, 1997) and masculinity (Connell, 1995). Doing so, however, has not resulted in either white people or white men loosening their grip on power. Until this happens, it is hard to see how egalitarian social relations can be established through the celebration of 'hybrid' identities. To me, this suggests that work needs to be done on altering hegemonic definitions of identity at the *same time* as challenging subjugated ones. In other words, the processes of redefining the self have to encompass and change the identities of both the 'oppressors' and the 'oppressed'.

Whilst useful, these postmodernist contributions to our understanding of identity are, in my opinion, inadequate. Part of the problem with the hybridity conceptualisation of identity is that the language used is reminiscent of biologised views of identity and culture and can play into dominant discourses that have essentialised identity (see

Radcliffe-Brown, 1952). Also, the language of hybridity draws upon verbal expressions of the oppressor which are conceptually sterile for taking self-definition into progressive future directions. And, hybridity discourses fail to either address or account for continuities in culture. Having the capacity to do so is particularly relevant to a world where, despite constant movement of peoples across borders and within them by both groups and individuals, certain facets of identity and culture are retained across time and space. Thus, for example, this approach cannot explain the persistence of many aspects of identity amongst diasporic groups such as people of Jewish or African origins. Nor can it shed light on people's desire to hang on to their antecedents, as in the desire of Gujerati Muslims in Britain to hold on to their previous language, culture and religion and still be accepted as full members of British society. Something new is created in the interaction between different people as they encounter and interact with one another, but some of the old also remains. Substantial numbers of these individuals and groups reject either/or reasoning that requires them to choose between one heritage or another, and instead endorse both/and logic (Brandwein, 1986, 1991) which enables them to retain the richness and complexity of their position of being both within and without the nation-state in which they currently reside.

Although the discourses of hybridised identities can cater for the description of multiple identities, they are unable to either explain or indicate the basis on which one individual identifies with other individuals on the basis of common attributes, suggest the grounds upon which solidarities are shared across a whole group of individuals, and elucidate the conditions in which they will reject identification with those like them to adopt the identity of those unlike them, especially of those in the dominant group. Additionally, hybridity discourses have failed to overcome the socially negative valuation of certain identities over others, whether or not hybridised. Fook (2001) argues that hybrid identities may be rejected by both the dominant group and the subordinate group. Similar claims of not belonging to either dominant or compatriot communities have been made by members of other ethnic groups in the United States, for example Italian Americans in the Bronx (Ciatu et al., 1998). As a result, the individual claiming a multiple identity may feel isolated and alone. However, in playing out the politics of naming the self or others, the concept of hybrid identities assumes self-definition, and that is a valuable insight into understanding the processes of identity formation bequeathed by postmodernist thinking that needs to be retained and developed further.

Identity in social work

Social workers have tended to treat identity in largely homogenising and essentialist terms. Totalising identities may be useful when advocated as 'strategically essentialist' categories to achieve a particular purpose or formulate political myths that establish a nation or create continuity in conditions of diaspora where the bases of both collective and individual identities run the risk of being undermined by the social conditions of their existence. The problem with this view dominating a profession such as social work is that it excludes those it sets out to include and denies the uniqueness of the individual or family within a specific social context as the basis of an assessment.

Totalising identities have focused on the ubiquitous citizen whose identity is a fixed, monolithic one defined primarily by those in charge of the nation-state. Investigations into who was included in the category have exposed the citizen as being a white, middle-class, heterosexual, able-bodied man who was married to a white woman who shared his cultural attributes but stayed at home to look after the children (Pascall, 1986; Dominelli, 1991; Lister, 1997). Consequently, social workers emphasise a familialist ideology which, despite its lack of relevance in a large number of cases, is constructed around women's role as nurturer within the family. This depiction has meant that women have not been considered human beings with needs in their own right, but as mothers with responsibility for their children, as carers looking after older dependent relatives and as wives who take care of their husbands and do the domestic chores. Familialism has also ignored women's actual role in the workforce – a feature that has long been evident in the lives of black women and white, working-class women. Moreover, it has downplayed women's strengths, focused on their weaknesses and pathologised individuals for not complying with dominant norms without questioning their relevance.

Familialist ideology has assumed woman's dependent status in the home and denied a woman her own specific voice in her affairs. Additionally, questions about the unequal distribution of resources within the family and the unequal burden of housework borne by women have rarely surfaced in social workers' considerations. Familialist ideologies have underpinned social workers' interventions and played a key role in silencing differences that do not fit with traditionalist familialist paradigms or ways of viewing the world. Whether a woman lives as a single parent, a part of an extended family, a learning disabled mother or older lesbian, their voicing of differences have been ignored.

Familialist orientations have also excluded black and white women by neglecting their caring roles within the wider economy and the home. And they have excluded men, black and white, from the role of homemaker. Whether the man is in the house because he is unemployed or whether he goes out to work is immaterial to practitioners who prefer not to deal with him. His absence from the home scene is accepted as a state of affairs convenient to both. In the process, a hegemonic world view that is rooted in a white heterosexual masculinity becomes the normative yardstick that shapes the ensuing intervention. The power of familialist ideology is particularly evident in social workers' neglect of men in cases involving domestic violence against women and children (Bhatti-Sinclair, 1999; Hester et al., 2000).

Identity as a totalising, static entity

Practitioners' essentialist attitudes to identity issues continue to dominate the field. Their approach can be portrayed as a totalising one which insists that there is one way of viewing any particular identity or culture. Although a plurality of identities and cultures is now accepted by some as part of a commitment to a pluralistic multiculturalism, each one is considered monolithic and fixed in both time and space. A good indication of this approach is the demand made by both practitioners and students that specific courses are laid on so that they can be taught about *each* different culture. By this they mean that they want a course unit on each kind of ethnic identity or culture (that they take to signify ethnicity) that they might encounter in their work, for example Asian culture, Islamic culture, Bosnian culture. Or they want to study what it means to be gay or disabled or old. In other words, culture is considered fixed and immutable and as standing for the whole person. The context and the personality are treated as an indivisible entity in which each part signifies the whole, and losing 'differences' in the process. Through this framing of the issue, their own involvement in reinforcing particular discourses about others and failure to acknowledge their own particular identities and the impact this has on their work are bypassed. I term their stance the *acquisition of information approach* to difference.

Being exposed to other types of identity can raise awareness and sensitivity about different ways of being and seeing the world. However, it does little to challenge relations of oppression. These static constructions of 'others' that social workers seek fail to acknowledge that the act of naming is itself a power relation in which they, as practitioners, are key participants. Moreover, in naming or viewing the other as different from them, they reaffirm their own identity as the norm and fail to appreciate the significance of its interactive capacity and exclusivity. In other words, power relations of dominance remain unaltered. It is for these reasons that I argue against the toolkit approach to either culture or anti-oppressive practice (Dominelli, 1994).

For practitioners, the acquisition of information approach to difference is reflected in the idea of 'cultural competence'. This is usually taken to mean that a social worker will have attended a course on a particular type of culture. On the basis of having taken this course, a social worker will be assumed to have acquired cultural sensitivity, learnt all the basic details of that culture and will then be able to apply these when a 'client' from that particular culture requests a service (see Lum, 2000).

The conceptualisation of power relations and knowledge in the 'give me info' approach is problematic because knowledge and culture are considered static. The social worker simply 'acquires' it by transmission from an 'expert' of the culture in question. In this construction of cultural reality, the 'expert' is never the client. Another key failure of this approach is its incapacity to consider power relations at the personal, institutional and cultural levels because power is seen as a zero-sum entity which weighs in the practitioner's favour. Furthermore, by conceptualising their relationship to privilege their knowledge position as experts, practitioners turn the client into a passive victim of their ministrations and ignore the interactive nature of their relationship. Another weakness of the 'give me info' approach is that the social worker's own identity is rarely interrogated and his or her own privileging on a number of different dimensions of identity and its impact on the client–worker relationship are ignored.

Moreover, this way of learning about cultures facilitates an alliance between the traditionalists in a particular culture who refuse to acknowledge the contested nature of that culture and the guilt-ridden practitioner who feels unable to judge any culture other than his or her own, and who may even be worried about the appropriateness of doing that. A further danger in this way of handling the matter is that the individual client's own way of responding to his or her specific cultural identity is assumed rather than sought or affirmed as part of the assessment process. Therefore, new stereotypes may replace old ones. And, through the process of applying these stereotypes, social workers deny the clients' agency, including their capacity to contest culture or engage in its creation and recreation. In doing so, practitioners treat clients as passive victims of their intervention within cultural terms that they determine. The work that they then do together becomes another way of asserting professional power and valuing the expertise of the professional at the expense of that held by the clients. Yet, in terms of knowing a particular client's culture, a more reasonable assumption would be that the client is better placed to know it than a practitioner who has been on a course. And it can be accessed by the practitioner through a sensitive questioning of the client him or herself.

The identity of social workers is itself a neglected issue that needs to be examined and deconstructed. The place of social work in the nation-building process and as part of the welfare state is a historical legacy that has been largely ignored (Lorenz, 1994). Linked to this is practitioners' position as middle-class professionals who are usually part of the dominant group and who have been socialised into sustaining the 'expert' voice. There is a history and a practice that both create and are created by each other. This historical context needs to be considered in terms of the specificity of any given social worker. This includes identifying the particularities of the individual practitioner involved, including his or her own or racial or ethnic grouping, gender, age, sexual orientation, status and so on, alongside that of the client.

Treating identity as a static entity within a hierarchy of worth that privileges people of white Anglo-Saxon origins has had a tragic history in social work. The subordination of racial identities has been crucial to the unwarranted taking into care of large numbers of aboriginal children in Canada, Australia and New Zealand (Armitage, 1996) and black children in the United Kingdom (Barn, 1993). In colonised territories, these actions have drawn on notions of white supremacy in which Anglo-Saxon culture has been glorified at the expense of the indigenous ones (Tait-Rolleston and Pehi-Barlow, 2001). The profession thereby became implicated as an instrument of social control and used to socialise aboriginal children into English (or at times in Canada under French patronage, into French) ways of life. By endorsing these practices, those carrying out social work tasks became complicit in preventing children with indigenous cultures from speaking their own languages or developing their relationships with their parents and extended families. Cruel physical and emotional punishments were meted out to any child contravening these injunctions or, in other words, exercising agency by resisting this definition of their persona (see Haig-Brown, 1988 and Furniss, 1995 for a discussion of the damage done by this approach to identity). In addition, commercial, religious and voluntary social work organisations were drawn into carrying out the state project of colonising land and making it safe for white European settlers to inhabit.

Identity as fluid and multidimensional

Failure to respond to identity issues adequately is currently exemplified in the work that is being done with children of mixed parentage or heritage. These children have a black parent and a white parent, but their racial identity has been simplified. They are usually treated as black children in their encounters with the helping professions – schools, health and social services in particular. Yet, if they have a white mother, the family is treated as a white family by workers in these groups, and the black father is rarely taken into account. Recently, mixed parentage children have demanded that they be given the opportunity to decide for themselves what their identity is (Tizard and Phoenix, 1993).

Social workers have also been implicated in eugenicist activities (Lorenz, 1994), seeking to preserve the best physical traits as defined by the dominant group and offering 'counselling' to those who have had to deal with the aftermath of imperfect bodies, thereby personalising the issue and missing its structural components. Thus, the body and its various parts have been major sites of work undertaken with women of child-bearing ages, older people, black people and people with disabilities. Similarly, people with learning difficulties have their bodies politicised through social work interventions. In *The Rejected Body*, Susan Wendell (1996) talks about her feelings of powerlessness when people decide that because she does not look ill or disabled, she cannot be. Or, if she is feeling sick and disabled, that she should look the part. People with learning difficulties are expected to have features that prove their intellectual inferiority in a unique combination of racism and disablism.

Age is another dimension in which practitioners following dominant norms ignore identity while simultaneously taking it into account. For example, a child is taken to be dependent on its parents. When they fail to do their job properly, the state is authorised to take over the role. But the state's role as parent is time limited – until he or she reaches the age of 18 or 19, depending on the jurisdiction involved – whereas in a biological family, the relationship is not automatically and arbitrarily severed. It can endure throughout life in a variety of ways. Furthermore, the arguments about what social workers ought to do when intervening with children and families are presented in the dichotomous relationship of parental rights over state rights, to do what is in the best interests of the children. Seldom do social workers construct the child as a person with inalienable rights that belong solely to him or her. Thus, they reinforce adultist power relations (Dominelli, 1989, 2002) in which older generations silence younger ones.

Dependency is also evident with regards to the construction of youths, although for them, the categorisation is also likely to be gendered. So for example, young (white) adolescent men are considered to be sowing their wild oats and getting into trouble as a normal part of growing up, while young (white) adolescent women are controlled so as to prevent their becoming sexually active (Chesney-Lind, 1973). Older people are also constructed in particular ways that depict dependency, physical deterioration and sexlessness (Leonard, 1984) unless they are part of an ethnic grouping that venerates old age (Shah, 2001).

In carrying out these activities, social workers have been products of their time, undertaking the projects of the dominant or ruling group, although often working within the spaces that they have been able to carve out to lessen the burdens that this has imposed on vulnerable people and sometimes challenging such approaches. More recently, their desire to speak out for oppressed groups has arisen primarily in response to pressures exerted on professional practice by oppressed peoples themselves.

Conclusions

Identity is constructed around roles – what people do – and physical phenotypes – what people look like. In hierarchically structured societies, each role is ascribed a status that reflects its social worth. Similarly, physical characteristics are also accorded particular social values. Both are (re)produced in and through social interactions and become the basis for differentiating between one person and another around a positive and a negative pole. These are configured around a binary polarity of acceptance and rejection. Thus, those who occupy allegedly valued roles consider themselves superior to those who are 'different' and hold socially inferior roles. As a result of the unequal valuing of 'differences' between them, those in the superior group are privileged and demand respect from those they deem subordinate. A similar hierarchy of ordering is evident with regards to physical appearances, with some characteristics being considered more worthy or valuable than others. Whether hierarchical relations work in favour of the allegedly 'superior' being depends on the reaction of those interacting with them, particularly the extent to which they question this way of organising social relations.

Much of the ascription of physical difference refers to the body, including its various parts or bodily attributes, for example skin colour, hair texture, body size and shape. These are assigned specific values in a continuum of desirability, in which those specified as belonging to the dominant group are accorded the highest rating, whilst those of the group they despise have the lowest. This social ordering has essentialised the body so that the idealised body lurks in the background ready for use in denouncing any individual that does not live up to its normalising features. Consequently, discourses about the body present it as having been essentialised in unhelpful ways. Bodies have become racialised, gendered, culturalised (and so on) in and through social relations in the same way that social divisions have been. In short, biological features have been ascribed values that rank them in descending order of desirability and, in the process, matters that could be taken descriptively become politicised, and, as symbolic representations, these are used to subject people to relations of domination. Moreover, these dynamics encompass physical, cultural and other social characteristics.

Identity issues are evident in interventions with a range of client groups, yet it is an important but largely unacknowledged ingredient of social work practice. Concerns about identity can often work to clients' disadvantage as the 'new' social movements made up of women, black people and disabled people have highlighted. Elements of identity can actively become used as bases of oppression. The potential for social workers to engage in oppressive relations along identity dimensions is particularly worrying because practitioners work primarily with vulnerable groups who are, almost by definition, not part of the dominant social groups. In other words, their construction as 'clients' or people in need is taken as indicative of their inferior social status and they are responded to as such unless the client challenges that construction. Thus, their passivity is assumed even before they meet a social worker. Anti-oppressive practice highlights the role of taken-for-granted assumptions in constructing individuals in ways that disempower them, and in doing so alerts practitioners to more egalitarian ways of reacting to those with whom they work.

Social workers need to become more attentive to issues of identity and engage their energies in contributing to the liberation of oppressed peoples throughout the world. Highlighting structural inequalities, exposing the links between these and individual behaviour, and mobilising people to counter their deleterious effects on individuals and communities are important roles for social workers to perform. However, their capacity to do so will depend on practitioners having a vision of citizenship that is globally inclusive – of all peoples, regardless of where they live, their physical or social attributes and the discourses of inequality in which they and their clients are embedded.

Chapter 3

Anti-Oppressive Practice as a Legitimate Concern of Social Work

Introduction

Practitioners adopting neutral approaches to their professionalism have, like many amongst the general public, deemed tackling oppression a political activity best undertaken within the political arena controlled by politicians (see Culpitt, 1992) and of little concern to them except in their roles as citizens. This position is best represented by the maintenance school of social work (Davies, 1985) which often sees itself as in opposition to the views posited by those in the emancipatory one (Dominelli, 1997). Those in the latter support anti-oppressive social work and question the relegation of tackling oppression to electoral politics because oppressive relations can be practised within professional relationships and activities as well as outside these. Oppressive behaviours and practices perpetrated by professionals in their work with clients have been well documented in a range of professions including social work (Corrigan and Leonard, 1978; Dominelli, 1988; Dominelli and McLeod, 1989; Langan and Day, 1989; Morris, 1991), education (Swann, 1985) and health (Fernando, 1991; Boxer, 1998). These may be intentional or otherwise. But if their impact on either clients or co-workers is oppressive, intentionality is immaterial.

I argue that professionals in social work have a responsibility to eliminate oppression from their own practice or field of endeavour as well as contribute to the eradication of oppression in society more generally, because their profession is concerned with enhancing people's well-being. For social workers, this task is facilitated by having a value system which has a change orientation of securing social justice for their clients within an egalitarian and democratic framework.

Notwithstanding a history of social work's concern with defending the interests of the underdog, mainstream professional practice has been reluctant to embrace an explicitly anti-oppressive mantle. Until recently, the idea that social work itself could be responsible for perpetrating oppressive practices was considered professional heresy. Addressing issues of oppression in and through social work practice has been deemed a politically subversive operation and not condoned by the protagonists of traditional mainstream social work practice (see Davies, 1985; Pinker, 1993; Phillips, 1993, 1994; Appleyard, 1993).

The position of those objecting to social work's avowal of a liberationist project for those generally excluded from social power and resources became less tenable with the advent of radical social work. This has re-emphasised the importance of working to achieve social justice through social work activities and highlighted the significance of the principle of social justice underpinning moral behaviour within a social work relationship. Although their concerns began with arguing for class-based justice (Corrigan and Leonard, 1978), others extended its range to incorporate 'race' (Dominelli, 1988; Ahmed, 1990), gender (McLeod and Dominelli, 1982; Hanmer and Statham, 1988; Dominelli and McLeod, 1989), sexual orientation (Hanscombe and Forster, 1982; Arnup, 1995), disability (Oliver, 1990; Morris, 1991) and age (Phillipson, 1998). However, a commitment to social justice will not on its own ensure that practitioners work in anti-oppressive ways.

The radical social work critique has once again brought to the fore the tensions between different ways of defining the appropriate roles for social workers to undertake on behalf of society. This conflict continues to be played out in the profession amongst what might be characterised as two main schools of thought: one arguing for liberation; the other for the status quo (Dominelli, 1997). The difference between them defines the basis for professional responses to calls for changes in existing social relations. The former embraces these; the latter does not. In questions of voice, the liberationist approach emphasises the client voice; the maintenance one favours the expert voice.

Radical social workers have contributed to the development of the liberationist school and structuralist approaches to social work (Mullaly, 1993). Anti-oppressive social work has developed in response to the limitations of radical social work, particularly its privileging of class over other social divisions, its failure to see clients as agents in their own right and inability to create and provide alternative services consistent with its analysis. Corrigan and Leonard (1978) provide a classic example of this approach.

The liberationist school acknowledges the political nature of the profession and makes anti-oppressive practice a cornerstone in altering inegalitarian social relations within the profession. Within the context of a globalising economy, its adherents are concerned about the deleterious effects that macro-level changes can have on the everyday lives that people lead. Their efforts aim to empower individuals by linking their personal predicament to structural inequalities and seeking to rectify both of these. Doing so involves identifying the impact of structural and macro-level forces, as mediated by social policies and practices on personal relationships, and advocating for widespread social change alongside others endorsing social justice (Cunningham et al., 1988).

The maintenance approach is more traditional in that it argues that social workers need to focus on keeping people going through their routine tasks, by concentrating on micro-skills at the individual level. Consequently, it ignores the larger structural and macro-level forces that also shape people's personal circumstances. For those following its precepts, enabling people to adapt to the status quo in more purposeful ways is a major preoccupation. They do not consider initiating changes in the existing social order as appropriate professional behaviour. Involvement in social change becomes an activity relegated to after office hours. Thus, the two schools may have analyses of social problems that converge with each other, but the liberationist one is committed to acting upon these as part of the job, the maintenance one does not.

In this chapter, I address the moral and ethical dilemmas that are inherent in each approach and demonstrate how liberationist ideals are an integral part of anti-oppressive social work practice. Moreover,

I suggest that this form of practice provides only one way of advancing universal human rights at both the individual and collective levels. In pursuing this goal, the liberationist approach to social work challenges the orthodoxies endorsed by those alleging the need to root out 'political correctness' in the profession, a view that has been gaining ground as part of the backlash against anti-oppressive social work as represented, for example, by anti-racist and feminist perspectives on the subject (see Pinker, 1993; Phillips, 1993, 1994; Appleyard, 1993). The 'political correctness' critique has sought to reassert the traditional expert voice by drawing on client dissatisfaction with bureaucratic forms of social work and the failure of those espousing liberation to actually deliver on their promises, while ignoring their critique of the inadequacy of existing mainstream services.

Bureaucratic social work practice had already been found wanting by those in the liberationist school. But the proponents of the backlash have politicised this issue in a way that directly links their aspirations for the traditional expert professional voice into the political processes of government. Consequently, ministers in the United Kingdom have argued for an end to the concern with 'isms' in social work, for example Virginia Bottomley, when Secretary of State for Health. Additionally, those purporting to advance client empowerment have failed to appreciate how the formation of their relationships with the people they worked with continues to draw on the context of bureau-professionalism in which they are embedded. This has enforced *power over* relations in that they have retained professional expertise and the right to intervene in people's lives as they deem fit. So instead of engaging in a dialogue across differences, they continue the monologues of old.

Ethics in social work practice

Ethics are the rules that govern or guide behaviours or interactions between people to accord with their moral direction. Ethics in the modern Western world have followed Kantian philosophy which accepts the separation between the body and mind, whilst locating rationality within the mind (Banks, 1994). This dualistic conceptualisation of ethics has endorsed white male supremacy by positing women (white and black) as incapable of rational thought and limiting their actions by defining them as the property of men and subject to their will. Men, on the other hand, have been cast as the superior rational beings who have responsibility for ensuring that women behave in accordance with the logic that they as men control and promote. Moreover, this conceptualisation of knowledge acquisition and people's place in the world promotes a dualism that extends to other social divisions, including 'race', sexual orientation, age, disability and other attributes which are characterised as having positive values for those deemed superior and negative values for those designated as inferior.

This conceptualisation of social relations should not be understood as essentialist, but rather as the way in which those who have the power to name some as subjects and others as objects channel discourses to normalise social interactions so as to privilege their ways of knowing and interests in contested domains at particular points in time. Part of this privileging rests on what is accepted as knowledge and evidence in resolving counterclaims, particularly those questioning accepted or already legitimated forms of organising social relations. (White) men's rationality, dualistic concepts and 'hard' evidence become the signifiers that include or exclude alternatives. This dualistic framing of knowledge valorisation and acquisition devalues women's (Belensky et al., 1997) and black people's (Asante, 1987) ways of knowing and the knowledges acquired by people in the course of their daily lives (Smith, 1987, 1990; Essed, 1991).

Despite the misogynist rationale behind the Kantian way of organising social relations and the submerging of other definitions of masculinity under a hegemonic white heterosexual one (Connell, 1995), (white) men have presented their approach as neutral and of universal relevance. Feminist scholars have been amongst the major critics of Kantian assertions and have demonstrated the gender-biased and temporal nature of the ethics based on Kantian principles. Feminists have identified the reliance on white men as the yardstick for measuring others in 'malestream' ontology and epistemology. However, white feminists have largely retained a Western bias in their own work (Mohanty, 1991; Mohanty et al., 1991). Black women (Basu, 1997) have subsequently questioned white feminists' claims and exposed the (false) universalisation of their own particular experiences (Badran and Cooke, 1990; Mohanty, 1991; Collins, 1991). Other feminists have highlighted the exclusion of other women along a range of other social divisions and set about articulating the validity and importance of their own specific experiences and voices (Wendell, 1996).

One of the problems with spelling out ethical principles is that they are usually expounded at a fairly high level of abstraction. Doing so helps to resolve the issue of broad relevance so that they cover a wide range of possible scenarios. But, at the same time, it can result in the removal of the social context in which these principles are embedded. And because they seek to represent points of agreement covering the greatest number of people, their contested nature is also obscured. Their contentious aspects become evident when it comes to *interpreting* the meaning of these principles in a specific situation, when various interpretations become explicit.

Moreover, there is a close link between the values that are espoused and the ethical principles that are derived from them. In modern social work, a Jesuit priest, Father Biesteck (1961), expressed the values that have been accepted as characteristic of the profession. These have included: respect and dignity for the person; confidentiality; and self-determination. Although these have been criticised as being Western-oriented and individualistic, they continue to influence heavily the codes of ethics propounded by a number of professional associations, including the British Association of Social Workers (BASW) and the American National Association of Social Workers (NASW), although other countries, including Australia, New Zealand and India, promote similar general principles (Banks, 2001). In BASW's *A Code of Ethics for Social Work*, its Statement of Principles claims that:

> Basic to the profession of social work is the recognition of the value and dignity of every human being, irrespective of origin, race, status, sex, sexual orientation, age, disability, belief or contribution to society. The profession accepts a responsibility to encourage and facilitate the self-realisation of each individual person with due regard to the interest of others. (BASW, 1996)

These examples give limited emphasis to the social context in which these principles are enacted. They focus primarily on the professional relationship between the worker and client, that is, they address primarily interpersonal interactions at the individual level.

NASW presents its core values as service, social justice, dignity and worth of the person, the importance of human relationships, integrity and competence. Each of these values provides the basis for an ethical principle that follows from it. With regards to service, the ethical principle is that of helping people in need and addressing social problems. When promoting social justice, social workers are expected to challenge social injustice (NASW, 1996). Whilst an attempt has been made to recognise the social context, it fails to do so in ways that spell out how this is to be done in and through the professional relationship. Consequently, ethics have become individualised as a personal matter to be activated by the professional. Additionally, the NASW Code does not see the practitioner as also embedded in a social context which may or may not enable alliances to be made across the myriad of attributes that divide the parties involved in the interaction. Social workers' lives revolve around a formally legitimated status to a greater extent than do those of their clients. This privileges the 'expert' voice and produces one set of differentials which can skew working relationships away from equality. Also, there is a lack of recognition of reciprocity in the interactions described by professionals. The practitioner assumes the role of doing. The client, in consequence, has been cast as a quiescent being who does not contribute to, challenge or reflect upon the relationship that has been established between them.

Acknowledging client agency

Despite this portrayal, clients do undertake action in their own interests. Moreover, clients 'work' on their relationship to secure what they want. In other words, clients, like social workers, exercise agency. Anna, a client I interviewed for an earlier piece of research, put the relegation of her work in asserting agency in the following terms:

> She [social worker] asked me to be at her office for 9:00. I had to get up at six to get me and the kids [a boy and a girl aged two and three respectively] there. It was an awful journey. We had to catch three buses. We missed one and had to wait half an hour in pourin' rain. We got to her office soppin' wet. The kids were ratty. I was exhausted. She said, 'Please sit down', but didn't offer us a drink. Shirley [the girl child] started acting up 'cause she was bored. She [social worker] looked at me like can't you control your children. She sat there all smug like. She didn't have to say nothin'. I knew she thought I wasn't doin' my job right. But I wondered how she'd cope with 'em if she had to drag 'em across town like I did. But then she wouldn't would she? She's got a car. I was getting so angry...But I thought, better not show it if you want your Section 1 money. So I carried on as if I felt and saw nothin'.

Anna makes it clear that she considers what she is doing is *work*. It involves expenditure of energy, time, planning and organisation. Pulling all this together requires her to be a social actor trying to establish her own terms for the interaction. Moreover, she is aware of the inequalities between her and the worker, which she relates to the practitioner's greater access to personal resources that ease her life (the car) and judgmental attitudes that could prejudice her case and deny her access to the social resources that would smooth her path (Section 1 monies). Her realisation of the power imbalance between them means she has to silence herself and keep her opinions and feelings under control so as not to directly jeopardise the relationship between them by *her* behaviour. In other words, she is exercising agency in the way that she thinks best suits her purposes, that is, will facilitate access to the resources she wants. In the process, she is configuring herself as a 'deserving' client and helping to reproduce the exclusionary dynamics she wishes to challenge. Meanwhile, the social worker is relating to her as an equal. But in doing so, when their ontological, physical and social realities are so disparate and unequal, she is perpetuating a 'false equality trap' (Barker, 1986; Dominelli, 2002), that is, ignoring their different starting points to assume that they are equals when they are not.

A code of ethics encapsulates the substance around which professional expertise is framed and the basis on which socialisation into professional practice occurs. In this capacity, it acts as a regulatory code for professional conduct. Professional performance is assessed against its central principles in the event of a complaint being launched by clients, co-workers or employers. But clients like Anna are unlikely to complain. The code does not cover the 'work' Anna does. And, except for feeling unappreciated, there is little evidence that Anna can use to show that her dignity as a person has not been respected. If Anna were to lodge a complaint, the absence of evidence would make it hard for those charged with investigating the complaint to pursue it.

Professional competence is usually determined by a panel of peers who sit in judgment on a practitioner using the code of ethics to assist in measuring a particular individual's deviation from established acceptable norms. The social worker's reaction to Anna lies outside its scope. Thus, it obviates the basis for Anna's complaint. A jury of professional peers is unlikely to label the social worker's actions as either unreasonable or dismissive. Another key limitation of this procedure is that ethical codes individualise both the client who is brave enough to make a complaint and the professional who is the subject of it. So the context within which they are embedded and which impacts on their behaviour is not subjected to scrutiny.

Responding in the simplistic manner in which ethical codes construct complaints exacerbates the problem of dealing with moral and ethical questions, for these are complex and difficult. They do not necessarily lend themselves to the fragmentation and decontextualisation that individualisation produces. Besides, there are differing interpretations of what the ethical principles mean in practice and competing interests and pressures that social workers are trying to balance in any particular intervention. The scope for role conflict between their activities as advocates, gatekeepers, enforcers of a particular social order and its regulatory statutes, and representatives of a public commitment to alleviate the plight of vulnerable social groups is substantial. The following vignette illustrates some of the complications that practitioners have to unravel in resolving the ethical and moral dilemmas they encounter:

> Christine, a white social worker, is visiting Andrea, a white single mother, on a run-down estate in an English inner-city. As she goes up the walkway, she overhears some of Andrea's neighbours complaining about the 'filth' that the young black family that has moved into the block has been leaving in the doorways. One of them, another white woman says, 'I don't know why the Council lets this riff-raff into this estate. We don't have enough decent houses for us, why should we have to share them with them?' 'Specially when they just mess up the place', adds one of the women. 'Yes', responds another white woman who is with her. 'Did you see the kids break them two windows? All their mother did was put cardboard over the holes.' 'It's shoddy and gapes out at you and lowers the tone of the whole neighbourhood', another replies.

> 'How should I respond to these comments?' Christine wonders. 'Their comments are obviously racist. But they are not being made to me, nor are they being made by my client as such. As a professional bound by a code of ethics requiring individuals to be treated with respect and dignity, should I intervene to reaffirm the respect and dignity of the unknown black family who is being stripped of it? This is an action which even a public-minded citizen might adopt, not least because there are human rights and legal issues about racist behaviour at stake. Or should I take the easy way out? And, although feeling guilty about not responding, carry on and ignore what has been said. After all, who besides me would know that I have overheard these women's conversation? No one except me knows what has happened. My professional association is unlikely to intervene in this kind of situation. Besides, countless examples of these kinds of comments must be being made throughout the country everyday without complaint. Moreover, if I were to intervene, the women who have made these comments would not thank me for doing so. They look a tough lot in any case, and I am a little afraid of them.'

Christine is trying to weigh up a number of possibilities, including taking into account the consequences of her action, either way. But whether Christine takes direct action or not, she is impacting upon the situation. By doing nothing, Christine is giving the women the silent message that what they are doing is acceptable. In other words, through her silence, she condones their behaviour. Consequently, she is colluding with the acceptability and continued reproduction of racist attitudes. If she intervenes, the women might respond aggressively to her. But she can tell herself that she has maintained her professional integrity, even if the women give her a mouthful and carry on with their racist conversation. Christine is being faced with a moral and ethical dilemma, even if, from an anti-oppressive perspective, the principles that should guide her response are clear. She should take the matter up, although she would have to think about doing it in ways that would ensure her physical safety. She might act directly or indirectly, immediately or at another time, depending on the personal resources she has to hand and the back-up she can expect from her employer and colleagues.

In some circumstances, trying to impose easy answers on a particular dilemma may create more problems than it solves. For example, in the case of the underrepresentation of black people in social services departments, the followers of both the liberationist and maintenance schools may agree that they should aim to increase the number of black employees throughout the organisation. Yet, how they go about realising this aim and the range of other activities that they accept as being relevant to achieving this end can vary substantially.

The supporters of the maintenance school might endorse the encouragement of applications from ethnic minority groups. However, the view that they are working within a basically sound system would result in not looking for other changes. Unlike their colleagues in the liberationist school, they would not be concerned with making changes to the agency's decision-making structures, policies and everyday practices to support black applicants, not only during the selection process, but in every aspect of their employment in the organisation including rising up the employment ladder. Those in the maintenance school would also be unlikely to set in train changes that impact upon both black and white people. Engaging in root and branch adjustments to an organisation are anathema to those seeking to affirm the status quo, so facilitating such moves would be difficult for those in the maintenance school to contemplate. Nor would they find it easy to take steps that would ensure that all employees, irrespective of 'race', are adequately prepared for the widespread changes needed to realise racial justice.

A central aim of the liberationist school is to draw people who have been excluded and marginalised into mainstream decision-making processes and procedures and then seek to transform these. They would be aware that the strategy of increasing the numbers of black colleagues requires wholesale changes in the culture of the organisation, the ways that work is carried out, and the groups to which the agency is accountable. Moreover, for their strategy to be successful, change would have to permeate the entire organisation. They would press for changes at the personal, institutional and cultural levels, involving all personnel, including their colleagues, management and policymakers. Ultimately, societal level changes would be necessary to transform the context in which social work occurs.

Calling for and initiating fundamental transformative organisational changes may create additional problems for the people who are already employed by the agency, particularly those who have other priorities in their work. They may have become used to a particular way of working and resent being asked to alter it. They may refuse to open up opportunities to those who have usually been excluded from a range of tasks that they have traditionally undertaken and consider 'theirs'. They may display little commitment to the work that needs to be done and erect both covert and overt barriers to progressing anti-oppressive practice. They may even accuse their colleagues, who are steeped in anti-oppressive practice, of imposing it upon them against their will. A crucial matter that the advocates of anti-oppressive practice have to address is their failure to change the minds of those who have not been keen to support anti-oppressive strategies. Working with them to persuade them of the need to do so can be a full-time commitment in itself. But it is a task that anti-oppressive practitioners should not avoid. Anti-oppressive policies, training and practice can assist in this work. But change will not happen overnight.

Human rights are a concern of anti-oppressive practice

One way of traversing the divide between the maintenance and liberationist groups is to look for points at which their interests converge. Professional ethics may provide a basis for bridging the two camps for specific purposes. In recent years, anti-oppressive ethics, central in promoting anti-oppressive practice, have linked realising human rights in social work practice as one of its major concerns. Being involved in implementing human rights may lead to their convergence around particular action. The United Nations' (UN) Universal Declaration on Human Rights may provide one such point. It has been universally acclaimed, for all nations in the UN have ratified it and committed themselves to observing its injunctions. Despite this, black people such as Fernando (1991) have critiqued the UN's approach for being Western-dominated and fostering individualistic understandings of human rights. The Group of 77 has also complained that as it stands, the Declaration on Human Rights does not make allowances for the resourcing that is required to comply with its dictates. To respond to these critiques and prevent human rights from becoming a means through which non-Western views are devalued, the enhancement of human rights has to be undertaken at both the individual and collective levels and some resource distribution from the 'haves' to the 'have nots' is necessary. Despite being flawed, human rights have become starting points for ethical responses to meeting the welfare needs of people throughout the world (Wetzel, 1997).

Social workers have sought to make human rights the base for a non-Eurocentric universalising discourse about the role and purpose of the profession (Wetzel, 1997). Legally inscribed rights are anticipated as enabling individuals to hold particular countries to account if these are violated and can, therefore, protect both individual and collective interests in them. However, this very strength has become a weakness. For, as many low-income, non-aligned countries in discussions around the follow-up to the United Nations Social Development Summit have stated, the realisation of universal human rights requires resources for the provision of food, clothing, shelter, health services and education. Money is needed to pay for them. But money in the national coffers of low-income countries is in short supply for their citizens. Third World poverty is a major barrier to the actualisation of social rights in the welfare arena, whether individual or collective.

Poverty is also linked to the massive burden that low-income countries carry with regards to Third World debt repayments which add to the resources of high-income countries (UNDP, 2000, 2000a). For example, more than 20 countries in Africa have debt burdens that even at a discounted value constitute 200 per cent of exports and are deemed unsustainable by the World Bank (Carlsson and Ramphal, 1995, p. 201). Yet Western countries are reluctant to make this connection and move quickly to address it in their own policy formulations, although agreements to discharge this debt during 1999 have begun to prise open this particular issue (Jubilee 2000). Social workers can argue for the elimination of this debt by presenting graphic information about the deleterious impact of poverty on the everyday lives of poor people and the enormous loss of human potential that retaining this entails.

Process considerations are crucial in upholding an anti-oppressive basis to the realisation of human rights. So, besides dealing with the context, another concern of an ethical anti-oppressive practice is to ensure that the way people are treated reflects the aim that is sought. In other words, anti-oppressive ends require that anti-oppressive means be used in achieving them. Thus, the guilt of those accused of human rights violations has to be established through due process. This becomes increasingly relevant in the task of initiating individual change amongst oppressors. Punishment has to fit the crime. Having an ethical base from which to proceed is a useful, but insufficient step for achieving this task. Where necessary, the resources required to obtain this state of affairs also have to be made available by those controlling them. Social change cannot be left as a matter of individual choice and struggle. Although individuals may need assistance in reaching their target through appropriate training and consciousness-raising endeavours, there is also a collective response for individuals to help one another implement the necessary changes. Society has to become involved through those who contribute to this overall enterprise by endorsing their activities and providing the resources needed to achieve these ends (UNDP, 2000).

Legitimating anti-oppressive social work

Mainstream social work has deemed adopting an anti-oppressive position a political act that runs counter to professionalism and outwith the bounds of professional solidarity with clients. Consequently, the profession has jealously guarded its alleged neutrality in the face of demands that it acknowledge its close ties to the nation-state, its being driven by social control considerations and its rationing of resources to those in need. Remaining neutral, rather than displaying a commitment to improving people's well-being in general, has enabled the profession to forgo challenging structural inequalities within the existing social order. This reality has become increasingly evident under the neo-liberal market culture (Kelsey, 1997; Ralph et al., 1997). Ignoring the collective dimensions of identity, pathologising individuals for failure to act in ways endorsed by the ruling regime and decontextualising their social existence have provided the mechanisms whereby the non-recognition of oppressive contextual domains has been achieved. Moreover, individualising social ills becomes a vehicle for practitioners to use in managing their clients, whilst their employers manage them through bureaucratising and monitoring professional performance.

The adherents of the maintenance school have endorsed this neutrality for what they consider valid reasons. A key one has been that the externally validated objectivity implied in neutrality protects users from the vagaries of either political intrigues or changing professional fashions (see Pinker, 1993). Avoiding becoming susceptible to political contingencies in the non-party political sense is considered a corrective to the likelihood of power relations being abused and thereby making service delivery unreliable and unamenable to bureaucratic rationality. Those in the maintenance school have combined ethical considerations with organisational exigencies to guide social work practice in particular directions and safeguard what professionals through their expertise define as being in the client's interest. An irony of this particular stance is that maintenance school advocates do not perceive their prescription of the paths that practitioners should follow as itself a political act. Yet it represents an essentially conservative position that supports current social arrangements.

Political relations permeate all relationships because the exercise of power and agency is involved in all interactions between people. However, my argument is not that one political stance is in and of itself 'superior' to another, but that the political nature of each stance should be made explicit, so that the individuals concerned have the information they need to assist them in making choices about how they want to live and which political positions they wish to endorse.

A further key difficulty which the maintenance school of social work has in demonstrating objective neutrality is that it ignores the contexts in which social work practice is undertaken. One of these revolves around the family. Much traditional social work with individuals has been conducted within the unacknowledged or taken-for-granted context of the Western nuclear family. But this, like the rest of the social environment in which a person is embedded, has often been taken as given. Moreover, it has been deemed immutable and enduring. These assumptions are further underpinned by the belief that if handled in ways that release its energies in an appropriate manner, the family is capable of providing the best forms of support to those in need. These views have been challenged by feminist analyses that have uncovered widespread emotional, physical and sexual abuse within its remit (Barrett and McIntosh, 1981). This is a contested view, with its applicability being challenged by rightwing ideologues arguing the sanctity of the (white) family in general (Murray, 1984, 1990, 1994) and black feminists who have revealed the importance of black families that operate as havens of support and safety in a racist world (Bryant et al., 1985; Collins, 1991).

Moreover, 'the family' has been given an additional lease of life as a conceptual tool in the social work profession, particularly through psychodynamic casework, as a result of the popularity of Freudian analyses. This trend has proved problematic, for although Freudian insights into family life have highlighted its *social* dimensions, these have been presented as timeless universal truths that apply to all societies and cultures. This bias has reinforced social workers' failure to acknowledge either the multicultural bases of societies or the diverse range of family forms that they encounter. Additionally, the static pictures of family relationships depicted in Freudian analyses ignore the changes that these undergo over time. Also, they do not recognise the differential power relations that feature within family life, even in its Western nuclear variant. The outcome of practice based upon Freudian precepts has endorsed traditional familialism or Western patriarchal relations within the family, even when these have been questioned by the client(s) concerned, or deemed inappropriate by those of non-Western social origins. Thus, Freud's concepts have been used to impose patriarchal relations upon reluctant users or in situations where they are inappropriate.

Despite the limitations identified in this critique, psychodynamic forms of social work have been particularly important in raising the professional status of social work. The domination of traditional professional paradigms by Freudian analyses has enabled social work practitioners to root their practice within scientific discourses. These have enhanced their power and prestige by lending greater credibility to practitioners' claims of professional expertise. However, practice has developed within bureaucratic parameters that have left little space for service users. Moreover, in relating personal woes to family dysfunction, these professional understandings have pathologised those who have needed help and individualised the social problems they face. Psychodynamic models of social work have allowed practitioners to blame clients for the problems they face. Thus, Freudian psychodynamic casework succeeded in dislodging the connections that C Wright Mills (1970) argues exist between private troubles and social ills.

Challenging the public–private divide

Maintaining the division between the private sphere and the public one is crucial to psychodynamic forms of intervention. It assists social workers to locate the focus of their interventions within the private domain. Without this division, the separation of individuals from their wider social context is not possible. Mainstream social workers' failure to address the fragmentation of social life, and their propensity to extract individuals from the broader social networks within which they are located, has been challenged by proponents of the liberationist school (Freire, 1972, 1974). They have utilised consciousness-raising to enable clients to make links between the personal and structural components of their lives. Additionally, they have interrogated the division between the private and public realms by examining the connections between these spheres. The popularising of the ensuing critique, and its potential to undermine the status quo, has worried mainstream practitioners and initiated a backlash that aimed to dismantle the questioning of social work theories and practices advanced by those in the liberationist school (see Phillips, 1993, 1994).

The capacity of liberationist-oriented social workers to expose inegalitarian social relations in the private domain has also been significant in raising awareness of issues linked to the emancipation of women and children as has occurred regarding domestic violence and sexual abuse. Feminist social action and scholarship have turned these private woes into social issues that require state intervention to respond to the specific needs of women and children who have been physically and/or sexually assaulted and change existing practices within statutory agencies (Mullender, 1997). Their endeavours have contributed not only to making shelters available for women and children who have been physically abused within their own homes by men who are known to them, but also to exposing the link between masculinity and domestic (Orme et al., 2000) and sexual (Dominelli, 1991a) violence. Without feminist inputs, traditional interventions on these matters have trivialised the nature of their complaints and have worked to disadvantage women.

At the same time, the issues of domestic and sexual violence have to be considered in more complex ways. To begin with, the category 'woman' has to be deconstructed and understood in its specific intricacies. So, for example, the realisation that the woman client who a (white) social worker is attempting to help comes from a particular ethnic grouping requires the practitioner to take on board in both the analyses and interventions the fact that the woman has specific ideas about her situation, the options she would like to explore and those that are possible for her, given that she is a woman from a particular ethnic group whose experience is contextualised by that reality (Mama, 1989; Wilson, 1993). This includes ensuring that the social worker addresses the *specific* needs of the woman in question rather than relying on stereotypes about set categories of women. The social worker also has to be aware of her own categorisations and identity. These too need to be deconstructed and reconstructed to facilitate sensitive anti-oppressive practice and enable comparisons across the different social divisions to occur.

Sensitive responses also involve the integration of theory and practice regarding any particular issue, for this enables the social worker to work more effectively with any client within the particularities of their situation. For example, if a social worker's support of a woman is not rooted in feminist principles of practice, it would be difficult for her to consider the impact that either the hegemonic definition of femininity or her position as a woman might have in her specific circumstances. And, operating according to stereotypical injunctions, she may end up imposing her views about what the woman should do with little regard for the woman client's own wishes. This can happen, for example, when a social worker advises a woman who has left a violent husband to go back to him because there is very little that she can do to help her. This response perpetuates an individualistic analysis and calls forth individualistic ways of addressing this woman's plight, even though the presence of many other women in a similar predicament has been well documented and is well known to social workers (Frankfort, 1972; Mullender, 1997).

In other words, individualising approaches fragment both the understandings of an individual's problems and the solutions proposed for dealing with it. They also disempower both the client and the worker by preventing the development of more creative and appropriate responses. These could focus on increasing the options available to a woman to transcend economic dependence on her partner, for example to offer the woman training to acquire jobs that offer more than the minimum wage, find appropriate childcare resources, and/or provide low-cost loans to extend her housing options.

Emancipatory and maintenance approaches to helping relations

The main basis on which emancipatory practice can be legitimated is that it prevents the waste of human potential that is caused by oppression and enables individuals and groups to realise their capacities to the full. This is both a moral and a practical position. The desire to treat all peoples as equals, regardless of their personal characteristics and standing in society, is a noble goal. Its realisation raises a number of ethical and moral considerations that need to be specified, for equality is a state of affairs that has to be worked for, that is, achieved rather than taken as a given. In social work, the adoption of a moral position based on equality is a stance that is shared, on some levels, by those endorsing either a liberationist viewpoint or a maintenance one. However, the meaning of equality and the basis on which it is secured vary for each approach.

In the maintenance school, equality is defined in formal terms. These aim to establish the procedures whereby individuals can approach organisations to gain their fair share of the social and material goods that are defined as available to them by virtue of their citizenship. These procedures also regulate relationships between individuals so that they can interact with one another within a framework of formal legal equality. For those in the liberationist school, equality is more than a formal requirement that focuses on access to social and physical resources through individualising procedures. For them, achieving equality requires that attention be paid to both processes and outcomes that are evident on both individual and collective levels. The liberationist school seeks to go beyond the individualisation of questions of access to resources and attempts to establish the parameters within which distributive forms of justice can prevail (see Rawls, 1973).

Consequently, the forms of justice that can be called upon to resolve a particular situation are not uncontested. There are considerable disagreements over the definition of justice, and what constitutes a just outcome. What is defined as just in one case may be considered unjust in another. Moreover, if the individuals involved feel disempowered, the process of securing justice in different arenas may be one that is in itself unjust, particularly if it causes 'innocent' individuals pain or suffering. An illustration of this is a nation's engagement in war in which civilians are killed even though they are not necessarily the ones whose behaviour initiated the war in the first place. Social workers may be called upon to work with both the initiators and the casualties of such processes, as recent events in Rwanda, Bosnia and Kosovo have confirmed.

The desire of its proponents to transcend distributive justice pits liberationist-oriented individuals against those advocating maintenance procedures. This sets the stage for conflict between them as one struggles for ascendancy over the other in a replication of the *power over* dynamics eschewed by those interested in emancipation. Part of the problem in engaging with this situation is that in defining their positions in diametrically opposed terms as part of an either/or logic, areas of commonality between them are overlooked. Yet, life is seldom conducted exclusively in polarised either/or terms. Both/and forms tend to co-exist in the messy realities of the worlds inhabited by individuals. Given their common goal of enhancing well-being, finding ways of compromising or bringing about convergence in their position would enable people to pursue social justice more effectively.

The backlash against anti-oppressive social work

Leading Establishment figures reject the idea that Western societies are oppressive because social relationships are structured around inegalitarian relations that exploit people who are deemed weaker or inferior (see Phillips, 1993, 1994; Pinker, 1993). They also support the premises underpinning the maintenance school of social work over those of the emancipation school. Their position has not assisted those promoting anti-oppressive practice to achieve their goals. In Britain, the struggle against anti-oppressive social work peaked in the summer of 1993, and focused primarily on anti-racist practice as promoted by the Central Council for Education and Training in Social Work (CCETSW) which had published Annex 5 in Paper 30 several years earlier (CCETSW, 1989). This annex outlined the importance of adopting an anti-racist stance in social work as part of the requirements of assessment in its qualifying award, the Diploma in Social Work (DipSW).

The backlash against initiatives aimed at overcoming structural inequalities, in countries such as the United States, has been more generalised and has affected intellectual thought in a wider range of subjects. In America, it became known as the 'cultural wars', in which anti-racism and feminism were labelled treacherous ideologies that unleashed the oppression of white men (Brooks, 1996). The placing of this debate in the cultural arena is important, for it is this site that represents what a society stands for. That is, it involves the values and norms whereby individual behaviour is normalised and judged. Culture in traditional anthropological texts has been presented as changeless, immutable and monolithic (see Radcliffe-Brown, 1952). In other words, these have acknowledged only one main way of defining culture – a patriarchal patriotic one – and cloaked it in unchanging garb. By ensuring that the dominant definitions of acceptable behaviours and norms acquire the clothes of culture, other competing claims are marginalised by these discourses. Consequently, other cultures are confined to being sub-cultures that either might be tolerated to some degree or deemed subversive elements that have to be destroyed before they impact on the broader society in a substantive manner. Within racist debates, culture has also been used to justify the separation of one group of people from another and to underpin what Barker (1981) has termed the 'new racism'.

The discourses of the 'new racism' turn cultural attributes into binary opposites which provide the basis for racialised discrimination. Islamophobia, which pits the tenets of the religion of Islam against those advocated by Christianity to argue that the latter are superior, is a current example of racialised oppression that takes culture, of which religious adherence is a part, as its core. Furthermore, a dominant group can use other social, economic and political resources to link religious exclusion with other forms of social exclusion and thereby marginalise the capacities of those they categorise as inferior to exercise their full rights as citizens – a case that is illustrated by the struggles for Catholic Irish autonomy in Northern Ireland. However, the struggle for ideological supremacy that it entails enables its advocates on either side of the ideological divide to dehumanise the 'other', cast them as enemies and perpetrate violent acts against those adopting another position.

The forms of racism perpetrated by the 'new racism' give less credence to biological traits as the basis of racial differentiation and instead emphasise cultural differences. Nonetheless, this continues to privilege the dominant culture over the others that can be found in any particular country. And, as Thatcherite discourses in 1980s' Britain have demonstrated, those advocating ideologies that do not endorse or legitimate the claims made under the 'new racism' have been (re)defined as 'the enemy within'. Conceptualising culture as an unchanging entity ignores the dynamics of culture which are rooted in interactions between and among people to provide a basis for its constant variation through change, renewal and affirmation.

Interactions between peoples result in their changing their cultures and being changed by them. It is not something that happens 'outside' them. They are participants in the processes of transformation that result in cultures as products of contested ideas and practices that yield patterns of continuity and discontinuity over time. The 'new racism' demands that the dominant culture be protected from change, particularly that emanating from those considered external and inferior to it. This view of culture is racist.

Policing cultural boundaries

Those who endorse racist ideologies with regards to culture engage in a series of activities that are aimed at patrolling cultural boundaries in order to retain their privileges. Sometimes this is overt, as in the case of the British National Party; at other times, it may be unintentional as happens in white feminist writing that excludes black feminists from its discourses (Bhavani, 1993). The end result of both is that inegalitarianism is reproduced through their interventions. Diagram 3.1 below indicates the range of behaviours that racist individuals resort to in policing their boundaries. These activities are aimed at intimidating those that are different, in the futile hope that in doing so they will ensure the survival of their own culture and protect it from change, particularly that which emanates from others who are considered inferior. Ironically, these responses indicate a failure on the part of those engaging in such coercive strategies to adjust to and cope with change, usually driven by macro-level forces that have rendered ineffective their previous accommodation to life events. Thus, they strike out of their own fears and uncertainties to impose them on others in the hope that they will find security and thereby prevail.

Diagram 3.1 indicates the range of strategies that those engaged in maintaining a racist hegemonic position utilise to reproduce *power over* relations, and against which subordinated individuals and groups can react according to acceptance, accommodationist and rejectionist responses.

Power over relations are central to racist ideological constructs and their proponents indulge in a number of activities that will create a climate of fear amongst those they refuse to admit into their midst so as to keep themselves on top. I have called the power relations operating along the 'race' dimension, 'racialised power relations'. These are aimed at patrolling racialised boundaries and constitute

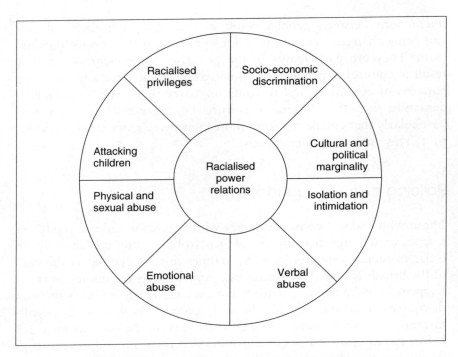

Diagram 3.1 Controlling racialised relations

a politicisation of 'race'. In the West, this revolves around a binary dyad that endorses white supremacy, that is, power is used to configure white people as the privileged group. Maintaining racialised privileges involves the adherents of racialised power relations in using various terrorising tactics, ranging from verbal to physical abuse and including emotional and sexual violence, to isolate and intimidate their targets and exclude them from socio-economic and political resources. Children are also subjected to attacks that aim to keep them and their parents in their place. Controlling racialised boundaries through acts that demean and imperil others both relies upon and is an expression of *power over* dynamics.

Racist individuals expect to privilege their own position and will attack adults and children to ensure their own survival, devising new strategies as required. Every aspect of life is subjected to the tyrannical regime that is required to sustain racialised power relations. The history of black–white relations in much of the Western world is littered with systemic examples of such treatment – black slavery and apartheid being two of the most horrific ones (see Fryer, 1984; Small,

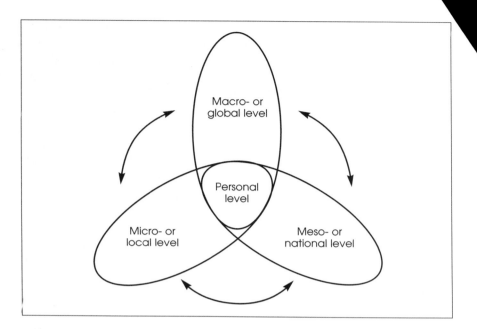

Diagram 3.2 Interconnected levels of interaction

1994; Gilroy, 1995). Once these tactics become systematised and generalised, we are no longer dealing with racist individuals, but racist institutions and systems. These may be local, national or international in scope, and operate at macro-, meso-, and micro-levels as indicated in Diagram 3.2.

Taking an anti-oppressive position means standing against racialised privileging and becoming involved in bringing about the demise of racialised power relations. This is unlikely to be either easy or straightforward, as those who have a lot to lose by allowing such developments to proceed will attempt to resist the changes that will be required to bring about this state of affairs. They will attempt to impede progress at all points, but are most likely to make the local community the site of their most intense interventions. In promoting their goals, they will establish clear boundaries between the local, national and international domains and will maintain their conceptual separation so as to target their activities more effectively. This will also ensure that the interdependency which exists between these levels remains masked, and facilitate the continued scapegoating of black people for macro-level changes that have disempowered white individuals within the localities they both

th groups have been disenfranchised by macro-level
ing upon local communities and could provide grounds
..s and alliances across racial divides remains invisible. To
..nter-racial action to take place, both groups need to share an
..alysis of social change that does not blame individuals for structural
weaknesses. Such a development is not likely to bear fruit as long as they
define the relationship between them purely in interpersonal terms.

Those struggling to reverse the agenda set by those promoting anti-
oppressive practice have ignored the impact of global forces upon local
developments. These have assisted in the intensification of processes
that promote various forms of inequality and individual culpability, as
many social problems are the outcome of macro-level trends. For
example, the loss of highly paid manufacturing posts for white men in
the West has been the result of capitalists' reorganisation of their
activities on a global basis to improve their capacity to extract more
profits from their ventures by locating them overseas (Wichterich,
2000). The decline of blue-collar jobs for men has little to do with the
limited gains that white women and black people have made in the
employment market. They are the outcome of decisions made by those
(usually wealthy white men) running multinational corporations and
government programmes in the countries involved (Wichterich, 2000).
The massive worldwide movements of workers are part of this. From
the privileging of white businessmen to the derogation of asylum
seekers who risk all to take up lowly paid posts in Western countries,
racialised and gendered class relations are at play.

Poverty is another social ill that has been aggravated by the loss of
highly paid, full-time posts. Both men and women lose out in these
trends. Women, as those employed primarily in a casual, part-time
capacity in the service sector, have also been losers through predatory
employment practices endorsed by globalised corporations, as reflected
locally through low-paid employment opportunities, the contract
culture, privatisation of public provisions and downsizing in both
public and private sectors. Under these employment conditions,
women's long-term interests such as acquiring pensions that cover
their needs in old age or their demands for financial independence
throughout the life-cycle are not taken into account. Consequently,
poverty impacts largely on women and children who make up the bulk
of those who are poor (UNDP, 1998) in both the short and long term.
Women are in the losing stakes because low pay today means little
capacity to purchase financial security for tomorrow. And children miss
the boat because the legacy of growing up poor lasts a lifetime.

Poverty eradication or alleviation schemes have been supported by large numbers of people in a range of countries. International organisations such as the UN are seeking to eradicate poverty in the near future. This aim has been considered achievable because people believe that it is possible to improve the position of poor people throughout the world, if all countries, whether recipients of aid or its donors, work together to realise this goal (UNDP, 1998). Without the eradication of poverty on a worldwide basis, it becomes impossible for all peoples to realise their human rights and participate effectively in the social, political and economic life of the country in which they live. Poverty alleviation measures are issues of concern to all peoples and constitute part of the global struggle against oppression.

Social workers have an important role to play in bringing this objective to fruition. If social workers are to have ethical responses to women and children, they cannot ignore poverty or blame being in this predicament on the individuals so affected without also understanding the problem as a systemic way of denying people access to social resources. Social workers have a key role to play in promoting discourses that promote social justice at the local, national and international levels and in taking action that supports poor people in achieving this goal. Those who define such questions as political ones that lie beyond the remit of social work increase the likelihood of little being done to change the plight of poor people. As a result, instead of advocating on their behalf, professional social workers will be called upon primarily to pick up the pieces and offer 'band-aid' solutions to their predicament (Bolger et al., 1981). And the structural causes of their difficulties will continue to be neglected. Fortunately, international social work organisations such as the International Association of Schools of Social Work and the International Federation of Social Workers have begun to mobilise the profession around structural issues, bringing these into policymaking discussions within the UN and its agencies.

Conclusions

Anti-oppressive practice seeks to eliminate oppression within professional practice as well as contribute to its eradication within the broader society. However, both of these aims are deeply contested ones. They are not shared by all professional colleagues or by all their fellow citizens. Moreover, even if all social workers were to agree with these objectives, the processes whereby these are to be achieved and the means to realise them would prove controversial and the participants would have to deal with these. Being clear about their principles, value base and ethical orientation will help individual practitioners in the decision-making processes about where and how they will direct their work. Endorsing social justice and human rights as the basis for their response is central to emancipatory forms of social work, of which anti-oppressive practice is one. And they need to deal with this issue as an integral part of their job, not during their leisure time.

The implementation of these goals is further problematised because anti-oppressive practice has to be anti-oppressive in all its dimensions – inputs, processes and outcomes – if it is to break with patterns of oppression in which one group of oppressors is simply replaced by another. Doing so places client agency as a central feature in anti-oppressive practice and has the impact of challenging expert knowledges and ways of working and promoting egalitarian partnerships that draw upon power-sharing and resource reallocation to foster equality between the two parties.

Moreover, anti-oppressive approaches have to address simultaneously the local, national and international levels. In addressing the needs of individuals, groups and communities, social workers will have to respond on a holistic basis that takes account of the different contexts in which they and their clients are embedded. Their interventions will have to focus on inputs, processes and outcomes in their interactions with each other as they negotiate over the plan of action that will form the centrepiece of their intervention. And they will have to beware of the potential for (re)producing 'false equality traps', where the desire to promote equality leads practitioners to assume that both they and their clients are at the same starting point in life's journey. These difficulties make the anti-oppressive project a complex and difficult one, but one that I argue is worth doing.

Chapter 4

Anti-Oppressive
Practice in Action
Working with Individuals

Introduction

To successfully address issues of oppression, anti-oppressive interventions have to encompass social relations at the personal, organisational and cultural levels, although a social worker may concentrate a particular involvement primarily on one of these. Social workers tend to work with individuals and include others when it seems necessary. Thus, securing individual change by working with individuals in therapeutic relationships has been a key aspect of practice. Traditionalists or proponents of the maintenance school of social work have worked with individuals in the hopes of getting them to adopt accepted social norms, and pathologising them when their endeavours fail.

Practitioners who follow emancipatory approaches seek to achieve anti-oppressive practice by focusing on the specifics of a situation in a holistic manner and mediating between its personal and structural components. To obtain this impact, social workers and their clients develop clear goals to pursue and use networking and negotiation techniques to secure change. Change usually occurs at the micro-level where interpersonal relationships are the target of the intervention(s).

But sometimes success in these requires change at either meso- or macro-levels or both. For example, if poverty is causing personal hardship, institutional (meso-level) and/or societal (macro-level) changes may be required alongside endeavours aimed at helping the individual to control its deleterious effect on his or her life. Profound movement in one of these three spheres may also produce changes in the others as they are all interconnected.

There are a number of therapeutic approaches that can be used in working with individuals, ranging from Rogerian counselling to feminist therapy. Each has its own theory and forms of practice which can be explored by the reader in the relevant literature as I will not be going into their details here. Instead, I focus on the dynamics that shape therapeutic relationships between professionals and their clients. In therapeutic interventions, the prime, although not only, focal point of the relationship is the interpersonal one. White (1993) argues that therapists working in one-to-one relationships draw on narratives that either draw upon or seek to resist dominant discourses to make sense of clients' experiences. In working with individuals in a therapeutic way, the anti-oppressive social workers' task is to open discursive spaces in which clients can develop their own interpretive story, that is, one that gives meaning to their experiences, and to understand how dominant discourses operate to suppress this story. In other words, it is about validating the clients' entitlement to explain their lives in their own ways and in doing so assist in their empowerment. This is in contrast to traditional therapy which attempts to 'reframe' the client's story in ways that assimilate it into the dominant discourses (White and Epston, 1990). That is, therapy becomes a means whereby deviant people can be made normal (Parsons, 1951). The normalising role of traditional therapy endorses the status quo and confirms the client as the source of the problem (White, 1993). In contrast, resisting the dominant discourses involves the unmasking of the power relations of normalisation and the telling of other stories that are more consistent with clients' lived experiences. Engaging in the validation of alternative stories enables clients to separate themselves from the totalising discourses that subjugate their experiences. According to White (1993), resistance is a legitimate goal of a therapy that seeks to empower clients.

I would argue that the ensuing action has to be further contextualised so that it encompasses more than the two people directly caught up in the therapeutic relationship. The intervention may involve only the practitioner and the client concerned, or a range of other people in networks or institutions that are relevant in a particular case. And they too have to be included within the unmasking of the power relationships that prioritise some discourses over others, because as significant others, they also have a role to play in legitimating or suppressing the story as the client wishes it to unfold. In an anti-oppressive situation, both the practitioner and the client would be fully engaged in making an assessment of the specifics of these contexts and the others who are meaningful in their lives. And they would both locate themselves within the contexts that apply to each of them in the specifics of the work they do together.

Intervening on a holistic basis includes paying attention to the power relations which are operating in any given interaction between professional worker(s), service user(s) and meaningful others. With regards to their own therapeutic position, their starting point is that power relations in the client–worker relationship are complex, but negotiated between the practitioner and the person asking for a service within particular social contexts. In other words, the relationship between them is mediated by the broader power relations and social structures within which they are embedded. Both parties to the interaction exercise agency within the constraints that impinge upon them individually and collectively. Consequently, the worker is not totally powerful and the client is not totally powerless. In this way, as Nancy Hartsock argues with regards to women:

> [They] build an account of the world as seen from the margins, an account that can expose the falseness of the view from the top and can transform the margins as well as the center. (Hartsock, 1990, p. 171)

Power relations are encounters in which power is enacted through a multifaceted set of negotiations that yield particular results. These are unstable in that any outcome can be challenged and renegotiated at any time if one party disagrees with the end result. Professional interactions are marked by a series of compromises that take into account a number of other considerations:

- the practitioner's opinions;
- the client's views and responses;
- the legal remit for the work they do together;
- the resources available for meeting a given need;

- their relative responsibilities vis-à-vis each other;

- the use of professional discretion;

- and the degree of ambiguity about the (de)merits of the range of options available for enactment.

Being clear about these possibilities and who pays the price for going down one road rather than another are important aspects of the decision-making processes for the practitioner to consider when working within an anti-oppressive practice framework.

Addressing process issues is an integral aspect of anti-oppressive practice. If its precepts are to be followed in a therapeutic or one-to-one relationship, the process within which the interaction between the client and the worker takes place has to espouse egalitarian ideals in how it is conducted as well as through its intended outcomes. The process between them is interactive. That is, it involves relationships which both of them create and recreate through the work they do together in a context in which the growth of globalisation, managerialism and competence-based approaches to social care, amongst other forces, impact upon the work they do together (Dominelli and Hoogvelt, 1996). The naming of these forces by the individuals concerned depends on their social position, theoretical sophistication, personal priorities, ideological orientation, personal attributes and a range of other factors specific to them. These are numerous and not always easily accessible, so individuals select those that are important to them and make sense to them from within their own framework of knowing. Their experiences of life are used to understand what is unknown and bring it into the realm of conscious action. According to White (1993), dominant discourses can hinder such knowing because knowledge is couched within socially acceptable narratives, and so some of the client's story may remain unarticulated – sensed rather than spoken – because that particular narrative is outside the realm of the dominant discourse.

In this chapter, I use case study materials to explore how anti-oppressive practitioners work at the individual level to transcend oppression and promote empowerment. Although a particular social worker may focus on a one-to-one relationship with a client, their interaction occurs within a broader societal and organisational context which cannot be ignored, even if it is not directly acted upon. The delivery of an appropriate service to an individual may also require that a number of practitioners work carefully together within the context of a multidisciplinary team. I also consider the knowledge, skills and values which make such work possible in the market-driven context within which social workers currently operate.

Working with individuals in anti-oppressive ways

Social work has long debated the extent to which it is responsible for initiating structural changes as well as individual ones. In recent times, radical social work which highlighted class dynamics à la Corrigan and Leonard (1978) has been castigated for concerning itself virtually exclusively with structural change. Jan Fook (1993) has argued that radical social work can be undertaken with individuals, and calls it 'radical casework'. Other feminist authors concur with Fook, although earlier work has located the individual more specifically in his or her social context (Chaplin, 1988) and insisted that the personal can be linked to the structural components of change. Anti-oppressive practice endorses the view that individual behaviour can be changed to a substantial degree. However, anti-oppressive practice departs from traditional professional approaches to individual change, in that the social context is addressed holistically to encompass the personal, organisational and cultural dimensions of a person's life. This looks at the relationships between these three spheres and examines the interconnections between them. In identifying these, anti-oppressive practitioners break down rigidities in the boundaries between the public and private domains. The resultant blurring of the borders between them inverts the established power relations to redefine what might be deemed a private trouble to be dealt with by an individual as a public one that requires a range of other interventions included in social policies in order to help one person (Dominelli and McLeod, 1989).

Feminist action regarding domestic and sexual violence is a classic example of this process. Here, to help many individual women experiencing the same problems, women have come together in self-help groups to mount a critique of the social relations that have underpinned and sanctioned the acceptability of such behaviour by individual men, usually in the privacy of the home, and, in the course of speaking out about the pain experienced by individual women, a private trouble was redefined as a social one (Frankfort, 1972). Feminists then created alternative services, based on this understanding of the situation, to empower women and provided resources developed and controlled by women who had been in these situations (Dominelli and McLeod, 1989; Horley, 1990; Mullender, 1997). Their critique has also encompassed the failure of other agencies, including the police, probation officers and the criminal justice system more generally, to cater for the needs of abused women. Hence, feminists have called for changes in the law, the treatment of women by mainstream agencies, particularly the police, the judicial system and social services (Mullender, 1997), and in the hegemonic definition of masculinity (Dominelli, 1991). The failure of gender relations, based on hegemonic masculinity, to meet the needs of men (Dominelli and McLeod, 1989), women (Dworkin, 1981) or children (Mullender and Morley, 1994) was highlighted and fundamental changes in the relationships between men and men, men and women, adults and children were also demanded (Dominelli and McLeod, 1989; Dominelli, 2002).

Anti-oppressive practice also emphasises understanding identity formation as a dynamic process and places its impact on human behaviours at the heart of professional social work interventions for both the practitioner and the client. An individual's identity is a state of being that is constantly in the making through interpersonal inter-actions. Identity is formed through processes that are rooted in a person's sense of self, or who he or she is or wants to be, and draws upon group or collective identities, particularly as these are depicted in their cultural components, using the term 'culture' in its broadest sense to indicate that it refers to those ingredients that are socially used to define or specify a way of life or being.

Although the processes of identity formation are in constant flux, a person's identity consists of both continuities and discontinuities that are both enacted within and extracted from his or her environment, including his or her cultural domain. The continuous aspects of this are those values, norms, knowledges and traditions that are institution-alised to ensure their survival across time and space. These may also be safeguarded by being passed down from generation to generation, often through word of mouth and through socialisation processes which are both institutionalised and individually oriented within the collective setting of a particular group. These continuities enable practitioners to clarify an individual's claim to belonging to a specific group or culture. Continuities are those cultural dimensions that individuals draw upon when they say, 'I am a...'. They aim to tell a story of being that defines the participants as they wish to see themselves existing across time and space.

Continuities and discontinuities in identity formation

However, these continuities have to be understood as selective and partial as well as being constantly contested and/or (re)produced in interactions with others through specific discourses, including those from the same group. Individuals choose which elements they will emphasise and which they will ignore in any particular encounter, depending on their reading of the situation, their understanding of the other person(s) relating to them and what they hope to achieve through their interaction with others. As in other relationships, the selection of information to be exchanged in a social work encounter will be shaped by these dynamics. What is revealed may also change as the relationship between them develops, or it may follow the same broad outline evident in the initial encounter. Identity is, therefore, socially constructed in and through social interactions with others.

Contestation provides the grounds on which continuities become transformed into new adaptions, are reaffirmed as continuities or become discontinuities. Discontinuities in the composition of an individual or group's cultural traditions constitute cultural capital that signifies the distance that an individual or group seeks to establish between themselves and what has previously been taken to *represent* them. Discontinuities indicate that change is taking place in an identity construct. Over time, discontinuities may become accepted enough to reach stability and become continuities until these are altered through further interactions. Although discontinuities occur within interactive processes, these changes may be self-initiated or imposed by others who exercise *power over* relations that may be reinforced through systems of reward (punishment) or socialisation processes. Individuals exercise agency when choosing their relationship to the continuities and discontinuities that exist in their particular culture(s) in configuring their own identity in their interactions with others.

Taking identity issues into account is an important aspect of working with individuals because these are integral to a person's sense of self. Relating to the particular person in their own terms is important if practitioners are not to use stereotypes to oppress individuals by treating them as set categories, thereby endorsing a pathological view of their skills and potential. It also has to be addressed if the stereotype has been internalised by the client. Anti-oppressive practice requires the practitioner to consider the individual's strengths and weaknesses as identified by *both* of them and ensure that identity issues pertaining to both the worker and the client are addressed in any intervention. For example, identity issues along the 'race'/ethnicity dimension can be racialised within the discursive space occupied by a worker from a dominant ethnic group working with a client from an ethnic minority one to underpin oppressive relations between them (Kadushin, 1972).

Racialised relations create and reproduce binary dyads containing both a dominant and a subordinate member. Racialised relations also interact with other sources of difference between the worker and client to further complicate whatever other oppressive relations are being enacted. Racialised identities are likely to undermine attempts to establish an anti-racist working relationship between them, if the worker does not appreciate that being a member of the dominant group will impact upon that relationship. They do so by reinforcing hegemonic value systems and ways of knowing and viewing the world, particularly at the level of taken-for-granted assumptions. If these presuppose superiority, they are crucial in reproducing relations of domination which cast an ethnic minority client as inferior. Once this occurs, it further disadvantages the client, who then has to work very hard to establish a position of equality or achieve a lessening of the power differentials that accompany an anti-oppressive approach to structuring relations between them. Racialised relationships are constantly being structured or created and recreated through personal interactions, so that dealing with oppression is not a simple one-off event that is dealt with and then forgotten, as is suggested below by Janice, a white practitioner of English descent who is based in a local authority that has participated in an anti-racism awareness training programme.

■ *Case study*

I attended an anti-racist training course and expected to find that at the end of it, I would be able to work with black people without diffi-culty. I thought I would learn about black culture and traditions, and that I would know what to do when I worked with black clients. Instead, I found that although I became more aware of the language that I used and how this could be racist, I did not gain in confidence on how to be a better anti-racist practitioner. I felt even less able to work with black people after the course than before it. I now avoid working with black clients whenever I can and often think that I'd be better off if I'd given it (the course) a miss.

Janice's comments reveal that she conceptualises identity as a fixed, non-changing entity that can be 'acquired' through intellectual effort on her part. Her failure to appreciate its fluid, interactive nature frustrates her and paralyses her capacity to either think her way through her predicament or take action to get beyond it. As a result, she is not even able to conceive of the idea that she can find out about a particular black client's culture, if that is relevant to the work she is undertaking, by asking her or him about it. In other words, even basic social work skills such as collecting information about a client by asking questions or taking a life history recede from her repertoire of practice. But her predicament indicates how she has been unable to get out of the dominant discourses which essentialise 'race' and culture as fixed and totalising entities. Janice would have to learn how to deconstruct this narrative to unmask how the discourse of hegemonic power relations is implicit in the way that she *understands* the problem that she has to deal with.

If they do not engage in deconstructing their own understandings and ways of conceptualising the world, social workers such as Janice are reluctant to explicitly address identity issues for fear of upsetting the other person, being thought of as ignorant and lacking in understanding and empathy, and being incapable of addressing the difficult complexities that are embedded within identity considerations. Consequently, the significance of identity in social work relationships is rarely openly discussed or commented upon by either worker or client, even when the issue is at the forefront of their thinking about their relationship.

The work entailed in structuring relationships and setting the boundaries within which professional interactions occur may be invisible to the participants as they focus their energies on other aspects of their relationship such as meeting practical needs. However, not exploring underlying identity dynamics may mean that the actors are unable to reach the goals they have set. Operating within the contexts of both public and professional questioning of how to work appropriately with black and ethnic minority individuals, families or groups, (white) social workers who struggle to deal with the ambiguities surrounding their position can end up relying on stereotypes (even well-intentioned ones) which reduce their capacity to critically engage with clients from backgrounds other than their own. This has happened on several well-publicised occasions regarding the death of black children in local government care. For example, in the case of Jasmine Beckford in Britain during the 1980s, a white social worker failed to insist on seeing a little black girl who was being abused by her carers on the grounds that she did not want to unduly intrude into black family relationships (see Blom-Cooper, 1986).

As a result, instead of demonstrating their ability to show acceptance of the other person while remaining critical of their behaviour, (white) practitioners become disempowered and unable to respond appropriately to the situation they are located within. In serious child protection cases, such paralysis may cost a black or ethnic minority child his or her life. And, although the particular social worker concerned might be castigated for her inaction, dismissed from her job, and the local authority's procedures tightened up, this has not prevented similar tragedies from reoccurring. Subsequent to Jasmine Beckford, the inquiry that followed it, and the changes in interagency working and other procedures in the child protection system, the deaths of Tyra Henry later in the 1980s and Anna Climbié more recently have demonstrated that white professionals including social workers continue to fail black children and are unable to work comfortably with issues of 'race' in difficult situations.

In Janice's case, a more empowering approach to her predicament would have been for the local authority to address her specific needs and find out how to respond to these more effectively than simply sending her on a general anti-racist course. In the interview, Janice revealed that a crucial reason why she wanted to attend the course was that she felt uncomfortable with 'being a white person from the dominant ethnic group', but this issue was never considered in either the course or the supervision sessions that she had to debrief her afterwards. Neither did she see herself as being all-powerful or not requiring support. Thus, her worries, her understanding of both her own identity or that of others and how the two intermeshed with each other were left to one side to cause her constant anxiety and fear. Fear that she would do the wrong thing when she did not want to was uppermost in her thinking, but she lacked the skills for dealing with it and was unable to identify and seek appropriate help.

Janice's story indicates how identity issues, including the practitioners' own, impact upon their understanding of themselves and others and how their absence from the agenda of explicit matters to be addressed impacts upon their work across racial divides. These practitioner concerns should be at the forefront of anti-racist training. Janice's failure to see herself as an all-powerful practitioner was a realistic appraisal of her position in some respects, but it was a state of being that had to be overtly addressed if she were to free herself of the paralysis she felt in relating to black clients. Working to respond to her own unmet needs and thereby empower herself as an individual would have helped Janice to recognise the messiness of answers to the questions 'Who am I?' and 'How does this impact upon my work with others?' It would have also facilitated her ability to move away from stereotypical responses to her own identity and that of black people, and given her confidence to look more reflexively upon her own identity (Bourdieu and Wacquant, 1992). To respond to these shortcomings – which she was aware of – would have required an open commitment to helping her understand herself alongside supportive resourcing from her employers. Had this happened, she might have felt strong enough to use her skills in taking life histories to find out in more specific and relevant detail the importance of culture and identity to the people with whom she intended to work.

This, alongside her deeper understanding of the dynamics of racism included in and through language which she obtained from the course, would have enabled her to relate more appropriately at the inter-personal level with the black people on her caseload. The issue of the lack of resources geared specifically to meet the needs of black people requiring services from her office would have had to be tackled through other measures aimed at dealing with its structural com-ponents, that is, institutional and cultural racism. An educational course can raise awareness of the issues but, on its own, it cannot deal with structural inequalities.

With regards to the client at the receiving end of these dynamics, if the practitioner imposes *power over* relations that exclude the client from the decision-making processes or delivers an unsatisfactory service, the client is initially without institutional backing for challenging an inadequate response to his or her position. Consequently, he or she has primarily his or her own personal resources to draw upon in resisting the professional's structuring of a given event in a particular way (Dominelli and Gollins, 1997). If the client lodges a formal complaint against the practitioner, institutional and legal resources may subsequently be brought into the frame. But they may not be used to empower the client by making resources available to him or her in order to pursue the claim. They are more likely to be ranged against him or her in defense of the practitioner's intervention. Until some sort of parity is reached in their interaction, the worker will not hear the client voice or acknowledge client agency; and is therefore likely to continue enacting oppressive behaviours and attitudes that (re)enforce the client's status as a passive and dependent recipient of professional expertise.

Endorsing client agency in practice

Providing individual clients with adequate resourcing to pursue their claims, acknowledging their agency and validating their own knowledge base as a source of expertise, despite institutional and legislative powers that favour the professional, is crucial to anti-oppressive practice. The worker has to recognise the interactive nature of the process in which he or she is engaged if the client is to work less hard at being heard. Clients cannot be treated as mere objects who simply respond passively to professional subjectivities.

When a practitioner acknowledges a client's agency, the capacity to oppress becomes a matter that is considered explicitly and as a central part of the intervention process. Thus, difference, rather than being ignored, is considered specifically in terms of its impact on the interaction. Difference becomes a key marker of identity attributes in interpersonal relationships. Ways of valuing and celebrating these have to be explicitly considered and negotiated, if differences are not to be treated as tokenistic attributes belonging to the 'other'. Focusing on agency and strengths rather than passivity and weaknesses to engage in a change-oriented relationship is one way of achieving this objective in an empowering manner. Reaching this objective also requires thoroughly involving the client in making decisions about the issues to be considered and how this will be done.

From the client's point of view, agency is a state that he or she enacts when taking decisions about exercising control over his or her own life and asserting his or her capacity to act as a subject. Acting in ways that acknowledge the client's potential to exercise agency requires an understanding of power relations and how power operates in subtle, covert and overt ways in a client–worker relationship. Conceptualising encounters as involving both parties as subjects who exercise agency is particularly relevant in anti-oppressive practice. Here, the professional recognises his or her greater contextual power and engages in power-sharing endeavours aimed at empowering the client by reducing power differentials between them. This response is more likely to impact on the interpersonal relations between them than on the broader social structures. However, practitioners can influence these to some degree by using their role as gatekeepers of social and material resources to alleviate client hardship, instead of curtailing their aspirations, and bringing these to public attention. In other words, identifying social shortcomings occurs as a result of individual interventions.

Clients' willingness to explore their decision-making capacities with practitioners cannot be assumed. So a white social worker who asks a black person whether or not they want a black worker to work with them cannot treat the matter as if it has been predetermined, that is, that the client does not have a choice and must have a black worker. At the same time, the issue cannot be left as simply a matter of personal preference. In acknowledging the right of a black client to choose a worker on ethnic lines, a white practitioner cannot let the issue of racism pass without sensitively considering the relevance of the unequal power relations that being embedded in racialised contexts reproduces.

For example, the impact of personal racism including internalised racism on a client's decision, and institutional and cultural racism expressed through the roles that the white agency and the white worker play in signalling that certain types of choice are preferable to others, has to be examined. This is because the value that white agency personnel place on the work done by black practitioners and the emphasis they give to meeting the needs of black clients become important factors in 'permitting' certain kinds of choices and 'disallowing' others. A client can pick up both verbal and non-verbal cues of validation and worth in reaching a decision that seems appropriate to that context and interaction. The practitioner who does not engage in conscious endeavours to become aware of these dynamics will miss them, and engage in totalising discourses to the detriment of his or her practice and the client's options.

A client will have good reasons for either accepting or rejecting ethnic matching. So, the black client's motivation in requesting a particular worker needs to be considered in terms of that particular situation. The response given to questions probing a specific choice may indicate that it is simply a matter of preference, part of a strategy aimed at safeguarding his or her position in a black community, or an attempt to play the game in the terms posited by the agency. The worker should be aware of and sensitive to racism as an issue *that applies (or not) to that particular situation*. Its relevance is a matter for discussion and deliberation, not of assumption. For instance, if an Asian woman chooses someone outside her ethnic group to discuss a problematic issue which involves family and community members, the worker should not assume that the choice is made because she fears that others in the community might find out about her requests for assistance and bring shame upon her and her family. Nor should the practitioner conclude that the client has internalised dominant racist views about black workers' abilities to offer a first-rate service.

The reasons that apply should be explored with the client concerned, and appropriate action should follow discussions about why
this particular woman has sought help in the way she has done. If internalised racism has been the basis for her choice, the worker should not
assume that client deficiencies provide the explanation. Rather, further
exploration may reveal that it is the agency's overt and covert racist
messages to clients that are responsible and these have to be tackled.
Equally, the worker's and agency's motivations in offering the client a
choice have to be transparent. Is choice being used to mask institutional racism? Could it be the failure of white workers and their agency
to work in anti-racist ways that causes the 'dumping' of responsibility
for dealing with racism upon black people? Or is it a genuine attempt
at working in an anti-oppressive manner?

Power relations in helping relationships

Whilst I have used racism as the vehicle for exploring the power
dynamics involved in the potentially oppressive dimensions of the
worker–client relationships above, similar *power relations* apply with
regard to other social divisions rooted in identity. This is because
agency and negotiated interactions are central dynamics in the power
relations that are enacted between those involved in working together.
Within the repertoire of top-down power relations involving identity-
based social divisions such as 'race', gender, class, disability, age, and
sexual orientation, client agency is often submerged under the cloak of
dependency. That is, traditional professional framings of worker–client
interactions tend to assume that the client is passive and dependent – a
person who must be helped by the professional using his or her knowledge, skills and goodwill. The presumption that the person asking
for assistance is 'defective' in some way percolates this configuration of
the person and sets the context for *power over* dynamics to be
(re)produced rather than egalitarian ones. As a result, dominant
discourses become reinforced rather than undermined.

As I argue below, such attitudes are particularly evident in
responses to people with disabilities who are cast as being dependent
on able-bodied people, women who are deemed to be dependent on
men, children who are dependent on adults, and older people who are
assumed to be dependent on younger relatives. In all these cases,
expectations about dependency structure the interpersonal relationships between them in ways that presume that the 'dependent' person

is incapable of making decisions for him or herself and is in need of help, that is, can arbitrarily or stereotypically be deprived of control over their own lives in a paternalistic assessment of doing so for his or her 'own good'. This conceptualisation of dependency promotes relations of domination rather than facilitating individual empowerment, and in the view of Memmi (1984) does a disservice to interdependency which acknowledges that a relationship of dependency that is not disempowering of the other person is one that involves both parties as mutual beneficiaries.

Disempowerment through paternalistic attitudes that inform social interactions with disabled people is an illustration of *power over* relations. The discourses that these social relations rely upon have been resisted by disabled people who have challenged the traditionalist approach to dependency that is favoured by the professionals working with them. This approach they term the 'medical model of intervention' and argue that it disempowers disabled clients (Oliver, 1990) because professionals make decisions *on behalf of rather than with* disabled persons. They have also denounced these interventions as patronising and disempowering. Moreover, in paternalistic interactions, disabled people are denied direct access to resources, for these are mediated through professionals who operate as gatekeepers. As marginalised people, they are excluded not only from accessing social, economic and political resources, but also from defining what these should be and how they should be made available to them. In denying disabled people full citizenship rights and a real say in matters that directly affect them, these processes marginalise them. In other words, society simply tolerates them rather than accepting them as full members and active citizens. Exclusion is a process and a state of being that disabled people share with other marginalised groups. The invocation of exclusionary dynamics by more powerful others becomes a mechanism for restricting disabled people's participation in wider social processes on the basis of who they are, that is, according to attributes associated with identity, and is experienced by other oppressed groups.

Instead, disabled people posit the social model of disability which locates the difficulties that they encounter in the way that social relations are organised (Barnes and Oliver, 1998). So they refer to the disabling society which includes disabling organisations or environments and individuals that prevent disabled people from exercising agency by minimising their capacity to make decisions and take action for themselves. Although critical of the dominant society, the disability movement, like other liberationist movements, has reflected dominant ideologies within its own organisation. For example, the disability movement of the 1990s had a tendency to present disabled people as a homogeneous group. But white women (Morris, 1991; Wendell, 1996), black women (Begum, 1992; Begum et al., 1993) and others have identified this shortcoming and begun to theorise differentiation amongst disabled people. In their critiques, they espouse forms of practice that recognise that disability is intersected by class, 'race', gender, age, sexual orientation and other social divisions which have to be incorporated into relationships and the analyses of these if individuals are to be responded to as whole beings. At the same time as highlighting difference, however, they have also argued that the commonalities of being a disabled person in a disabling society should not be forgotten (Wendell, 1996).

Furthermore, disabled women have included process issues, that is, how relationships are enacted, as a critical dimension that has to be addressed in the client–worker relationships involving disabled people (Wendell, 1996). In paying attention to processes, respecting the person, a traditional social work value (Biesteck, 1961), cannot be left simply as intellectual knowledge held by the practitioner. This is because the practice of professionals who stick to that level only will do no more than show a tokenistic appreciation of the matters to be addressed. Acting along tokenistic lines lays the basis for an experience of exclusion that the client working with them will feel, experience and *know*, even if they do not verbalise it at the time that it happens. Anti-oppressive practice is about integrating knowledge that is held in the head, with feelings one has in one's heart and the skills that one has to implement one's ideals, or realise one's professional aspirations (Dominelli, 1994). That is, there is a unity between the hands, head and heart, or skills in practice, intellect and emotions – what I have called the 'PIE' component of anti-oppressive practice. If a practitioner does not understand its complexities, is not committed to working as an anti-oppressive professional at all these levels, and is incapable of realising these interlinkages in their relationships with clients, their interventions will be experienced as oppressive. Anti-oppressive practice is about a dialectical relationship between feeling, thinking, and acting in empowering ways, and reflecting upon the outcomes to evaluate the achievement of its aim of empowering people.

Part of the key to success in these endeavours is the social workers' capacity to empathise (Egan, 1998) effectively with the client. This means engaging with the client in such a way that, for a moment, the practitioner virtually is the client. At this level, the practitioner can draw on bonds of solidarity, an acceptance of humanity for what it is and link it to the desire for social justice. Once an empathetic connection is made and understandings of the complexities of the situation are realised, the practitioner will be moved to action, often tinged with anger at the injustice of a client's predicament. If channelled appropriately, this anger provides the basis for critiquing a social order that creates such injustices in the first place, without losing track of the knowledge that through his or her behaviour the client has also had a role in producing the particular situation he or she is embedded within. In other words, the personal and the structural are connected and can be understood as such by both practitioner and client. For the social worker, this becomes a defining moment in which he or she begins to appreciate the importance of contextualised practice and acting holistically when engaging in processes of change at the personal, institutional and cultural levels, even if he or she chooses to focus primarily on one aspect of these. The implications of this approach for practice are explored in the following vignette.

■ *Case Study*

Carole is a 15-year-old young woman of Afro-Caribbean descent living in Britain. She attends a large comprehensive school in a small city. She is one of three young women who have come out as lesbian. She and her white English partner, Mandy, were caught kissing in the school grounds and distressed several pupils who saw them embracing each other. The headteacher, an older (white) Englishman who had been in the profession for over two decades, called an Education Welfare Officer to help deal with the issues that Carole and Mandy presented. He insisted that whatever Carole and Mandy did outside the school premises was their business. But he was not having 'this kind of behaviour' going on during school hours.

The social worker who became involved in this case, was a young (white) English man in his mid-30s, called Tony, who, unknown to the headteacher, was himself gay. Tony asked the headteacher, 'If this had been a case of a young man and a young woman who had been caught kissing, what action would you have taken?' The headteacher replied, 'None.' And then added, 'But I would not have had this pile of letters of complaint to deal with, either.' He picked up a stack of letters an inch thick and shoved them at Tony, saying 'You read these. I've never had this kind of correspondence to deal with when a boy and a girl kiss.' He then looked at Tony and said, 'I have my league tables to maintain. If I don't deal with the matter in a way that keeps majority opinion happy, I won't get the pupils I need to keep the school open. Then where would we all be?'

Tony was finding responding to the headteacher difficult. He made him feel distinctly uncomfortable and didn't leave Tony any space for discussing, let alone questioning his preferred way of dealing with the issue. So, Tony simply stood up and said, 'I'll go and speak to the young women. Where are they?' The headteacher said, 'I'd prefer it if you talked to them outside school hours – in their own homes, with their parents present. They may have something to say about their behaviour. 'Here,' he continued, 'this is the case file with all the information the school has collected. You might want to read this and talk to the form teacher before going to see the girls at home.' With that, he gave Tony a nod, indicating that he had been dismissed.

This example illustrates a classic shutting down of discursive space. It shows how social structures and individual behaviours rooted in different value systems interact with each other to produce closure in an investigation rather than open up possibilities that can be explored through the social worker's practice. It also reveals how the headteacher has structured the issue in *power over* terms to handle it in ways that would be acceptable to majority opinion which was antithetical to the open expression of a lesbian identity. In doing this, the headteacher has linked his personal behaviour to the dominant discourses and cultural norms. And, in being able to exercise his authority as the person in charge, he has institutionalised these understandings in his practice and interaction with Tony. The headteacher's framing of the 'problem' to be addressed also engages with the institutional concerns he has – maintaining his relationship with the parents who have written to complain and ensuring the financial and physical survival of his school. The young women's views are not relevant in this framing of events, and indicate one way in which adults act to disempower young people and children, or at least exclude their opinions from the intervention agenda. Similarly, Tony's wish to work with the young women in a different way remained covert. This framing of the matter also submerges the importance of addressing issues of homophobia.

The headteacher's unwillingness to face homophobic reactions could have drawn on personal values, but they have also been reinforced by legislation that prohibits discussions of sexual orientation in school in ways that promote homosexual relationships as being equal to heterosexual ones, as has been the case in Britain under Clause 28 originally introduced under the Thatcher administration. The oppressive homophobic framing of the interaction between him and the headteacher has disempowered Tony's capacity to act and reframe the situation in an alternative manner. So it was not possible for Tony to examine his reactions in the above scenario at the time. Moreover, it has also shaped the subsequent intervention between Tony and the young women and their parents.

In this situation, it is crucial that Tony has a support group amongst whom he can discuss his predicament, if he is to empower himself in further negotiations with the headteacher and be able to work effectively with the young women and their parents. Being honest about his own feelings, learning how to deal with these and addressing his failure to raise the importance of finding out what the young women want to do about their sexuality rather than having it imposed upon them by the headmaster, their parents or Tony would constitute key issues for him to consider within this support group.

To be further meaningful to him with regards to this case, the support group would have to engage with the issues as Tony has experienced them, a process that would be facilitated if its members share identity attributes with him. In other words, if he is going to explore issues of homophobia with the group, it should contain practising homosexual men and women. Given that there are a number of other concerns for Tony to explore, for example his feelings of disempowerment as a professional working in a setting controlled by other professionals, he may need to consult other support groups. If he has a team where dilemmas encountered in practice can be openly discussed and support given, this can be another source for bouncing off ideas, reflecting upon his behaviour and considering the range of options open to him. Although Tony could draw on a number of different kinds of support groups to overcome his feelings of inadequacy as a practitioner, at the end of the day, he has to reach his own conclusions about the best way forward. Additionally, he has to be able to act in a way that he can defend when held to account for his behaviour and the judgments he has made, whether this be to the headmaster, his employers, politicians taking an interest in the case, colleagues, the young women's parents, or the young women themselves.

Sometimes, the structural components of an interaction are not so visible to those involved. This is evident in the case materials considered below where Zak is unaware of how his father's acceptance of the views of hegemonic masculinity have shaped his relationship with his father and contributed to his feelings of inferiority at school.

■ Case study

Zak was a 14-year-old boy who hated being at school. He was generally a loner and did not have many friends. He did reasonably well in most subjects, but was especially good at maths, which he loved. His least favoured activity was physical education, and he detested football. Zak's father, Ben, was a senior vice president in a bank and was hardly ever home. He earned a lot of money and felt that this was his main contribution to the family's well-being. He showed little interest in Zak, but made it clear that he expected his 'quiet' son, as he described him, to be a model of good behaviour.

In his youth, Ben had been good at amateur football and had been extremely disappointed in his son's failure to excel in the game. Ever since Zak had embarrassed him on the football pitch at age five, Ben had refused to play any game that required physical prowess with his son. And, as Zak grew older, he found he had even less in common with him. Eventually, it got to the point where, even on those rare occasions that he saw Zak, Ben hardly ever spoke to him.

Zak, on the other hand, adored his father. He constantly tried to gain his approval, but without much success. He had hoped that his being 'good' at maths would at least be recognised by him. But whenever Zak's ability in this area was highlighted, Zak's father always said, 'It's no more than I can expect from someone who has had all the chances in the world.' As Zak grew older, he stopped trying to please his father and began to look for other sources of affirmation.

When he was 14, he made friends with a gang of older boys that had been getting into trouble at school and had dabbled in drug-taking and dealing. Initially, the gang saw Zak as an easy source of cash, for he was given a substantial allowance each week. As the friendship grew, they began to involve Zak in their exploits. One day, the gang leader dared Zak into selling a small amount of 'crack' to a couple of schoolboys to prove that he was a man like them. The boys' parents found out and called the police who promptly went to Zak's house where his father answered the door and let them in. He could not believe what they were telling him about his 'quiet' son.

When asked why he had sold 'crack' to young children, Zak replied that at least his friends had been interested in him – what he thought and what he wanted. He had simply wanted to be tough so that he could be accepted by the gang. As he said, 'No one else gives a damn about me.'

This case study exposes the importance of feeling accepted by important others and acquiring a sense of belonging somewhere, issues that are intricately woven into a sense of personal identity – who a person is and what he or she stands for. In the instance described above, the issues revolve around dominant discourses of masculinity and manhood in men's identity formation processes. The dominant definition of hegemonic masculinity has been found wanting whilst at the same time being constantly reaffirmed (see Connell, 1995). Zak's predicament reveals the inadequacy of macho formulations of masculinity for sensitive men and the importance of having nurturing notions of masculinity guiding relationships between a father and son.

Zak's father was disappointed in his son because he had failed to excel in 'manly' activities represented by being good at playing football. And Ben could not see fatherhood as anything other than that of being the economic provider (see La Rossa, 1995). The complexities of a father–son relationship escaped him, and he had a tendency to see his son as an extension of himself, thereby affirming dominant discourses of masculinity. Ben's emotional underdevelopment was further reflected in his inability to deal with either his own feelings or the emotions that his son had – his need for affirmation as a worthy person and good son whatever he did. So, in perpetuating hegemonic masculinity in his interactions with Zak, Ben had cut himself off from being able to guide his son in the difficult process of growing up to be a man who was a caring and useful member of society.

In the absence of other alternative views of masculinity and manhood, Zak had found the daringness of the gang attractive. The gang also reinforced dominant views of masculinity, seeing toughness as a badge of manhood. In relating to Zak in terms of his capacity to take risks and prove that he could act as a man, the gang had succeeded in making Zak feel that if he could meet their requirements for becoming a man, he would belong somewhere, that is, his need for approval and acceptance had been recognised, if not met, albeit under exploitative conditions. Accepting the dare had been Zak's way of gaining access to the ranks of 'real' men. By successfully meeting the challenge, he would have been able to prove that he too was a 'man'. Had he been able to complete his mission, Zak would have also affirmed hegemonic masculinity as the way of being for him. Unless he is supported in exploring this situation with regards to his identity as a sensitive young man, Zak might easily become convinced that he is a 'failure as a man'. And, in engaging in other behaviour aimed at proving that he is one, he would follow masculine precepts for behaviour including violence, drug-taking and otherwise using other people as objects, behaviours endorsed by the lads in the gang. However, following their guidance is likely to land him in further trouble without confirming his worthiness as either a man or person in his own right, as many young offenders have demonstrated time and time again (Graef, 1992).

This example demonstrates how hegemonic masculinity has failed all the men involved in the above scenario, filling their lives with empty exploits and the absence of real emotional engagement with others. It also shows how important it is to have a social work service that is not stigmatised and aimed at dealing only with problems of poverty or only with meeting the needs of marginalised groups. Rather, it indicates that social services should be made available to anyone that needs help in dealing with difficulties in their lives. Had Zak been able to go and talk to someone outside the family setting about his feelings of worthlessness, the poor relationship with his father could have been addressed early on, and Zak spared the misery of feeling isolated and alone.

He would not then have felt a need to form friendships with young men who could lead him into further difficulties. Masculine identities, particularly the need to display one's manliness by behaving in particular ways – playing football or being tough – also underpin Zak's difficulties. He needs alternative models of manliness which can affirm his own skills and talents without his having to prove that he is a tough guy. Again, having a social worker who could explore these issues with him would have spared him much angst and helped to validate him as the person that he is and to become the best that he can be. This case also highlights the inadequacies of hegemonic masculinity for both his father and the lads in the gang. Ultimately, society's endorsement of hegemonic masculinity would have to be questioned and replaced with a more nurturing one, if more men are not to (re)live experiences similar to those thwarting Zak's and Ben's relationship with each other.

Conclusions

Identity attributes underpin individuals' understandings of themselves and the world they live in. Particularly important in this regard is clarifying what is expected of them, for identity considerations have a direct impact on their ways of relating to their physical environment and other people. This chapter shows the significance of situating individual behaviour in the broader social environment and appreciating that there is an interactive relationship between the social structures that a person locates himself or herself within and their behaviour towards and interactions with others. To work in anti-oppressive ways, social workers need to be able to address these issues directly in the work they do with individuals, if they are to deal competently with the links between social structures and individual behaviour.

At the same time, social workers have to develop an awareness of their own identity and sense of who they are, for these affect their sense of the world, their place within it and their relationships with others, including professional ones. Unless they locate themselves and who they are within the context of a working relationship, practitioners are likely to engage in stereotypical behaviour that can damage the work they do with clients. Crucial to this positioning of themselves is social workers' ability to address their own needs at the personal, institutional and cultural levels. Social workers who are comfortable with dealing with their own identities will be more effective in responding to the needs of others who have different identity attributes.

Working with individuals across a range of behaviours to enhance their capacity to interact effectively and appropriately with others also suggests that social work should not be limited to being a residual service dealing only with the needs of poor people. If social workers are to facilitate society's responses to all those in need and safeguard the human and citizenship rights of all those who might approach them for services, the profession as a whole has to be destigmatised and taken out of the realm of being a residual service that only the most desperate of human beings would willingly access. This requires practitioners, policymakers and the general public to have a more open debate about the role and purpose of social work in society. If its remit is to ensure that social justice is realised, everyone will have to accept that social workers will highlight distressing situations and hold society to account for the injustices that it perpetrates.

If the profession is to respond to anyone in need at the point that this is identified, social workers will require the skills of being able to work with anyone who walks through the door, regardless of their identity attributes, and provide a relevant service. This will necessitate that social workers undertake high-quality, extensive training that places citizens as social actors at the centre of the work they do, whatever social divisions are relevant in any given case. They will also have to have a level of resourcing that is currently missing from the personal social services in most countries, even when all the contributing sectors are considered – the state, the commercial, the voluntary and the domestic. Engaging in self-empowerment and self-help initiatives cannot be more than part of the response to human need. Social, political and economic issues are also important elements in developing an effective social work response at both individual and collective levels. Proficiency in the profession is a combination of individual knowledge, skills and values working within a well-resourced, regulated framework that simultaneously promotes personal growth in individuals, groups and communities. I will now turn to exploring these other dimensions of a forward-looking, progressive social work practice that holds empowerment to promote equality amongst individuals and communities as a core value.

Chapter 5

Anti-Oppressive Practice in Action
Group Interventions and Collective Action

Introduction

Oppression individualises people in ways that isolate them and fragment their experience, leaving an individual feeling uncertain, without alternatives or incapable of taking action to change his or her situation. Coming together in groups is a major way of reversing this fragmentation. Realising their power within a group setting engaging in collective action can be a response that empowers an individual and enables him or her to work with others to redefine their state of being and develop a greater range of options within which to live. By coming together to enact *power of* relations, group dynamics enable people to enlarge the scope of activities within which they can accomplish their objectives. Where appropriate, social workers can assist in the process of mobilising people into collective entities that aim to improve their living environment and well-being as part of the normal process of their work.

In this chapter, I explore anti-oppressive practice in group and community settings, arguing that whether action is taken at the collective level or not, the individual must also feature in these activities, and that social workers who become involved in organisations dedicated to such objectives have a duty to work at both the individual and collective level. This is because group action involves individual participation, and so his or her needs at the personal level should feature in the group discussions at some point. Without links between individual and collective experiences, group activities can become sites for further oppression rather than leading to the creation of emancipatory behaviour and frameworks for action. This holds whether the group is formed as a formal one such as a trade union or professional association, an informal self-help group, a campaigning group or a lobbying group.

Organising around identity

Identity issues can provide a powerful foundation for individuals to utilise in the creation of collective organisations that endorse *power of* relationships and move oppressed groups in liberationist directions. Black people, white women, lesbian women, gay men, disabled people and older people have each organised around their identities, using common aspects of these to unite them in groups ready to take action aimed at changing their situations. Decisions to focus on their commonalities are taken tactically and strategically to achieve agreed goals. It does *not* follow that they are unaware of differences and divisions between them. They may have chosen, at least for the moment, to disregard these when taking specific action about a particular aspect of their lives, or to define these differences in ways that privilege some at the expense of others. Black women have consistently emphasised these points when discussing the intersection of gender relations with those of 'race' and prioritising the latter to unify their communities in struggles against racism (Collins, 1991).

Groups can also be considered as entities that are formed to reflect a community of interests. These may be based on identity attributes, geographical location or finding common cause around particular issues. In the context of organising around particular interests, a group can become a 'community' of people who share common aims, objectives, space and other features which can be used to consolidate their interactions and promote shared activities. Groups can become vehicles for coping with change as well as become sources of change.

Groups can be created around any aspect of life. The group may be self-formed as in the case of a number of people coming together to take action around a problem that may be personal to them, for example a self-help group around substance misuse. Its main emphasis may be self-help initiatives that leave group members in control. Groups may also be facilitated by experts, as in the case of groups established by probation officers to assist offenders in overcoming domestic violence. Or, a group may be one that exists prior to the individual's arrival on the scene, as is the case, for example, with the family that one is born into. Social workers will be working with all kinds of groups during the course of their work and should have a basic understanding of group dynamics and their facilitation (see Brown, 1992).

Identity-based groups

Another significant feature of identity-based group initiatives is that identity becomes an axis around which support networks can be developed. Through these, people support and learn from one another, thereby strengthening each other's resolve in resisting oppression and exclusion, and finding ways of participating more fully in public life. Their demands for action are often linked into the realisation of their potential as full citizens of the country in which they reside. Engaging in such action can be extremely liberating and exhilarating, as the stories of oppressed groups reveal (see Basu, 1997). Although antioppressive practice concerns itself primarily with oppressed individuals and groups, oppressors can also utilise similar forms of organisation, that is, identity-based groups, to retain their privileges and power, as did, for example, the Nazis. Thus, it is not the form of organisation that determines whether it promotes liberation or oppression, but the ideological underpinnings, the aims and objectives the group sets itself and the processes or means whereby they intend to achieve these.

For identity-based groups to work together in anti-oppressive ways, their determination to challenge oppression has been particularly important, by redefining in positive terms identity attributes that more powerful others have degraded and used to keep them in subordinate positions and deny them access to social and material resources (Cleaver, 1971). Through self-affirming actions undertaken on a collective basis, each group attempts to set a new discourse that will successfully turn a characteristic that has been cast in a negative light by ruling elites into a positive validation of their existence, thereby reversing the power dynamics that have previously seemed impregnable. The redefining of 'black' as a trait to be proud of during the American civil rights movement is a classic example of this redefining, that is, reclaiming a name and investing it with positive meaning. In redefining its members and their situation, a group empowers itself in ways that enable it to begin to shape the social agenda in its own terms.

Struggles for self-definition and affirmation are ongoing, particularly when structural relations of inequality remain firmly in place. There is no one-off battle to be won. Oppressed groups constantly have to negotiate and renegotiate their social status. But, through collective action, they are able to do so from a position of greater strength. Social workers can support them in their struggles both directly through membership of such groups and working to realise agreed group goals and indirectly through various forms of support which can include funding or services provided for those more actively involved. Additionally, social workers have an important role to play in raising public consciousness of the position of subjugated groups within society.

Moreover, by constructing alternative discourses around their identity attributes, oppressed groups have been able to tackle the internalisation of oppressive relations amongst their own members who have accepted the 'naming' of their traits as inferior by the dominant group. Internalised oppression is an important dimension of self-policing by oppressed people who regulate their own behaviours to sustain relations that are consistent with their subordinate place in the social order. They do so by limiting the range of the possible to that authored by the dominant group.

Self-affirming activities reauthor dominant discourses by challenging the view that it is not possible for oppressed peoples to ameliorate their situation. Placing affirming role models in the public domain, developing individual self-confidence, promoting positive images of the group and endorsing self-directed programmes of action form part of the repertoire for building confidence in who they are. Through this process, individuals who have previously been excluded and unable to participate in expressions of citizenship in public arenas have found their voice and capacity to act in accordance with their own interests. These actions have been crucial in redefining the meaning of citizenship to make it more inclusive, although ironically they are simultaneously engaged in excluding those different from them in the broader society. Maintaining equality whilst celebrating difference is essential in not (re)producing a new set of *power over* dynamics in their relationships with others, and the challenge for oppressed people is to find ways of achieving this.

Although empowering when acting against their oppressors, the dynamics of identity-based group activities can be disempowering for some individuals within the group, particularly those who wish to assert identity characteristics that are not endorsed by others in the group. In these circumstances, they may find that they have to suppress their aspirations for recognition of their position. Having dealt with identity issues in the process of establishing itself, an identity-based group can then act in ways that ignore identity issues to ensure that its activities are carried out. Thus, the problem of oppressing individuals within the group is often neglected, as the group's internal dynamics become overwhelmed by the preoccupation of realising their agreed plan of action. Many groups work on the basis of submerging individual identities in order to focus on getting the work of the group done. The assumption that they are all the same and hold identical views lies at the root of this dynamic and contributes to the lack of attention given to this matter. Leaving personal considerations to one side may be a belief held by many group members and often requires individuals to behave as if they have no feelings or views that diverge from those formally associated with the group.

Groups that operate on this assumption provide fertile ground for the 'false equality trap' to spring. Proceeding along these lines does not address the needs of those individuals who may very well endorse the end-point of the action, but have reservations about both the strategy and tactics for achieving it. This may include questioning the means and or the methods employed and who undertakes each particular action or part of it. Approaches that ignore individual responses may easily endorse relations of inclusion and exclusion simultaneously, and group heterogeneity, most evident at the point at which the individual interacts with seemingly similar others, is lost. Melucci (1989, p. 18) argues that groups should not base themselves on a false unity and warns that a collective reality has to exist as a real phenomenon.

Inclusionary and exclusionary dynamics

The inclusion of marginalised peoples occurs when individuals who are generally excluded from the broader society come together in a group for specific purposes and have their experiences and existence as individuals validated in the course of doing so. At the same time, the dynamics of exclusion are fostered internally within the group, unless the individual is also given space to be such within the collective setting. Ironically, the group acquires a life of its own, and an unintended consequence of collective action can be the exclusion of those it intends to include. This can happen because a group is simultaneously greater than the sum of its parts, and less than all the individuals who comprise it.

This problem does not have to be insurmountable, as the women of the Greenham Common Women's Peace Movement were able to demonstrate during the mid-1980s, when they opposed the deployment of cruise missiles in Britain (for more details of their activities, see Cook and Kirk, 1983; Dominelli, 1987). By focusing on process and emphasising that each individual could contribute in whatever form they found personally acceptable, because every single effort added to and became part of the overall endeavour, the women at Greenham were able to be inclusive while allowing individual choices as to what activities they participated in and the extent to which they would do so. It also maximised the number of people who were willing to become involved in their protests.

Thus, women involved in Greenham Common activities found processes whereby each individual woman was enabled to participate according to her own preferences without incurring stigmatisation and opprobrium from the others (Dominelli, 1987). This method of involving others on their own terms marks off this group's relations to those in its midst from the more normal authoritarian ways that activist groups have traditionally treated their supporters. The activist in the Greenham Common Women's Peace Movement was relatively autonomous, in that the decision about what action she would personally undertake was always left in her own hands. The only proviso was that she had to let the other women know what she intended to do. This method ensured that each woman was accountable to, but not constrained by, other women. It meant that women could participate in some activities, but not in others where they felt uncomfortable. So women could support and contribute to the movement in myriad ways.

At the same time, this approach enabled each woman to know who was doing what, so that plans could be made whereby the lives of others were not endangered by not knowing who was committed to undertaking a particular action at any given point in time. Women were also linked into supporting each other on the basis of what each one wanted to do. Being respectful of other women's contributions, rather than expecting each one to behave in a fixed way, meant that women's emotions and fears could be openly discussed and strategies devised for dealing with them. This was particularly important for those involved in the Greenham protests because imprisonment, attacks by those hostile to the movement and being trodden under the hooves of powerful police horses at chaotic moments during demonstrations were real worries.

The search for new methods of working alongside others in non-oppressive ways is a continuing one that calls for constant (re)appraisal of existing endeavours if differences amongst group members are to be catered for rather than being dismissed as irrelevant. However, the energies required for continuously being in responsive mode can result in emotional exhaustion for some members of the group. But this is indicative of how commonalities have to be worked for, rather than assumed. Although it is easy to simply leave the valuing of difference at the point of accepting that there are parallel universes which each person inhabits, this leaves little scope for resolving difficulties at the points at which these universes intersect and interact with each other. The concept of interacting or intersecting universes bears more fruit for analytical purposes because it more closely approximates the realities in which people live. No person is an island, but is rather a subjective being who interacts with other subjective beings in constantly shifting configurations that have elements that change and others that remain the same.

Without specific attention being given to issues of inclusion and the processes for facilitating agency, traditional group organisation carries the danger of reinforcing the passive views of individuals who have little or no capacity for self-directed action. This can be particularly problematic in social work where organisational exigencies often turn clients into bureaucratic objects whose subjectivity is downgraded or devalued. Consequently, the personal strengths of the individual users can be ignored and their weaknesses amplified. This approach usually results in professionals establishing paternalistic relationships with service users whether as individual or in groups.

Relations established on this basis emphasise expertise and the services provided by practitioners, rather than endorsing a real partnership in which professionals take a back seat while 'clients' take control of the group formation processes, create the group's agenda, acquire the skills of working with others in this setting, implement its plan of action and secure its future, or not, depending on the purposes of the group. A number of groups are formed with time-limited, specific goals, and are dissolved when these have been reached. Validating 'clients' as subjects individually and collectively enables service users to move out of the bureaucratic object role and exercise their agency as people with the right to make decisions for themselves. In short, I would argue for empowerment as a user-centred process that integrates professional expertise with promoting social justice and overcoming social exclusion. Social workers working with groups can pay attention to such processes and ensure that a group creates spaces in which individuals can be themselves.

Focusing on process issues

At the micro-level, group skills need to accentuate process issues and focus on their meaning for the individual and impact on group interactions if participation is to be more than tokenistic. Process matters because it projects attention onto how the ends are to be achieved. Process considerations encompass rules and procedures whilst transcending them to include how people interact with one another. Process also provides the means whereby private issues become public ones. Turning a private woe into a matter worthy of public notice or matter of concern to a number of people can be important in integrating an individual into a group.

Personal isolation is overcome when a private trouble is redefined as a public one. Isolation is critical in the dynamics of retaining a public issue within the private domain and having a person feel that she or he is the only one experiencing a particular problem. In these circumstances, group processes become an important vehicle for valorising personal experiences and legitimating their value as worthy of public concern and action. The valorisation of personal life stories through public discussion becomes a basis through which personal knowledge becomes more than anecdotal evidence that tells the story of one individual.

Experiential knowledge becomes accepted as empirical evidence once it falls under the public gaze of the group. In other words, it moves out of one person's subjective experience to become objectified knowledge that moves on to a different plane of recognition. Group discussions also provide a vehicle for linking individual experiences with structural positions and the opportunities and limitations accompanying them. Once knowledge creation is recognised as a constant process of accumulating information, reflecting upon it and amending it in light of experience from a number of sources, it becomes a dynamic force with which service users can engage to become full participants. Knowledge is not something that is acquired on a once and for all basis, but is continually being (re)created.

Empowerment as process

Empowerment becomes an important dimension of group processes. As a process, empowerment is about negotiating with others to influence the decisions that will impact upon one's life. Within the group, empowerment has to occur at the individual level as self-empowerment and at the group level as collective empowerment. The two levels interact with each other and are interdependent. However, empowerment may not occur at both levels simultaneously. An individual may feel personally empowered at a point when the group as a whole does not feel this. Such an outcome is possible if a group leader emerges who usurps group dynamics to achieve his or her own personal goals and enrichment. Equally, a group can be empowered in terms of achieving its overall objectives, but leave people feeling disempowered as individuals. This can happen when each participant does not feel ownership of the group processes and decision-making instruments. In these circumstances, they will experience group dynamics as exclusionary rather than inclusionary. Exclusion is likely to result when difference, including differences of opinion, is either ignored or treated as immaterial. It can also be produced when group members are cast as passive consumers of group activities. Social workers who lead groups need to be aware of such dynamics and ensure that they do not skew group processes.

Empowerment also involves mainstreaming the concerns of marginalised or dispossessed groups. The contested nature of people's realities must be acknowledged if empowerment is not to submerge difference. Valorising difference requires those who hold formal power to have a respectful attitude towards the rights of others to voice their own opinions and work towards realising their own objectives. At the same time, those in marginalised groups have to acquire confidence in themselves and their skills in order to change social arrangements so that they more appropriately serve their needs. People have to support one another in working towards the creation of an agenda for action that meets their needs while at the same time not oppressing each other. In other words, the value of equality has to infuse all their interactions with each other. As explained earlier, *power of* relations can convert to *power over* ones, if sensitivity to, or valuing of, others who are different is lost and their capacity to act is ignored.

Empowerment cannot be considered as a question of the powerful giving power to those who are not powerful, that is, conceptualised as a zero-sum game. Empowerment is a two-way process that involves dialogue between opposing groups, a commitment to sharing power and a recognition of the power of 'the other' (Dominelli, 1986). As Matshilo Motsei claims, 'You don't give someone power. They must claim it for themselves' (quoted in Kemp et al., 1995, p. 158). Empowerment is the realisation of that claim. Kuyek (1990) also suggests that creating a culture of hope is an important dimension of individual and collective empowerment, for it provides a spur to action and endorses the belief that conditions can change and the quality of life improved. People need to believe in the possibility of being able to change their situation in order to engage meaningfully with others.

Values as organisational issues

Empowerment is also a value, but there are other ones. Values should be visualised as dynamic entities rather than as fixed and immutable objects. Values develop over time, being modified through interaction, including conflicts about them. People may remain committed to their values, or they may change their mind about them. Moreover, values are subjective, although some of them may be presented as absolute because they are recognisable or persist over space and through time. Thus, values are not 'given' or fixed, although they may be passed down from one individual or group to another and across generations, and constitute an important aspect of a group's cultural and organisational heritage, that is, they acquire stability in being told and retold. Values emerge through interactions that may be either conflictual or consensual in outcome, thereby giving them fluidity as well as substance. That some values endure across the span of time and geography reflects their relevance in different contexts, and reproduction through interpersonal interactions.

At this point, it is important to consider the value systems which underpin empowering action. Are clients self-directed agents, or objects reacting passively to plans for action set by others? Values of affirmation underpin attributes that endorse the former and support individual and group empowerment, while dependency relationships inform the latter. But modern social services are also responding to clients with a different, more market-oriented system of values. However, the empowerment of welfare 'clients' as consumers is difficult when access to money rules certain choices in and others out. Despite this, individuals are encouraged to think of themselves as having rights to present themselves in the marketplace and choose what it is they would like to purchase.

The assumptions of freedom of choice underpinning this picture are very appealing, but these also mask some unpalatable realities, particularly the lack of purchasing power amongst social work clients, the majority of whom are poor. An individual's entry and exit strategies are constrained by financial resources, regardless of what they might want or need. A market system is predicated on having the potential to choose, and exercising choice underpins individual autonomy. But people who lack the wherewithal to participate in this arena because they are poor, marginalised and/or excluded from the monied economy, as are most social work clients, cannot participate in market mechanisms. In these circumstances, suspicion of the market's capacity to respond to identified needs can be influential in undermining its relevance to large swathes of the population (see Rank, 1994; Zucchino, 1997; Ralph et al., 1997; Dominelli, 1999). Within this reality, positing choice as the way forward is disingenuous. Addressing the structural inequalities inherent in this situation is a prerequisite to individuals taking action on an equal basis with those who have the money to play the market and choose what they want.

Additionally, consumerism produces other sets of problems in that it individualises the persons who 'go to market'. Their choices are made as individuals. They are personally expected to find the money they need to participate as individuals. Thus, there is no connection between them and other consumers even when they undergo similar problems and limitations. They do not engage in collective actions with one another. Nor do they necessarily make the connection between the choices that the producers make and the options that are open to them as consumers. Thus, it is difficult for clients as consumers to envisage options other than those that are given to them, nor can they hold producers accountable for the 'choices' that they make when deciding what becomes available for them as consumers to choose from. In other words, choice occurs within a range of possibilities defined by others. At the same time, the relationship is one that is embedded in the interdependence that exists between them. However, the relationship is a market-based one that endorses *power over* dynamics that favour the provider and is reproduced through the power of money and not a reciprocal affiliation. Social workers have a role to play in questioning the exclusion of poor people from accessing social resources in this way.

Citizenship in practice

Consumerist arrangements increase clients' experience of passivity, for they are not involved in either the decisions about eligibility or the processes that result in a particular product or service being made available. In the social welfare arena, this arrangement also disguises contractual power. The power of the commissioner who purchases the services from which the individual will be able to choose is substantial and influential. The purchaser often dictates what is produced or provided and can act to curtail or limit choice (Clarke and Newman, 1997). As their decisions are made contractually behind doors that are closed to clients, those creating the services become invisible and, more importantly, unaccountable to the people who end up 'consuming' or using the services they produce. These dynamics can impede the citizen's capacity for active involvement in creating provisions whether individually or collectively.

Moreover, any complaints the individual may have about the options on offer can only be raised through an impersonal, routine or bureaucratised process. This can increase his or her sense of alienation and isolation, because the options for action are only a technical procedure that can frustrate rather than deal with their concerns. The inadequacy of bureaucratic proceedings as a vehicle for protest cannot be challenged within this configuration of the professional–client relationship. For the complainant, the relationship has been constructed not so much with access to the practitioner, but to the impersonal mechanisms that an unknown figure has put in place. The person dealing with complaints is equally remote and distant. Additionally, the creation of the client as a bureaucratic object has as its counterpart the professional as a bureaucratic object, for the worker is also restricted to procedural interventions. As bureaucratic objects, clients and professionals may discover that they have more in common with each other, if they form an alliance of groups aimed at resisting their objectification as consumables or objects at different points in the service delivery process.

The fragmented individualising of professional and client in modern social work practice in Britain undermines the key principles of citizenship, particularly those of interdependence, reciprocity and solidarity. The interdependent nature of the relationships between professionals and clients is fairly obvious. Without clients there would be no professionals. Clients need professionals to obtain services otherwise inaccessible to them. Reciprocity involves both the worker and the user in responding to the issues raised by the other, with each of them taking responsibility for resolving the problems that they encounter together. Reciprocity also suggests an element of mutuality, or a commitment that each party to the interaction is giving and receiving. Solidarity is linked fairly generally to the interdependent nature of modern society and is the acknowledgement that no individual is self-sufficient, but reliant on others for a range of things. It provides the basis for altruism – a commitment to caring for others. However, its impact on welfare is different because solidarity in these instances draws on values rooted in the willingness of one person to commit him or herself to ensure the well-being of another with whom they have no direct relationship and for whose welfare they have no direct responsibility. Assuming a share of collective responsibility towards others depends on values which endorse the rights of others – altruism, equality and social justice and also require a person to take action that realises these values in practice. Groups can provide important forms for organising around these values.

Social work can be seen as the collective expression of such solidarity. Unfortunately, the implementation of what seems a simple ideal is not clear cut. None of these principles can be put into practice in a straightforward manner, because they are realised in specific contexts that are and have been shaped by the interplay of power relations involving both those who are interacting with each other and historical developments that have influenced a particular milieu, including that of the welfare state of which social work is part. Part of the reason for this is that the ideal is a contested one. Some people do not subscribe to it, particularly if their values endorse a competitive individualism (MacPherson, 1962), and are interested only in thwarting its fulfilment at every point. Others are only committed to it in part. They will support the principle in the case of 'deserving' individuals, particularly children and older people, but not for others (Thane, 1996). Consequently, social workers have to work with the ambiguities and contradictions that its contested remit imposes upon them in practice. This can make service delivery extremely difficult and reconfigures professional or even technical endeavours as political ones. The politics of practice circumscribe the role of social workers as professional beings, and are negotiated and renegotiated in each intervention with either individuals or groups within the context of legal, social, political and economic exigencies set up by their employers and politicians on behalf of society.

Practitioners manoeuvre within their professional remit by managing the tensions inherent in their role as employees within a particular setting. In engaging with practice as a political exercise, social workers utilise their commitment to promoting individual or group well-being within an empowering context as creators of their own realities. In doing so, practitioners are aware of another set of complexities – conflicts of interest and direction between the different stakeholders who may demand a say in the way they work and the interventions they undertake. With regards to enabling individuals to become self-empowered, clients' assertion of their personal autonomy may place them on a collision course with a social worker's commitment to normalise their behaviour so that it is consistent with existing social relations, even when these might be oppressive. The history of the profession is littered with examples of social workers oppressing women, black people, indigenous people, disabled people, people with mental ill health – the list can easily be extended – with the aim of making them 'fit' more readily within the existing social order. This has occurred because social workers have uncritically accepted their role as 'normalisers' promoting the interests of those advocating dominant discourses.

The requirement that social workers operate within a particular nation-state with a given definition of who counts amongst its citizenry has contributed to difficulties in practising in inclusive ways. Those who do not meet national criteria for inclusion have been excluded from the category of citizen and denied its entitlements. Citizenship in the Western world has been framed within the context of a universalism which denies diversity in order to create a homogeneous group of people who can swear allegiance to a common set of institutions and be bounded within a given territorial domain (Lorenz, 1994). The nationalist project only recognises a universalism in which the ideology that 'we are all the same' prevails. Making homogeneity a basis for accessing welfare makes it easier for professionals to manage these provisions and take advantage of the efficiencies of scale. In a homogenising context, both activities can be taken for granted rather than having to be measured as an outcome of services received. This solution *ipso facto* excludes those who are different from the assumed stereotype of the citizen. When social workers treat populations as homogeneous, their differences can be denied or subjugated, thereby making it easier to assimilate them within hegemonic social relations. In other words, one aim of citizenship within the nation-state has been submission to existing norms and not a wide-ranging inclusion across differences and geographical boundaries.

In a context in which inclusion of difference is not an overriding concern, means-tested benefits and restricted access to entitlements make sense. Exclusion of those who are deemed 'undeserving' for a whole range of reasons, a number of which are identity-based, becomes readily accepted as a reasonable way of rationing scarce resources. This rational response to demands that the needs of all those entitled to services be met contains an irrational element. That is, it divides claimants into 'deserving' and 'undeserving' groups, without dealing with the problems that need to be addressed. This division does not do away with the needs these people have, regardless of the category they fall into, it simply rules out society's responsibility to respond to them either adequately if 'deserving', or at all if 'undeserving'.

This rationing dynamic is being replayed in Britain under New Labour's modernising agenda, where a commitment to work one's way out of poverty, rather than being someone at the receiving end of services which are a right of citizenship, becomes the key to rising above one's status as a marginalised citizen. Casting claimants as unworthy of support ignores the contribution that they make to social well-being through the work they do, usually without a wage. Whilst the figures are unavailable for Britain, Wichterich (2000) has calculated that 70 per cent of the world's work is performed by women who are not paid for it, a reality that excludes them from wage-based benefits. The United Nations Development Programme has valued their contribution at $US11 billion compared to $US7.3 billion as the total of manufactured goods produced. Yet, 70 per cent of the world's poor are women, 35 per cent of whom are sole parents (Wichterich, 2000, p. 124). So, gendered inequalities linked to the non-recognition of non-waged work done by women form an important part of this problem. As many of these women are also located in 'The South', their experience of gender is also likely to be racialised, and many will be located amongst the rural poor. Additionally, poverty is rising amongst the working poor in industrialised countries, where low wages and inadequate, if any, benefits also fail to draw them out of poverty (Rank, 1994). Despite these well-known statistics, the modernising agenda in Britain excludes those who

rking poor or those unable to work and their needs have
l by the government (Jordan, 2000).
king poor form a large proportion of marginalised and
eople. To transcend the poverty trap inhabited by the
or, working one's way out of poverty requires that work is
reconceptualised and restructured so that decent salaries are paid to
everyone, and higher levels of quality education are made freely available to all. It also necessitates overcoming the capability gap that
accompanies income poverty. This latter point is particularly important
in what has become known as the 'knowledge-based society'. Solving
the problems encountered by the working poor also requires that welfare provisions are shifted away from Elizabethan Poor Law ideology,
which insists that benefits should be targeted only upon the most needy
people and not exceed the lowest wage paid to workers in a particular
society (Dominelli, 1991; Rank, 1994).

New Labour's modernising response focuses on what an individual
can and must do to help him or herself. However, it does not tackle the
links between structural inadequacies and the transmission of poverty
across generations. Rank (1994) challenges the personal deficit view of
poverty and argues cogently that the failure of children to achieve is
attributable to: parental poverty; inadequate employment opportunities; and educational underperformance. These, rather than parental
failings including offering their offspring poor role models, account for
persistent poverty and exclusion. The structural causes of poverty also
need to be addressed if the person is to develop to their full potential
as an active citizen in the society that he or she lives in.

Increasing poverty worldwide has also intensified the processes
leading to the internationalisation of social problems (Khan and
Dominelli, 2000). For example, the loss of jobs for women in Poland
has exacerbated poverty amongst women and, in the absence of alternative forms of employment, pushed many of them into prostitution. A
significant number of these women become enmeshed in people
exploitation as they fall prey to people smugglers who engage in the
lucrative trafficking of women and children across international
borders, adding to the stream of undocumented migrants, refugees and
asylum seekers (Wichterich, 2000; Kyle and Koslowski, 2001). In
others situations, women become involved in low-paid jobs in
wealthier countries, even when they are highly qualified. For example,
70 per cent of Filipino workers abroad are women. This has enormous
implications for the demography of the home country and those left
behind, particularly their children (Daenzer, 1993). Social workers will

end up working with people in these circumstances and will require quality training to equip them to work effectively with them.

Sadly, what is happening in Britain and elsewhere is that wealth is being concentrated in fewer and fewer hands and work is becoming more and more casualised for the majority of people. Thus, 358 individuals can own 45 per cent of the world's wealth (UNDP, 1996), whilst over a billion people struggle to survive on one dollar (US) a day (Wichterich, 2000). At the same time, political discourses in Western democracies are casting citizenship for the majority of people in terms of responsibilities and duties, rooting the idea of entitlements in self-sufficiency and looking after themselves, in accordance with neo-liberal dictates (Teeple, 1995; Dominelli, 1999) which say little about what the state is obliged to do for its citizens. Little interest is being shown in people demonstrating solidarity by taking responsibility to contributing to the well-being of unknown others as well as those close to them. Within the context of world poverty, this solidarity has to have a global reach (UNDP, 2000, 2000a). Social workers can play a significant role in mobilising civil society organisations in power-sharing initiatives and mount a critique that highlights the casualties of neo-liberalism and advocating on their behalf in both national and international policy-making forums.

Also missing from traditional neo-liberal explanations of this problem of world poverty is accountability. Accountability, on the one hand, involves holding governments responsible for allowing many of their people to go hungry, become homeless and remain uneducated. On the other, it endorses demands that corporations pay adequately for the work that they extract from individuals and repay the public funds that are channelled their way through public subsidies and tax breaks linked to the job opportunities that they provide at a given point in time. Despite its being an important consideration in these discourses, extracting accountability from powerful elite groups engaged in running corporations and governments has seldom been achieved (Wichterich, 2000). Social workers can form alliances with others concerned about enfranchising marginalised people to hold governments and corporations accountable. They can also engage in consciousness-raising endeavours that are aimed at ensuring that the population more generally accepts the idea of being responsible for others unknown to them as part of their own explication of citizenship.

Social workers, as the professionals who deal with suffering people and the misery emanating from the current (re)structuring of social relations, can influence public debates on these issues. Particularly important

s the issue of poverty – its deleterious impact on individual
y well-being and the importance of ensuring the swift real-
rty eradication measures. Social workers can collect infor-
xposes the harsh realities in which many people live in
light the structural nature of many of their problems and
empower the people they work with to speak for themselves.

In this context, social workers can engage in community-based
research that paints pictures of the grim realities of people's lives and
offers new ways of dealing with social problems. As Ristock and
Pennell argue (1996), community research can be used to empower
people. Knowledge is power, and social workers can facilitate the
processes that make knowledge available to groups who might otherwise lack access to it and ensure that it is shared amongst participants
in the groups and communities that they mobilise. With regards to
world poverty, social workers have begun to raise some of these issues
in the international policy context of the UN as well as with their own
governments. For example, the International Association of Schools of
Social Work and the International Federation of Social Workers, who
represent social work educators and practitioners respectively, were
involved in highlighting issues of social exclusion and integration at the
Copenhagen Plus 5 deliberations on social development on these issues.
They have also been involved in discussions about poverty eradication
in a number of different forums.

Working in accordance with poverty eradication goals requires
social workers to foster collective responsibility and solidarity amongst
individuals. In other words, the individual cannot be considered an
island, but a member of a group to which he or she is expected to
contribute, and from which, certain forms of support will flow. Thus,
mutuality and reciprocity become the keywords for the interaction
between them. In this context, resources will have to be used efficiently
and wisely, but their prime purpose becomes one of meeting human
needs, not simply that of lining the pockets of the wealthy few. Effi-
ciency is meaningful in responses to alleviating poverty if it is not used
as a bureaucratic procedure that overrides all else, but as a way of
ensuring that full citizenship rights are enjoyed by society's most
socially excluded and vulnerable groups.

Ironically, welfare recipients who endure their situation as atomised
individuals accept the 'blaming the victim' ideology that permeates the
broader society when it comes to holding claimants personally responsible for requiring public assistance (Rank, 1994). Groupwork offers
opportunities to get people who have become atomised individuals to

rethink their approach to life (Mullender and Ward, 1991). Besides being invaluable in helping people to help themselves, groupwork can ensure that professionals become accountable to the people they serve, and challenge political inaction on social problems which have become individualised so as to pathologise individuals and hold them personally responsible for their plight without also considering the structural contribution to their woes. By working in groups, individuals can create alternative discourses and move towards their own empowerment. Social workers can facilitate group formation and support their activities.

Strengthening communities

Groups are formed as individuals come together to undertake collective action around an agreed issue or goal. Group-based activities assist community workers to take advantage of political opportunities for mobilisation at the community level (McAdam and Snow, 1997). Repressive measures against community groups can themselves encourage mobilisation, as often occurs against oppressive regimes (McAdam and Snow, 1997). This occurs because, as Naples (1997) demonstrates, resistance is about creating the basic conditions of life and is not necessarily oppositional. For instance, liberal feminists have a tradition of organising to find new spaces and forms of resistance that are not necessarily opposed to existing social relations (Naples, 1997), although they may challenge society's failure to include women on the same basis as men (Dominelli, 2002).

Groups tend to be goal-specific and often dissolve when they have reached their objective(s). Groups campaigning around a particular objective are good examples of these and include road closure and environmental groups. Many of these groups are effective in lobbying for particular points of view around a specific concern, but disperse quickly afterwards. A key difficulty of these groups is that of maintaining morale and interest in action once a specific crisis is over (Dominelli, 1990). These groups are also often voluntary, made up of activists committed to a particular cause. This has advantages in taking direct action, but is less able to deal with the continuity of the group. Professional intervention could be used to address this issue, as paid employees can continue to work on matters of continuity between crucial campaigning or lobbying moments. Success in these activities is a crucial aspect of maintaining momentum within groups.

McAdam and Snow (1997) argue that institutionalising successes provides one way of ensuring that these last across generations. Although difficult, this objective can be achieved. Naples (1997, pp. 258–74) discusses in detail how people change their demands when they lose their battle for community autonomy in order to continue the fight for their objectives and maintain continuity.

Groups can also be used to secure changes in individual behaviours, for example sex offenders' groups organised by the probation service. These aim to get the offender to take responsibility for his (sex offenders are usually men) behaviour and assume an acceptable place in society. However, a problem these groups encounter is that they have few direct links for integrating sex offenders back into the communities into which they will eventually return (Cowburn and Dominelli, 2001). People in these communities remain suspicious of the extent to which these men have changed their behaviour and refuse to accept them into their midst. Thus, it is important to formulate groupwork activities that will develop relationships between them, especially if this form of intervention is to be used to encourage the development of healthy communities in which people take responsibility for each other's welfare. For sex offenders, this will require the community to invest in their rehabilitation as useful members of society (Dominelli, 2002), while each sex offender has to engage in personal change including attitudinal reorientation to treat other people as subjects in their own right and not objects for them to manipulate at will (Dominelli, 1992).

Developing a community's commitment to each person's welfare will require specific actions to realise this, particularly in a world that is currently marked by a market-based individualism in which each individual is exhorted to look after him or herself and his or her family. Social workers can play a leading role in reasserting notions of solidarity that are rooted in the idea of communities as groupings of people that come together for specific purposes. These communities can be based on identities, interests or geographical location. The practitioners' main contributions will be to:

- assist in the processes of mobilising people;
- collect evidence that indicates the need for mutual systems of caring;
- and help to mount the arguments for reciprocated, solidarity-based welfare provisions.

Working in anti-oppressive ways will involve the social worker in linking the individual to their physical and social environments, to bring together the personal and structural components that are to be tied into the action.

The social workers' efforts are aimed at ending fragmentation by bringing people together to control developments in their communities. They need to recognise the fluid basis of community formation when these are being created to bridge differences during the formation of tactical alliances for specific purposes. Differences have to be taken into account and worked upon if unity is to be built across various divides. Undertaking this kind of work requires practitioners to transcend their bureaucratic professional roles and enhance the development of services that support the community's well-being. To do this effectively, social workers will have to be multiskilled in working with both individuals and groups. They will also have to be aware of different power relations and how inegalitarian power dynamics are enacted through routine behaviours that aim to keep people in their place and encourage them to negotiate with each other on an egalitarian problem-solving basis. To facilitate community groups in taking action, social workers will have to strengthen their capacities in working together with community participants for change. Their training and socialisation processes will have to incorporate this concern and forgo the emphasis solely on the decontextualised individual.

Identity, agency and power become tools for challenging the fragmentation of individualism, as these draw upon collectively acknowledged attributes to overcome isolation. In other words, social workers will utilise an alternative vision of society and interpersonal relations that can unify people whilst recognising their differences, responding to the implications of these for their action together and valuing the contributions that can arise from bringing these differences into the foreground. Social justice for all rather than profit-making for the few will be at the heart of their concerns.

Alternative developments in strong communities

Giddens (1994) offers concepts linked to his idea of 'utopian realism' which are useful in this regard. These are:

- combating both absolute and relative poverty;
- reversing the degradation of the environment;

- challenging arbitrary power;

- and reducing the role of force and violence in public and private lives.

Attending to these will assist social workers and community activists in mobilising for a broader social and economic justice that links local situations with global developments and in formulating demands of both governments and corporate entrepreneurs at their various levels from the international to the local. Foremost amongst the items to be given attention is the demand that the economy be structured to meet human needs, that is, that social policies should not be subordinated to economic policies (Dominelli, 1991).

'Utopian realism' also provides a framework for working to build new definitions of culture that will question the perpetration of social divisions based on the unequal distribution of power and resources, and the idea that improving one person or group's well-being can only occur at the expense of another. Central to putting this idea into practice are creating reciprocated power relations, and not treating the individual as a unit of resource that can be discarded for another replacement unit. This latter option is dominant in capitalist working relations, where insecurity rules and commodity relations establish the price of everything and the value of nothing. Instead, each individual should be treated as a valuable human being in his or her own right; someone who realises his or her specific talents and potential through social interaction with others in a collective or community context.

In formulating this alternative vision, social workers will also have to take care that they do not raise expectations that they are unable to fulfil. Failure to live up to these expectations will further fuel mistrust and antagonise local communities (Ng, 1988). Narayan et al. (2000) discovered that poor people view authority figures with hostility and suspicion. They do not want to participate in projects that have been designed by other people and reflect their priorities. Thus, social workers who seek to mobilise residents in such communities must ensure that they do so on the terms set by poor people themselves and work to earn their trust and respect. This holds whether they are involved in mobilising people for action or for research into their communities.

Working with multiply disadvantaged communities requires social workers to engage in social development strategies. Social development becomes an important part of the social worker's repertoire that is as relevant in high-income countries or neighbourhoods as in low-income ones. Social development is a process of intervention that locates the individual in their physical and social environments with the aim of improving individual and community well-being through collective action (Dominelli, 1997b). It aims to develop people as well as their localities and often involves extending local resources through networking initiatives and campaigning to secure social and economic justice within national and international jurisdictions.

The social economy in social development

Social development is rooted in the social economy, that is, an economic arrangement that is created locally to respond to *people's* needs as they define them (Donati, 1996), rather than one that pursues profits and meets people's needs as a by-product of economic development. The social economy is predicated on a reversal of traditional capitalist economic relations which subordinate social to economic exigencies (Dominelli, 1991, 1997b). Kuyek (1990) insists that a full costing of capitalist development should include the environmental and justice costs of both development and non-development.

The social economy also aims to redistribute resources to those who would not otherwise gain access to these. Unlike capital in the global marketplace which invests in financial and speculative activities and acts to lower wages, social sector employment seeks to look after the interests of the workers, the community, the physical environment and the users of the goods and services provided (Donati, 1996). In further contrast, the social economy enables activists to find funds from the community to procure resourcing that goes beyond the individual's capacity to acquire (McAdam and Snow, 1997).

The social economy has developed from a critique of the inadequacies of capitalist development in meeting people's needs. Contained within this has been a concern that the state, and the public sector investments that it controls, has subjected much of its social responsibilities to the dictats of private accumulation. As O'Connor (1973) argues, the development of the state sector has been useful to capital. Private companies have been able to draw on public resources through privatisation measures and are ready to be financed by public funds to manage hospitals, prisons, homes and health services as the state withdraws from these (O'Connor, 1973). The restructuring of public welfare provisions under neo-liberal regimes in Canada, the United States, New Zealand and Britain is an apt illustration of this point (Clarke and Newman, 1997; Kelsey, 1997; Ralph et al., 1997; Teeple, 1995; Zucchino, 1997).

However, one of the difficulties of the social economy centres on its inadequate theorisation of individuals and their position in its infra-structural assumptions. They are not so much self-sufficient and compliant as interdependent, reliant on the activities of others and relatively autonomous. Through the social economy, an economy of solidarity which is formed of many disparate individuals and organisations can arise. Each may have different objectives and the organisers of social economy initiatives may find that these are in conflict with one another and that their differences require resolution. In other words, a coalition of like-minded individuals and enterprises has to be created and maintained, not taken-as-given or taken for granted. Therefore, it is important not to idealise the potential of the social economy and to find ways of resolving disputes amongst its constituent parts by non-violent and inclusive means. Creating public spaces that are readily accessible to all and in which dialogue can take place is an important aspect of the process of facilitating such discourses and social workers can help to bring this about.

Kuyek (1990) argues that rooting social development in the social economy facilitates the reclaiming of economics through community economic development, as these kinds of initiatives are grounded in meeting local needs (Dominelli, 1997d). The process of organising for social development can be exemplified by the Desjardins financial network. Based in Quebec, it comprises credit unions, insurance mutuals and investment firms which are located in the social economy sector that draws on community support including social workers and community activists. This network has been highly successful in promoting development initiatives whilst ranking amongst the top suppliers of Canadian financial services (*Canadian Business*, 1997). As part of the social sector, the Desjardins network seeks to meet those community needs not addressed by either commercial or state enterprises, and at the same time involves community members in its formation and growth. In other words, the Desjardins experiment has carved out a niche in the market that had been left by other providers. Social economy networks such as the Desjardins one draw heavily on notions of community-based solidarity and reciprocity to release their people's energies in the creation of a better world (Donati, 1996; Shragge and Fontan, 2000). The capacity of the social economy to develop 'social capital' (C 1988) or release local potential for development, by en community activists in non-commercial and non-monetary ver is also exemplified by the Desjardins network.

The self-sufficiency approach advocated by those who support social economy initiatives is unlikely to tackle deep-rooted, major social problems such as poverty or crime, because it is too deeply embedded in the idea of self-reliance as the way out of capitalist exploitation and assumes a 'beneficial' dynamic as the basis for capitalist development. In other words, it does not propose an alternative to capitalist development, but rather carves out a niche within it. Thus, it can end up competing with more traditional capitalist alternatives, albeit effectively, as the Desjardins network has demonstrated. But such dynamics may reduce the capacity of local activists and communities to challenge capitalist social relations overall.

Lunghini argues (1995, pp. 74–6) that the social economy occupies that area outside the market that provides the space that can be used to create 'democratic forms of needs assessment, local control of demand, and a decentralised organization of supply'. Moreover, Lunghini (1995, pp. 74–6) maintains that communal and reciprocal relations can be recreated in a modern form by taking autonomous individuals as their starting point for action. However, I would argue that in focusing on autonomous individuals, the social economy is likely to replicate the inadequacies of capitalism with regards to meeting the needs of individuals and groups for a better quality of life, as autonomous individuals are not linked to their compatriots and are not likely to engage in solidary commitments and reciprocal arrangements with others. Thus, there is little to encourage him or her to become part of a collective endeavour aimed at benefiting all.

Managing poor people

At the same time, a market-based, self-reliant individualism presumes the worst of people, particularly if they are 'poor' or different from the dominant definition of who counts in society or those categories taken as the norm. Workfare offers a classic illustration of these views of people in need. Workfare advocates depict poor people as lazy individuals who must be forced to work (Rifkin, 1995). Such assumptions are integral to neo-liberalism and can readily destroy the social fabric that has been carefully created over the years (Rifkin, 1995). Yet, the evidence provided by countless opinion polls indicates that poor people would rather work than be on benefit. The catch for them is that the work must pay more than the minimum wage if they are to be able to pay the bills incurred in daily living. Sadly, most workfare schemes prepare people for casualised, low-paid jobs that no one else wants (Ralph et al., 1997; Zucchino, 1997; Wichterich, 2000).

More recently, some jurisdictions, for example Canada and the United States, have begun to use voluntary organisations to police workfare (Ralph et al., 1997). This type of work changes the nature of voluntary work and organisations, and brings them into the more controlling elements of the care relationship. These bodies have also been subjected to making binding contractual agreements with both funders and users. Such arrangements give the funders or purchasers of these services – usually the state – enormous power in dictating developments in these agencies. They have also altered the meaning of partnerships as relationships between free and equal parties with congruent interests. Also, they may undermine the principles underpinning the ethics of service to the community, by providing services to others for profit. The loss of more altruistic ethics and the idea of solidarity with others which nourishes them have diminished the concept of the common good. Those advocating business ethics have also become embroiled in redefining mutual assistance and state operations as commercial transactions. This approach in turn has degraded citizenship to an exchange relationship that consumes public services without contributing to their formation and development.

Neo-liberalism lacks a critique of the *costs* that ordinary people and the environment carry for its present and future growth. As a result, neither firms, corporate leaders nor financial institutions are held accountable by government for the *consequences* of the decisions they take on behalf of people's, the community's and the planet's well-being. Indeed, state responses tend to be reactive and defensive, as happens when multinational corporations decide to take their jobs elsewhere. The Blair government's reaction to BMW's sell-off of Rover cars is but one case in point. On a smaller scale, Benford's threat to close its Leamington plant in favour of Manchester is another case in point (Sales, 2001). Replacing the loss of well-paid, blue-collar jobs with largely low-paid, service sector ones (Wichterich, 2000) is not an adequate response from the ordinary working person's point of view. Because most of those who lost their jobs in these instances are men and the cheaper replacement jobs attract women, gender relations are complicated at the local level. And, the large sums of money that the state has provided to attract private enterprise fail to generate the anticipated long-term growth in the economy (Bartlett and Steele, 1998).

In the neo-liberal world, a small minority carries out skilled work and wields all the power, whilst more and more individuals are consigned to undertaking increasingly marginalised, contingent, 'servile' work in the low-paid service sector (Gorz, 1988). These jobs fail to provide working people with sufficient income to meet their needs, and impair their capacity to provide for themselves, even if they wanted to (Zucchino, 1997). In other words, such developments promote negative social equity. In pursuing the self-sufficiency agenda and ignoring the ties of social solidarity, society becomes more irresponsible as business corporations and the market gain hegemony over well-being (Titmuss, 1963). Without the development of well-paid job opportunities for people once they come off welfare, workfare provides one example of such irresponsibility. That people will leave the welfare rolls in the majority of cases is well established, so this eventuality, that is, the need for well-paid work for poor people, is predictable (Morris, 1995). The existence of such jobs must be planned for. Social workers have a role to play in advocating for these types of opportunity for poor people.

The critiques of utilitarianism, statism and bureaucratism have led to new political responses which attempt to reconcile corporatist interests with community ones. On the official level, this has been termed 'communitarianism' or, as promulgated politically in Britain and Germany, the 'Third Way' (Jordan, 2000). However, communitarian approaches (see Bulmer and Rees, 1996) fail to problematise the idea of 'community', taking it as unitary and given. That is, it is conceptualised in an idealistic, normative, conservative manner rather than addressing its unstable, fragmented nature. 'Communities' have to be built or configured by dealing with the divisions which are masked by the inclusive language that is conveyed through communitarian discourses. Without such endeavours, communities do not exist.

A further critical issue here is that the fundamental rationale driving economic decisions within communitarian approaches cannot be challenged within the Third Way (Jordan, 2000). Despite the mass of evidence that indicates the high price paid by individuals who are excluded from mainstream society's remits, the Third Way endorses capitalist relations as providing the most appropriate ways of organising social relationships at the level of the community. So, the British government can only look at how to minimise the devastating consequences of the loss of livelihood on people's lives, rather than questioning why communities should be in this position in the first place and considering how to avoid its reoccurrence in future. Thus, when various mulitnational firms such as BMW decided to take their business elsewhere, there was no co-ordinated response that integrated the local, national and international developments with human well-being at its centre.

Failures of this magnitude identify the importance of having a holistic approach that stands outside the immediate relations within which it is enmeshed. At the same time, being rooted in democratic accountability and solidarity amongst peoples enables government to attempt problem-solving that transcends the narrowness of any one particular issue. Despite its rhetoric, the Third Way has failed to achieve this goal. And, although committed to 'joined-up' thinking, it is unable to hold corporate decision-makers to account. Furthermore, its response in practice is weakened by the failure of its analytical model to conceptualise an equality of interests between the contending stakeholders. Consequently, some economic interests and decision-makers remain privileged over others, thereby ensuring that their particular framing of the questions shapes the possibilities open to others who may sit around the table with them.

Maintaining private accumulation and the employment associated with it has engaged the state in, on the one hand, safeguarding the conditions for accumulation and, on the other, maintaining a social consensus (Ruffolo, 1985). Moreover, the state has been significant in removing the requirement that business should contribute to people's general well-being through the welfare state (Ruffolo, 1985, p. 239). In other words, the state is in the contradictory position of being both engaged in perpetuating the problem and seeking a solution to it. And, in spite of well-founded critiques on the inadequacies of the neo-liberal approach to economic development and social welfare espoused most thoroughly by Reagan in the United States and Thatcher in Britain, newly elected governments in the West continue to promote a corporatist agenda, for example Gordon Campbell's Liberal government in British Columbia in Canada.

A key dynamic in neo-liberal approaches to economic and social issues is that the market and bureaucratic organs become increasingly costly and unable to meet social needs. But, as their capacity to respond to their citizen's welfare concerns diminishes, their bureaucratic voraciousness increases (Ruffolo, 1985, p. 197) and the value accorded to self-sufficiency and looking after one's own needs rises. This dynamic is unlikely to be broken until people's limits for self-sufficiency are reached. Then, the discourses around the need to organise collectively to look after each other will again occupy public space. Social workers can assist in the process of bringing these discourses about and link up with others who have alternative visions about how to organise social relations.

Meanwhile, the privatisation of welfare services has been extended to encompass the management of poverty by involving the private sector in overseeing a broad range of services formerly provided by the state, including social security, income support and pensions. These initiatives run the risk of intensifying exclusion for they cannot adequately address structural issues. Nonetheless, they reaffirm the strategy of the state in managing poverty by using professionals, including social workers employed in these organisations, to manage poor people, while its officials in turn regulate the practitioners. As a result, social workers have become central in controlling poverty by focusing on the individuals living in poor neighbourhoods, while their own performance is governed by their line managers whose control of the new information technologies enables them to amass considerable data for the purposes of monitoring their attainments. Individual pathology has thereby been given a new lease of life. Without an alternative vision of the possible and a mobilisation of the people to take control of their own communities, social workers will be unable to resist being accomplices in the acts of controlling poor people.

Alternative envisioning

However, while the state has been busy preparing communitarian responses that have not challenged the fundamental basis of capitalism, others have sought to do so, albeit primarily through less formal organisation. Informal responses have sought to establish communities along less orthodox lines, bringing together a range of disparate individuals and groups from different corners of the earth, employing the new computer-based technologies and the internet for their purposes, for example the Women's March, anti-globalisation protestors and Attac. These groups can be seen as postmodernist configurations as they lack the shape and forms usually associated with groups. The airwaves provide their meeting space and a keyboard their means of communication. Nonetheless, they have proved to be powerful forms of getting people together for specific, if brief, moments to make their views heard. In this sense, they have offered a new version of 'community' – one that transcends time and space by not being geographically bound, but loosely structured, fragmented, and without specific cultural ties, united only by their rejection of the established world order. A critique of neo-liberalism, the desire to develop local economic initiatives in the community, a concern to develop environmentally sustainable forms of development, and the attempt to raise standards of living in poor countries in 'The South', have brought them together in various forms of direct action aimed at challenging the social relations endorsed by corporate capitalism. As their concerns have crossed borders, so have the 'communities' that they have established. Their permanence is their transient nature which can be mobilised in various forms of protest around these themes as the occasion demands.

Despite short-term gains, reflected largely through the airing of their vision in the media, these informal responses to social and community development are, in my opinion, unlikely to succeed in the longer term for the following reasons. Its adherents are unable to:

- attract the majority of people to their worldview;
- take on corporate capital in terms of what it has achieved;
- win the media war regarding their message of the shortcomings of capitalist development;
- and assure the general public that they are not led by a small cadre of violent individuals who seek to acquire power and control over the activities of less active others.

However, creating communities by following the guidelines proposed in official discourses is also likely to fail. This is because their propositions do not:

- address the messiness that is an integral part of collective mobilisation;
- deal with the hierarchy of positions that different social actors occupy;
- seek to stem the tyranny of control that self-appointed leaders of a 'community' can perpetuate;
- respond to the need for capacity-building amongst those policy-makers and officials who embark upon community development

initiatives with little understanding of what it is they will have to deal with in practice and have few solutions to the problem of how they will work with difference in non-tokenistic ways.

However, social workers, because they are embedded in these messy realities and are used to working with contradictory positions and messages, can offer insights that can help people to develop communities that mobilise more effectively in support of the goal of social justice.

Conclusions

Market discipline and regimes have had a significant impact on welfare provisions in the industrialised world and have contributed substantially to redrawing the role of the state, particularly with regards to the provision of welfare resources. No longer acting as a provider, its new functions have contributed to a lessening of the ties of solidarity that can bind individuals in society to each other. Fragmentation and personal self-sufficiency have loosened reciprocated caring and replaced these links to the detriment of communal well-being and civic ethics. Social workers can assist in mobilising people who seek to empower themselves and orient their activities in providing assistance for one another and meeting their collective welfare needs. Group interventions and collective action through various forms of organisation provide vehicles through which the fragmentation of individuals can be overcome. By channelling their energies in altruistic directions, they can work together to ensure the well-being of both individuals and the communities within which they are embedded.

Enabling collective action to facilitate both individual and group development requires creative ways of organising social relations. Although inadequate in resolving all the social problems facing contemporary societies, the option of social development and the rooting of economic forces within a social economy are more likely to achieve this objective than existing capitalist forms of organisation. Social workers have a key role to play as professionals who can mobilise communities to look after each other and make the most of the resources that are contained within them, and to raise the issue of a more equitable distribution of resources in society more generally. By doing so, they may facilitate the development of new alternatives that have yet to be devised and which may be more successful in responding to the pressing problems of today and prevent exacerbating the difficulties of tomorrow. Mobilising people in their communities is a good place for embarking upon this project. Social workers, with their considerable experience of working with people in their localities, have a crucial role to play in bringing such a vision to fruition.

Chapter 6

Engaging in Organisational Change

Introduction

Globalisation is having a substantial impact on the personal social services (Dominelli and Hoogvelt, 1996; Dominelli, 1999; Khan and Dominelli, 2000). Much of its impact on the social work profession has been articulated through the 'new managerialism', which has subjected welfare states in Western countries to market-oriented, regulatory regimes including that of becoming cost-effective businesses. The pressures emanating from market discipline have profoundly altered working relations in the welfare arena. These include having practitioners:

- make better use of existing resources within a residual welfare framework;

- target provision on those designated as the most deserving of poor people;

- become more accountable for their use of resources, time and expertise;

- exercise fiscal responsibility;

- negotiate with a broader range of service providers; and

- engage their clients more fully in the decisions made about their lives.

As organisations, voluntary sector welfare providers have become more business-oriented and the state's role has focused primarily on purchasing services and, through that, enabling services to be created and accessed.

These changes have altered the organisational context within which the personal social services are embedded. Some have been deemed desirable and welcomed, others have not. The requirement to make the best use of existing resources and ensure that they are used effectively is not unreasonable in any organisation, whether private, public, voluntary or domestic. Holding professionals accountable for their actions and demanding that they explain their decisions to both managers and users are also to be applauded. However, accountability is potentially contradictory and contested. It cannot simply mean being told what to do and then doing it. If excluded people are to be facilitated in challenging an inadequate welfare system and participate fully in developing more appropriate alternative services, accountability has to incorporate acting within a recognised code of ethics and a value system that endorses social justice and enables the enhancement of human well-being. Also, accountability ought to mean having the confidence to protest against social injustice when it is identified. Sadly, becoming business-oriented does not guarantee that those in need will receive the services they require; that working conditions for employees will become worker-friendly; or that employees will readily criticise their paymasters.

Commodification and the 'new managerialism' in social work

Part of the reason for this is the commodification of people and their needs occasioned by capitalist social organisation. In casting clients as consumers or customers who are subjected to bureaucratic imperatives, the 'new managerialism' turns clients and their needs into commodities. In short, they become incorporated into a profit-making enterprise that private entrepreneurs can exploit. The commodification of clients in this regard means that they are in danger of losing their dignity as people with a voice which is their own. Instead, they are obliged to frame their concerns within the tramlines established by policymakers, professional experts and entrepreneurs, whose ideas about which services are suitable dictate what becomes available. This construction of the situation positions client discourses in reactive mode, where their views are responses to the provisions designed by others who claim to act benevolently on their behalf – a kind of best-intentioned paternalism that leaves little scope for service users to intervene proactively in the decisions that affect their lives. In this process, client knowledge and expertise are easily devalued in favour of bureaucratic and fiscal rationality.

A further danger in the 'new managerialism' is its tendency to bureaucratise professional judgments and decision-making so that professionals cease to:

- consider the specific merits of a particular case;

- provide a holistic service that starts where the clients are now and seek change from that position; and

- facilitate the decision-making capacities of clients in contributing to their empowerment.

The 'new managerialism' also refocuses employer–employee relations in ways that further advantage management and the employers. The use of competency-based approaches for defining professional expertise, performance indicators and other forms of technological surveillance become tools to control and curtail professional power and channel the workforce in particular ways.

In the ensuing power struggle, the 'new managerialism' downplays the needs of professionals – as workers who are also people with needs relating to their employment in a difficult career – in favour of accounts and balance sheets that treat each practitioner as a unit of resource. In a people-oriented system, practitioners' ability to maintain high levels of motivation, job satisfaction and standards of excellence in the services they provide would be key concerns of managers rather than a side issue. Relationship-building is central to a people-oriented system. But the 'new managerialism' eschews relationships as counterproductive and unnecessary. Their devaluation presents a serious gap for social workers who have traditionally used relationship-building as a prime dynamic in changing people's behaviour and inspiring them to build a better future for themselves.

A social worker interviewed on a project conducted by Khan and Dominelli (2000) had this to say about the 'new managerialism' and the changes it had wrought in professional working lives:

> I feel that managerialism and market forces within a supposedly mixed economy of welfare are destroying professional social work practice. Increasingly the organisation is driven towards creating an expensive, callous bureaucracy, which prides itself on delivering resource-led policies as prime measures of its effectiveness and efficiency. Not content with deskilling a professional workforce, the organisation appears to have effectively distanced itself from accountability/responsibility towards social workers, preferring to devolve such responsibilities to the shoulder of individual workers. This has invariably caused untold stress and perpetuates a culture of 'fear' in the workplace. Social workers, in my opinion, are one of the most marginalised professionals within public service. The organisation has a poor record of adequately supporting/protecting social workers, doing little to promote the positive achievements of social workers, many of who are female residential level workers. Social services departments are usually predominantly managed by white middle class men. This perpetuates the patriarchal, conservative nature of the organisation. I think academic gazes should be geared towards finding out how a social service organisation enables social workers to achieve effectiveness and efficiency.

This social worker's comments reveal a sophisticated understanding of recent developments, and a depth of critique rarely articulated openly in the residential sector. However, they also expose a feeling of powerlessness amongst those who are expected to protect vulnerable people in this society, and they call for intellectuals to provide more guidance for practitioners in their day-to-day working routines.

The experiences of practitioners such as the one quoted above show that enforcing market-led regimes has turned social workers into units of resource. In other words, professionals have now become commodities, or exchangeable units of labour power whose skills have to be flexible and redeployable. That is, their skills have to be generalisable so that they can be transferred from one setting to another. The move towards competence-based practice with its fragmented, professionalised labour process is an apt instrument for this transformation in social work. In simplifying complex professional activities, competence-based social work makes it possible for any unit of resource to be replaced by another provided that all that is required of the worker involved is the ability to follow specified procedures in completing identified tasks. Thus, the commodification of clients' choices is parallelled by the commodification of professional labour. In the process, professional autonomy is effectively curtailed, and the practitioners' capacity to exercise professional discretion in responding to individual need is thereby limited. It constitutes the proletarianisation of professional labour and typifies a major shift in the culture and practices of social work. A social worker in the Khan and Dominelli (2000a) study put the changes that had occurred in the following words:

> If we become purchasers only we will need to change our title and will no longer be social workers but social welfare brokers.

Reining in professional autonomy is not, in and of itself, a negative act. It becomes so when it promotes routinised bureaucratic responses that are unable to address effectively an individual's unique circumstances and needs. Additionally, the customary bureaucratic methods that managers use to organise the labour process do *not* prepare the workforce for the complexities of practice. These include:

- dealing with the unexpected;

- addressing the multiple and interlinked difficulties of the people they are working with;

- making the myriad connections between the focus of their intervention and the multiple contexts that individuals, organisations and networks operate within; and

- the impact of the varied connections between different types of need upon their interventions.

In other words, in being turned into a commodity, the worker is no more than a technocrat or bureaucratic functionary following instructions. The capacity of a professional to exercise independent judgment after having made a thorough assessment of the issues to hand and relating to an individual in need in a holistic way becomes irrelevant to managerialist prerogatives. Yet, it is around the practitioner's conclusions that clients and professionals negotiate their relationship with each other, as clients attempt to win professionals over to their way of thinking and vice versa.

The problematic nature of market-driven changes carries the risk of exacerbating existing social inequalities. In contrast, changing the inegalitarian social relations, which are currently being propagated in a society that is guided by market principles, and repackaging social meaning in ways that are consistent with egalitarian norms are crucial dimensions of anti-oppressive practice. Anti-oppressive practice offers an alternative vision to the market-driven provision of the personal social services (Dominelli, 1996) and aims to empower individuals and communities. It does not target downwards to a residual model of welfare in a state that is preoccupied with recycling resources amongst and within those groups that are most needy. Instead, it operates within eligibility criteria enshrined within the notion of entitlement that all people have human rights that apply to them unconditionally – a universality of outcome in which the end result is equality. Thus, anti-oppressive practice goes beyond a world-view which is rooted in cultural relativism, for human rights belong to all, not just the privileged few. Human rights become a vehicle for guaranteeing all people, individually and collectively, the basic essentials of an egalitarian system – freedom from what Beveridge called the five giants of want, squalor, disease, idleness and ignorance – to develop people to their full potential individually and collectively.

ʕ Anti-oppressive practice adds to these the concern that inequalities are eliminated whilst taking account of the environment, the whole person and the differences that give people unequal life chances (Adamson et al., 1988). It also uses the idea of interdependence between people as a basis upon which diverse peoples can organise together to change their social situations for the better. This requires recognition of their different starting points and working at identifying common goals that can be pursued jointly. In anti-oppressive practice, organisational change is geared towards the realisation of this vision. Social workers can play a crucial role in this process by mobilising people, particularly poor, excluded or marginalised peoples, and facilitating organisational and cultural change. They also have a major role to play in transforming their own workplaces and can organise to change these. ⱽ

Organising in collective entities is important if substantial organisational change that is to promote equality for all is to be attempted. It is difficult to overcome the fragmentation and isolation brought about by the individualisation of social relations under capitalist globalisation without the collective sharing of aspects of personal experiences and the taking of collective action. Doing so is also important in realising the potential for formulating social problems as other than the outcome of inadequacies on the part of the individual concerned. The consciousness-raising activities of the feminist movement have provided a classical illustration of the practical enactment of this objective.

Its strength in demystifying social relations has made consciousness-raising a powerful tool in initiating changes in social structures. The unique potency of consciousness-raising with regards to mobilising women is that it has changed a woman's emotional and intellectual understanding of herself and her world, as well as changing her perceptions of the social relations within which she is embedded. She also becomes aware of the ways these are constructed through social interaction to achieve certain ends. As a result, she can make connections between her personal plight and that of others similarly placed, and between personal dissatisfaction and the organisational confines within which social relationships occur. Through this, the relationship between the personal and the political becomes obvious and susceptible to being challenged at both personal and structural levels (Frankfort, 1972). Similar points can be made about the ways in which other social movements, for example black activists (Collins, 1991), disabled people (Oliver, 1990) and poor people (Freire, 1972), have used consciousness-raising techniques to unpack their own specific forms of oppression.

Radical social work began the process of tackling such oppression in recent practice. It has argued for widespread structural change in the social work profession by demystifying the class relations which have structured interpersonal relations and enabled middle-class professionals to control working-class people (see Corrigan and Leonard, 1978). However, this school of thought did not consider consciousness-raising as a process, but as an act in a zero-sum display of power, whereby individuals and groups become aware of the dynamics through which they are kept subjugated by those who rule over them. Consequently, when transposed to the organisational level, this analysis left managers on one side of the fence as 'them' and workers and clients on the other side as 'us', with antagonistic 'either/or' relations between them. Their interaction was depicted as one of two parties contesting each other's claims. Whilst helpful in clarifying and speaking about class oppression – a topic that had been submerged in professional discourses up to that point – and exposing non-radical professionals for failing to side with their working-class clients, this analysis has presented social relations in simplistic terms that have neglected the complex nuances embedded in these relations in practice. Although alliances between opposing groups were posited as possible, how these were to be achieved in day-to-day routines remained more than vague. They were outside the framework of analysis and hence it proved difficult for its adherents to either conceptualise these differently or develop strategies for addressing them in reality.

With regards to the issue of organisational change, radical social work practice to date has been predicated on the notion that there are dichotomous relationships between those who manage the personal social services and those who work in them; and between those who work in them and those who use their services (see Bolger et al., 1981). Such attitudes between the managed and those who manage heighten the antagonisms that exist between them and create an impression that there is little point in seeking approaches which enable them to work together in any capacity. This pre-empts the potential for either strategic or tactical alliances that are rooted in understanding the specificities of their position and the myriad sources of oppression that impact upon both these groups differently. In other words, in defining the situation in *power over* terms, the managers are positioned as all powerful whilst the clients or workers as employees are portrayed as powerless. The same dichotomous relationship applies to workers who are posited as all powerful over their completely powerless clients. This view has failed to capture a reality in which power is created and embodied in social relations in more complicated and subtle ways. Anti-oppressive practice has endeavoured to address this limitation through a holistic approach that acknowledges the interconnections between the managed and the manager.

In this chapter, I challenge dichotomous definitions of the change process and issues to be addressed in producing organisational change. I use case study materials to demonstrate that there are situations in which managers can work alongside those they manage around the achievement of certain specified goals; and that practitioners can work with service users to secure agreed ends. This more complicated approach involves considerable negotiation and dialogue between the parties engaging with each other. But, it is more likely to initiate second-order organisational changes which can in turn raise questions about the ways in which social work and society are organised and the necessity for social change even at this level (Broadbent and Laughlin, 1990).

Organisation(s) matter(s)

Organisations are sets of social arrangements that people create in order to achieve certain goals. They form important spaces that are both contextual, in that they are constituted as particular sites in which social interactions occur, and structural, in that they configure the pathways within and through which social relations take place. Moreover, these structures are constituted by the social relations of which they are part. So, the potential for change and flux is always present, although realising this can prove extremely difficult, for people can be very resistant to the idea of change and settle for remaining in well-known, comfortable ruts. Achieving change depends on the actors involved, their aims and intentions and the 'allocative and authoritative resources' that they bring with them when they interact with others.

Social and material resources, policies, legislation, routines, regulations, a code of ethics and practices are part of an organisation's structure. They also constitute part of its resources and are part of its capabilities in supporting its employees and users. People's relationships with one another occur in and through these capabilities, and they become reproduced or challenged as part of their interaction with each other. People also use structural contexts to guide their behaviour. These form the backdrop against which their conduct can then be judged as organisationally appropriate or not. Organisational contexts become important tools in the repertoire of managerial control and can be utilised to either discipline or reward workers; or to meet client needs or not.

Professional social workers, like other workers, are bound by their agency's constraints as part of their employment contracts. Workers accept organisational constraints and commit themselves to working within them to a significant degree as part of their terms and conditions of employment. Their agreement to these is conditional, for the strength of their commitment to them will depend on how far their personal value system coincides with the organisational one, how pressing their desire to secure a particular job is, what other options for employment are available to them, their relationships with management, co-workers and clients, and what they expect to achieve in their work. These conditions will influence the extent to which they adhere to organisational norms and values and how long they will remain attracted to a particular job.

Legislation is also part of an organisational structure. In some areas of intervention, for example child welfare and mental health work, specific legislative acts impact on the types of activity that an organisation and its practitioners can lawfully undertake (Bayes and Howell, 1981). But, unlike many other employees whose activities are bound by legal constraints, social workers are also required to act in the interests of their clients who often challenge the very organisational norms which social workers as workers are obliged to maintain. These contradictory expectations lie at the heart of social work relationships and have provided the space that radical social workers have sought to prise open in order to shift the balance of power away from agency representatives and onto clients.

Their success in altering this state of affairs has been mixed, for power, as a key negotiating force created through and arising from myriad interactions in a particular context, is not readily conceded by any of those interacting with each other. And, although radical social work has made some gains by placing the issue of oppression on caring professionals' agendas, its concerns have not been mainstreamed to any significant extent. So its impact on statutory social services in particular has been peripheral, except for profiling the contradictory nature of helping relationships and exposing its controlling elements.

As long as maximising one's power to achieve one's ends is the basis for the negotiation, contested relations will continue to be the norm in the professional client–worker relationship. Contested relations are not necessarily conflictual, although they often may be. But they are constantly being challenged to open up new possibilities and directions for change. The outcome of the challenge depends on whether or not those involved in them agree to pursue similar ends by agreed means. Thus, people can continue to challenge one another on the details and their understandings of these, even if they have consented to a specific set of objectives and how to reach them in general terms. The net effect of these contested relations is that people can form temporary alliances with one another, including with those they normally do not consider as allies, if they seek the same goals. Recognising the potential for doing so is important if an individual or group of workers or clients is seeking to engage management in altering a particular state of affairs. Thinking along these lines allows for the formation of strategic alliances amongst those they would usually position as being on the other side. Participating in such alliances can also assist workers in empowering themselves when questioning existing policies and seeking to change their current thrust.

Tactical alliances of this nature have been evident in the implementation of equal opportunities policies. Workers, their trade unions and professional organisations have worked with sympathetic managers to convince others in the organisational hierarchy to support the recruitment and selection of underrepresented groups, for example women in managerial ranks and various ethnic minority peoples throughout the organisation. A principal shortcoming of this approach to change has been the tendency of those involved to assume that a limited action stands for more than that, that is, widespread social change. This attitude has resulted in practitioners taking managers' involvement in changing only one element of their larger strategic vision as signifying a broader commitment to egalitarian relations in every aspect of organisational life.

Proceeding according to this definition of events produces complacency amongst activists who go on to think that their entire programme of action has been accepted by management. And so they fail to continue raising demands for further transformational change once a specific goal in their wider strategy has been secured. An example of this has been assuming that ethnic monitoring will lead to the creation of more ethnic-sensitive services rather than merely describing the present state of affairs. The movement from one position to another requires further action, not the assumption that the part stands for the whole.

Furthermore, the managers' own position of relative powerlessness has not been addressed in this formulation of the relationship between workers and their managers. For example, practitioners making strategic alliances at team level tend to ignore the contradictory pressures to which middle mangers are subjected when they are being held accountable for their responses by both those who are higher in the labour echelon and those supporting the demands that emanate from those below. Yet, without considering and addressing the structural position of managers as allies in a more holistic way, their support of change initiatives in the longer term may be obviated.

To form allies in tackling oppression, activists should acknowledge and deal with the various forms of oppression that impact on every individual taking part in change-oriented activities (Bishop, 1994). Their participation may indicate dissent or dissatisfaction with the existing regime, but this is usually contingent and limited to specific circumstances and issues and should be taken as standing for no more than that. An illustration of this process is an organisational commitment to equal opportunities in recruiting and selecting staff, particularly those from ethnic minorities. Taking this limited action to represent the eradication of racism ignores the many other sites and practices in and through which racist social relations are produced and reproduced. So, whilst more black people may have become employed by an organisation, little else has changed in terms of either how the organisation is run, or how managers organise their relationships with employees and service users. This, I call short-termism.

Short-termism is the belief that changing either a part of an organisation or a particular practice at a given point in time will transform the whole, and not understanding that such action may indicate only the partial or conditional nature of an ally's involvement in a broader change effort. Short-termism produces patterns of action that are relevant to any alliance, regardless of whether or not it involves managers, workers or clients. Indeed, whatever aspect of identity is emphasised, organisers and activists should be aware of the two limitations of short-termism – its conditionality and limited scope. These pose dangers for the duration and strength of their activities, and their capacity to ensure that long-term or sustained changes in organisational structures take place.

Another important aspect of engaging in change is recognising that not being involved in an activity also has consequences. In other words, not taking action has implications for any change process. It can become part of the dynamics of the process of incorporation or resistance to change. That one of these responses may be an unintended consequence (Giddens, 1990) of not taking action is irrelevant for those seeking to change existing inegalitarian social relations. In this context, there is no such thing as not taking sides. Doing nothing is supporting the other side. That is, the 'them' over there becomes part of the 'us' over here, or vice versa, as a result of not taking a stand. Consequently, change is not a simple either/or process, but one full of complexities and ambiguities, each of which has to be understood and negotiated over if progress in achieving egalitarian ends is to occur.

These difficulties can make becoming involved in change seem a daunting prospect, a possibility that discourages many people from even beginning to get involved in challenging existing social relations. In these circumstances, remembering that not participating in action still results in being involved may be helpful. Being aware of the consequences of remaining detached can encourage an individual to engage in what is going on and thereby influence more unequivocally the direction that events might take. In other words, taking conscious action enables the individual to shape what is happening so that it is more in line with their particular values and wishes, thereby making them feel more empowered in the change process rather than being overwhelmed by it. This point is examined in the practice illustration that follows.

■ *Case study*

Angela was a white manager in a small agency within a national network of community associations providing services for disadvantaged people in predominantly white, working-class communities. The agency had equal opportunities policies of which the team was very proud. Angela was very committed to establishing egalitarian relations. She worked hard to involve her team in decisions about their work. Angela was also emphatic that only those who merited their posts were on her books.

However, she was rather timid when it came to exercising managerial power in support of what she considered 'radical' suggestions or ideas that had the potential of initiating conflict within the working group. It was not that she was afraid of responding to challenging proposals as such, but that she worried about not knowing all the risks that she would be signing up to if she went along with any particular proposal. It never occurred to her that sitting on the fence could have a similar impact. Appreciating this point proved a hard lesson for her.

The possibility of her learning it arose one day when she was recruiting a community organiser. The two candidates who were interviewed proved extremely able and were closely matched in terms of organising experience and performance during the interviewing process. The main difference between the two of them was that Bella, a woman of Afro-Caribbean origins, had higher educational qualifications than Angie, a white woman.

The majority, although not all, of her team supported Bella's candidature. Those who did not believed that the white woman would more readily identify with the community they served and be able to form relationships with the residents fairly easily. Angela found it difficult to make up her mind which candidate should get the job. She was concerned about which candidate would serve the community more effectively and did not wish to create a 'bad' environment in the office by making a group of people unhappy with her decision, and thereby 'split' the team. Moreover, she did not want to make 'race' an issue in the appointment. So she refused to facilitate discussions on this matter when asked to do so by those she saw as Bella's supporters.

As she was required by national policy to consult with the national office over appointments as part of the equal opportunities monitoring process, she told the team that she would let head office make the decision without a recommendation from her. The group who wanted Bella appointed felt unsupported by Angela at that point, but said nothing. Those endorsing Angie's application felt similarly and acted likewise. No one sensed that they could ask to examine the dynamics of 'race' and racism during the meeting. Later, over coffee, when they were amongst those they trusted, several expressed their frustrations about being unable to do so.

The silences of both groups did little to enable Angela to make a decision about the appointment. Part of Angela's problem was that she neither knew the precise nature of the workers' views, nor did she feel capable of taking action that might alienate either group by taking an option that she felt would leave a section of her team unhappy.

The outcome of head office's intervention was that Angie was appointed. Those supporting her candidature were elated. Those who expected Bella to become their colleague felt let down and extremely angry. Angela was surprised that she did not feel comfortable with the decision. However, she refused to accept the view of those who had supported Bella's application that, through her inaction, she had been complicit with what they experienced as a racist outcome.

Angela's inaction in this situation could be deemed an abrogation of her responsibilities as a manager, for in failing to act, she had been influential in producing the final result. In doing nothing, that is, by asking head office to make the decision for her, she had allowed a less qualified candidate to become one of her employees, and enabled the violation of several of her key principles in running the office to occur. In other words, she ended up with precisely the scenario she had sought to avoid.

This case indicates the complexities that have to be negotiated in any situation if cycles that reproduce inegalitarian relations are to be broken. There are a number of different levels at which racist attitudes are likely to be operating in this case. A racist formulation of Angie's skills assumes her capacity to work across racial divides while at the same time denying Bella's. In the realities of practice, it is more likely that a black person living in a largely white society would have acquired the skills necessary for working with white people as part of their life experience and training, whilst a white person who has always lived and worked amongst other white people is unlikely to have acquired the skills necessary to work with black people (Maxime, 1986). In meritocratic terms, all workers in an organisation should be capable of working appropriately with any member of the public demanding a service, regardless of their ethnicity, gender or other social status. Angie was *assumed* to meet this criterion whilst Bella was not, thereby inadvertently perpetuating a racist casting of the two candidates.

This case also demonstrates the importance of having a more holistic vision of an egalitarian society to which people can aspire, and the significance of following through with action aimed at realising it. It also reveals the need for alliances to be made across and within status hierarchies for a common objective to be achieved. For this to happen, open and meaningful dialogue that respects differences of opinion as being significant to an outcome has to occur. If the issues represent important matters, dialogue may provide novel opportunities for reaching agreed objectives. Although the end result cannot be guaranteed, had the team been able to speak their silences, it may have been easier to ensure that the most qualified and capable candidate was in fact appointed.

The silencing of dissenting views when social differences are at the heart of the matter is more likely to affirm than to challenge existing inequalities, and it promotes bad feelings amongst colleagues who have to work together in the interests of providing appropriate services to those requiring them. The ensuing atmosphere of being unvalued and disenfranchised would impact on service users as well as adversely affecting relationships within the team. If Angela's team had felt more able to discuss issues of racism in an open and supportive environment, the issue would not have been covered up and the outcome might have resulted in people being fully cognisant of the dynamics of both intentional and unintentional racism and its consequences for all of them. Being able to converse about this topic would have required both groups of workers and their manager not to speak from positions of superiority about their particular definition of the situation, but to really listen to and unpack the significance of what was being said and not said by all those involved in the matter.

Had they been enabled to embark on such a process, they might have discovered that they could express their anger with each other and the frustrations they felt about the way the matter had been handled. This would have been painful but, if handled well, it would have freed up their emotions to begin to invest in the situation on a more honest basis with each other, and possibly even to grow stronger as a team. The task of facilitating this process was up to the manager, who, if unable to undertake it personally, as Angela seems to indicate, should have brought in someone who could have helped them speak to each other across their own differences without posturing about them. Moreover, in not dealing with the feelings aroused by this outcome, further problems would be stored up for the team and those who would use their services. So, this outcome should be considered for its impact on the team's future working relations. Even without considering them, team dynamics will not be the same after this appointment.

Angela is intuitively aware that 'something' is amiss, as witnessed by her 'not feeling comfortable' with the decision taken by head office. Yet, she does not follow through on this to examine its significance or ask for help in understanding the situation and the role that she has played in creating it, even after the event. This allows the antagonistic feelings aroused to smoulder away and further poison relationships amongst those involved by intensifying experiences of mistrust and betrayal. Part of the problem Angela faces may also be her own unsupported and vulnerable position. She does not come across as an empowered and empowering manager. Her own powerlessness fuels its continuation, for she does not feel that she can identify and seek help in addressing her own shortcomings, including her fear of conflict within the team and inability to take, defend and manage difficult decisions.

Issues of identity, power and agency are also relevant to this case study. Angela's personal identity as a manager was one of being competent and interested in power-sharing. Her behaviour above suggests that she is also fearful of conflict and that her attempts at power-sharing can turn into an abrogation of managerial responsibility which can thwart agency policies and also disillusion those employees for whom she holds supervisory responsibilities. Additionally, it shows that she is a manager who does not really engage with the views and feelings of her team members. Hence, they feel disillusioned and disempowered by her behaviour. Angela's situation exemplifies the interconnectedness of the relationships between the managed and the managers. It also highlights the dependent and interdependent nature of the relationships between them. Both have roles to play in producing a particular outcome, even in a hierarchically structured organisation.

Angela has attempted to reduce the impact of organisational hierarchies by 'consulting' with her team and involving them in decision-making. But it is extremely difficult to flatten hierarchies to free decision-making potential, or facilitate power-sharing in institutions that assume power differentials are important. At the end of the day, the hierarchical organisational structure leaves Angela with the ultimate decision about what to do. And, here, Angela's position as both manager and managed becomes clear. Neither Angela's colleagues nor her team have recognised or questioned the constraints that this structuring of their relationships imposes upon them. And so the issue of Angela's needs as an employee who is a manager never arises, and she remains unsupported and isolated. Additionally, there is no recognition of her needs as a *woman* manager, even though research indicates that the manager's experience is a gendered one (Hallett, 1991; Grimwood and Popplestone, 1993; Dominelli, 1997c), and racialised as well as gendered for black women (Durrant, 1989; Dominelli, 1997c).

Additionally, there is the issue of the team's isolation from the communities they serve. Had they taken steps to engage with people living within their catchment area, they might have been able to develop partnerships that would enable them to treat clients in more empowering ways – as people who have a contribution to make in the creation of services that they would like to use. Such actions would have also enabled team members to develop skills in dealing with difference and the uncertainties that would challenge their knowledge and traditional ways of relating to community groups. They would have also had the opportunity to learn how to work in more co-operative ways (Shragge and Fontan, 2000) and engage ordinary people in bringing about organisational change.

Challenging the organisation

Angela's organisation also reflects institutional inequalities. The one relating to 'race' and racism is evidenced by the failure of working practices to value the contributions that might have been made by someone with a different identity from that of the dominant group. The organisation's institutional racism was reflected in its routine practices which were not open to valuing difference because they simply reproduced trusted routines, despite these having been found wanting from an equal opportunities point of view. For Bella to have fitted into this particular organisation, she would have had to have been indistinguishable from the existing members of the team, that is, assimilated into and by it. Had she been employed, this would have exacerbated the difficulties that Bella, as a black person, would have to address because the onus for 'fitting in' would fall onto her.

The responses to her application suggest that a number of her proposed colleagues would have found it difficult to accept her difference as a strength. Without making a big issue out of it, they are likely to be constantly testing Bella in the hopes of thwarting her so that their belief that 'she is not up to the job' would be confirmed. The configuration of the office means that the likelihood of Bella being able to question behaviour that is largely emotional and therefore fairly intangible and gain support from her manager in doing so are slim. And, as Bella would encounter these obstacles because she is a black person, they are caused by racist practices and show another unacknowledged burden that a black person carries as an employee. Organisations such as this one would have to challenge their workplace culture in order to initiate changes that would improve the chances of a black employee being treated as a valued colleague with much to offer the team and the service users.

Fear is another important aspect of the social relations and dynamics evident in this case study. Angela's fear of being proven wrong or making a mistake in a sensitive issue such as racism is one element of it. Her employer has a responsibility in addressing this matter because it hinders Angela's capacity to act according to her own expectations and become the sort of manager she desires to be. Providing support groups for managers would be an important approach that could be used to sustain those in charge of the office. This would require the organisation to cease thinking about managers as isolated personnel who must resolve the problems that they encounter themselves.

Another difficulty is the team's fear of being branded racist. This blocks them from knowing how to welcome someone from a different racial and ethnic background into their midst on equal terms, particularly when doing so might require that they do things differently. In other words, they could not just carry on with their old ways of working, and these would have to change along with their old ways of thinking. Yet they are uncertain about what to do. Fear of the unknown is debilitating to their capacity to act in the present and so they do not welcome changes to trusted routines. It is important that employers address such fears and provide opportunities where their employees can discuss their concerns openly, with the aim of improving their ability to engage on equal terms with those who are different from them.

Another avenue for improving the team's capacities to interact more appropriately with people in Bella's situation is for either management or members of the team or both to have developed outreach activities and develop links with the communities which their organisation serves. In this case, the team could have formed partnerships involving both black and white communities on their doorstep and found out what services were needed by their constituent groups and how they might best respond more effectively to their needs. Had team members established such types of relationships with these communities, they would have been better placed to respond to Bella joining them and have discussed issues of racism without feeling disempowered by the idea of even raising the issue.

Conclusions

Initiating organisational change in welfare institutions is not easy, nor is it a short-term proposition. The complexity of the issues and different actors involved requires a holistic perspective that covers both short- and long-term objectives, skilled negotiation and the ability to reach across and bridge differences between people. For social workers, organisational change has to occur within their own organisations, in their relationships with clients and in the broader society within which they are embedded.

Engaging in organisational change means that social workers have to subject their own agencies to scrutiny and find ways of making good the shortcomings they find within their own institutions. This becomes a major task for practitioners to undertake and they need to form alliances with others who can assist them in carrying their plans forward. Collaboration with managers can become an important source of support in facilitating change. However, the management role cannot be taken as simply a more powerful one. The ambiguities and contradictions in these roles can become a basis for joint working as well as sharpening the divisions between managers and those they manage. Along with having powers to make decisions for those in their charge, managers are subjected to pressures which may leave them feeling disempowered. However, if a manager is unable to help him or herself, he or she is unlikely to be able to support the workers in his or her team. So it is important that managers are supported by their organisation if they are to effectively support workers and service users.

Securing organisational change also allows practitioners and managers to form alliances with service users and can act as a positive way of engaging all stakeholders in an agency in improving the provisions that are being made available. Creating a more facilitative and egalitarian institution is an objective that can bring disparate groups together in a manner that can produce innovations in the services that are delivered, a working environment that promotes workers' skills and sense of well-being as employees, and services that clients can be proud of accessing.

Chapter 7

Beyond Postmodern Welfare

Establishing Unity Between Content, Process and Outcomes

Introduction

Postmodern welfare values diversity but, in eschewing meta-narratives, it fragments and individualises society to produce atomised persons, each of whom looks after him or herself. Postmodern theorists argue that it is no longer possible to change society in substantial ways, if doing so relies on having a grand vision that requires meta-level analyses, changing macro-level structures or asking people to organise collectively to undertake change in these arenas. Consequently, providing welfare on an individual basis is inappropriate in an inter-dependent world, regardless of the tenets of neo-liberalism. In my view, postmodern welfare can be appropriated easily for profit-making by unaccountable entrepreneurs and the vagaries of the market. Post-modern critics of modern welfare states have engendered a sense of despair in people's capacity to alter their environment, if it is based on dreams that seek to encompass everyone or encourage them to work in solidarity with each other.

In this chapter, I examine postmodern postulates for welfare and its conceptualisation of society and social change. These I find pessimistic and unhelpful to the task of eliminating oppressive relationships. Instead, I argue for a new basis for collective action that is rooted in the principles of accepting responsibility for each other's welfare, ensuring that those who are excluded through social processes are integrated into broader social networks and the realisation of a full citizenship that holds even when an individual crosses borders. The principles of interdependence, solidarity and reciprocity are central to implementing this alternative vision.

This approach recognises the interdependence that exists between people both individually and collectively in the local, national and international domains. Interdependence becomes important in embedding networks of solidarity that traverse social divisions and provides the framework within which more egalitarian relations can flourish. Changing oppressive relations has historically required people to share a vision for a better world on a collective basis and organise together to realise it (see Brinton, 1966). In other words, oppressed peoples improve their general life circumstances by acting together with others, even if their decision to do so is a strategic choice aimed at dealing with a specific situation. Acting as a group enables them to secure change and/or obtain compromises from those who have constructed social relations not to take their views and requirements seriously. In this manner, they challenge those who have succeeded in acquiring dominance at a particular point in time and undermine *power over* relations that privilege the needs of elites over those who may or may not live in their particular locale.

I suggest that macro-level change aimed at establishing egalitarian relations is possible if people can organise together on the basis of acknowledging their different starting points vis-à-vis society's allocation of power and resources and work together to identify the grounds upon which they can subvert inegalitarian social relations and express solidarity over specific agreed objectives. Making such a project possible will require agreement over the content of their action, the processes whereby it will be conducted and its outcomes. In other words, a unity that integrates objectives, processes and outcomes is central to working together to create a better world for all, not just for a privileged few. Understanding who stands to gain and at whose expense, if relationships deteriorate, to reinforce *power over* dynamics is an important component of such action. By pursuing this line of argument, I attempt to make the case that anti-oppressive practice can take us beyond the pessimism of postmodernism.

Postmodern insights

Despite this pessimism, postmodernist critiques of the existing social order contain a number of useful propositions about the modern condition. Some of these provide valuable insights which anti-oppressive practitioners can utilise to promote individual and collective well-being (Leonard, 1997). Postmodernists base many of their criticisms of social work on what they term its 'modernist' tendencies. These centre around the:

- propensity to treat clients as homogeneous objects;

- uncritical acceptance of scientific developments as progressive;

- futile search for absolute truths;

- fixed and totalising notions of identity; and

- other aspects which I have identified earlier in this text.

The inadequacies that postmodernists have identified in modernist or traditional analyses of social work have received a mixed reception in the field. However, one failing that they have highlighted is particularly important for anti-oppressive practitioners to note. That is the capacity to ignore differences in a presumed unity around a homogeneous subject. Lessons for an anti-oppressive practitioner to draw from this analysis are to value difference and not take unity for granted, focusing instead on creating it.

Another understanding that postmodern thinkers have identified that anti-oppressive practitioners can ponder upon is the modernist professional's assumption of the *passivity* of clients and the paternalistic approach to them that this fosters. Assumptions that privilege professional expertise have been integrated into the type of social work that has developed in the post-war welfare state and constitute an essential feature of discourses about the caring professions generally (Lorenz, 1994). Deconstructing the homogeneous passive subject has been central to the postmodern critique of this form of practice (Nicholson, 1990).

However, postmodernists have not been alone in identifying social workers' incapacity to meet client needs. A number of others – radical social workers, critical theorists and social activists, who may not share the concerns of postmodernists – have also raised similar limitations. Yet, these other critics have continued to reproduce unitary, if somewhat active, subjects within their analyses of whatever social division has preoccupied them, whether this has been class, gender, 'race', disability, sexual orientation or age (Healy, 2000), and thereby failed to transcend modernist conceptualisations of the problems and, in the process, lost the complexities of the individual situations (Parton, 1994).

Postmodernists have also highlighted how modernist paradigms of partnerships with clients privilege those who control social resources (Pease and Fook, 1999). In these, the parameters within which the sharing of power occurs have cast the client as an object who does the bidding of those who are more powerful than he or she. This construct further negates the client's capacities as a social actor (Rojek et al., 1988). Anti-oppressive practitioners promote client agency and voice to create more egalitarian working relationships.

On a more mundane level, postmodern insights indicate that clients' lives are rooted in everyday routines and interactions. Clients do not set out to challenge macro-level power relations. Focusing on micro-level interactions is empowering to clients because this is the site in which they can exercise the most control, a point that those bent on large-scale changes seem not to notice. Anti-oppressive practitioners cannot ignore either dimension. Unless they link the macro- and micro-levels in both their analyses and practice and begin from where the client is now, they are unlikely to get far in the change process.

Anti-oppressive practitioners are unlikely to embark on an enterprise aimed at securing wholesale social change through an individual worker–client relationship. Were he or she to do so, the clients are likely to feel even more disempowered than they do already, when facing a welfare bureaucracy and its representatives with requests to meet their daily needs and are rejected. Marcus, a young unemployed man of Scottish descent who had lost his partner and their kids through drink and violent behaviour, hinted at his rootedness in the everyday during his interview, when I asked what he thought he could change as a result of being a social work client. He laughed and said:

> Change? [more laughter] Do you really think I can make a difference to anything? Just look at this place. Next to no furniture...Nothing works properly. Hasn't seen a lick of paint for years...I get by. Denise has left me.

Can't get my kids back from the social. Bloody officials. You don't know them. They come at you all nice like, but lie through their teeth. Don't mean a word they say. Never listen to you. They're always right. You're always wrong. As to giving me money, forget it. Skint, that's me. No help from anybody. Rage. That's all I can do...Maybe if Denise and I got back together, the two of us could do something to make them listen. If we could get the kids back, that would be a major start.

To someone paralysed by being embedded in day-to-day concerns, change at any level seems facetious. Marcus does not see macro-level change as being at all relevant to him. It is only as an outsider listening to his story that I can see that macro-level contexts have had an important impact on his life and can account for a large part of the problems he faces – poverty, unemployment caused when the shipyards downsized, poor employment options in the locality, lack of training for other well-paid jobs, hegemonic masculinity becoming a barrier when he is no longer the provider for his family and resorts to violence to control members of his family, and a general hopelessness that pervades the estate that he lives in – to name a few. To some degree, even the social workers' failure to help Marcus can be understood as the result of a particular type of social work practice that does not deal with macro-level issues when working with individuals. Indeed, not doing so is a basic tenet of mainstream or maintenance social work.

Marcus's narrative makes it clear that he sees himself as a victim – primarily of the social workers who represent 'the system' in his life and whose interventions he experiences as oppressive. He does not abstract his situation from the immediacy of the micro-level. The only change he is interested in is getting his family back together, despite his inertia in dealing with some of the problems that he could, at least in theory, do more about, such as improving his physical surroundings so that these would be more welcoming to women and children and seeking help in curbing his violent behaviour. His fatalism has been constructed out of his refusing to accept responsibility for doing something about his situation himself, despite his victimhood. In other words, he has created his own situation within contexts that have not been of his own making, which is why, ideally, both the micro- and macro-levels need to be addressed to initiate substantial changes in Marcus's position.

If Marcus were to take responsibility for those elements that are under his control, he could begin to control some of his circumstances. But, given his current understanding of his situation, following even this more limited course of action would require some external input into Marcus's life. The aim of such intervention would be to enable him to feel hopeful about his prospects and more personally in control of his life, advise him of the opportunities that he can use to solve his difficulties, and assist him in accessing other social resources. Although Marcus is primarily embedded in his local circumstances, some of the problems that he has to address do have links to more global and structural deficiencies, for example unemployment and the ideology of a hegemonic masculinity that endorses violence as a way of responding to stress and relating to men, women and children. Social workers could help Marcus to make the connections between these and his particular circumstances.

Once he understands the dynamics of how macro-level forces shape the routines of his everyday life at the micro-level, Marcus can begin to understand the connections between structural changes and his feelings of worthlessness as a man. Reaching this understanding will make it easier for him to begin to deal with his oppression of Denise and the children, take responsibility for his behaviour, and address his feelings of being oppressed himself. Making headway in carving out a better life might be more readily facilitated if he were to engage in action with other people with similar problems and who share his understandings of the world. Then they could engage in discussions and/or activities that would enable him to make sense of his life and his lack of success in it.

If these activities helped him to link both macro- and micro-contexts to his behaviour, he might be able to begin to take some responsibility for the part he has played in getting into the position he is in at present. This would in turn support him in rising above his victim status and help him to tackle some of the broader issues that impact upon his life. He might even be moved to either directly or indirectly endorse the work of others engaged in securing macro-level changes. To address his own particular problems, Marcus would have to participate in action that goes beyond the (inter)personal front, at least by benefiting from the activities of others who are involved in understanding and securing social change at the more macro-level.

Without support in his current predicament, the actions that are needed to achieve wholesale change in his situation would be overwhelming for clients such as Marcus. Covering the entire range of tasks would also be impossible for any one individual to undertake on his or her own. Without social organisation of a collective kind, individuals have little option but to rely on interpersonal relations to 'get by'. So, in client–worker relationships, they concentrate on getting the best deal they can from the professionals that deal directly with them and use their own sources of power to enhance their negotiating capacities and secure what they want (Dominelli and Gollins, 1997). And, as he is without external assistance, this is the point at which Marcus is stuck, to the detriment of his own welfare and that of the meaningful others who have interacted with him.

Clients 'work' at their relationships

Client resilience, strengths and skills are downplayed in most professional discourses. Being client-centred involves appreciation of the contributions that clients themselves make in sustaining client–worker relationships. In other words, clients *work* at their relationships with professionals. Focusing on client agency helps anti-oppressive practitioners to value the efforts that clients make in securing the services they need. The activities involved in seeking help from social workers constitute *work* for the client (Callahan, 2000). Such work is constantly devalued and taken for granted by professionals, who simply assume that clients will put in whatever effort is required to meet their demands regardless of the costs that they have to bear in the process of doing so. An action such as coming to the office for a meeting may require a client to demonstrate considerable organisational skills and expend resources such as time and money, neither of which are automatically remunerated by the welfare agency. This in itself sets up inequalities between the worker and the client. The worker's time and transportation costs when doing a home visit are paid for by their employer; those incurred by the client in visiting the office become personal burdens to be borne in an individual capacity. In this situation, the work of one party to the interaction (the professional) is acknowledged, that of the other (the client) is not.

Clients constantly have to jump through hoops to obtain the services they need. This is work and requires the skilful navigation of official systems, procedures, personal relationships and networks. Service users have to become experts at finding ways in which they can maximise the likelihood of achieving their goals. And although they may feel that what is expected of them is unfair and operates to their detriment, their experience tells them that they have to become skilled at playing the system to make it more responsive to their aspirations. A commonly recognised ploy in this regard is that of a mother who finds her children a handful and would like some family support services. Because these are not usually available without a child protection issue being at the forefront of a social work intervention (DoH, 1995), she may claim that she will abuse her children if something is not done to help her when she has no intention of harming them, or she may just leave them in a social worker's office if getting support seems unlikely without such action. These responses to bureaucratised services on the part of these women should not be constructed as irrational in professional discourses, but as strategies of empowerment, even if these are misguided from the point of view of her children or her own aspirations to be a good mother to them. Moreover, these approaches to securing resources are often ineffective in securing the ends women desire and their label of being 'bad' mothers may be reinforced (Strega et al., 2000).

The 'games' that claimants and professionals play to find spaces within unresponsive bureaucratic provisions to address client needs are attempts at dealing with structural problems as if they were personal defects that can be overcome through the application of individual ingenuity. These strategies are ineffective because the structures that the actors are embedded within remain intact. Sadly, postmodernity offers little by way of tackling the issues raised in practice by the experiences of clients whose life stories indicate that alongside reorienting their own behaviour, structural changes in their social conditions are also required if their position is to truly change for the better, or for empowering relations to become the norm.

The failings of postmodernism

Postmodern analysts acknowledge structural limitations and abuses in professional power but do not seek to provide suggestions for tackling them. In these circumstances, I am inclined to agree with Young (1990, p. 19), who argues that postmodern theory is 'European culture's awareness that it is no longer the unquestioned and dominant centre of the world'. As such, postmodernism signifies the desire of Western intellectuals to come to terms with their own historical relativity by developing a theoretical construct that accepts their being subjectively decentred without challenging existing hierarchical power relations in any substantial way. These adherents of postmodernity can retain their privileged existence without calling for wholesale social change that upsets the privileging of some social groups over others. Moreover, the postmodern position allows them to focus instead on individual activities which can give one the impression of self-empowerment in a fragmentary and isolationist existence.

Both the analysis and the practice that follows from this approach result in corporate capitalism escaping critical scrutiny, despite the enormous impact that the decisions of its corporate elite have on the lives of countless poor people who become social work clients. Corporatism represents the current hegemonic global ascendency of capitalist relations in the social, political, economic and cultural spheres, and it is absolutely essential that it is subjected to a critical gaze and action, if the disempowerment of those whose lives are restricted by its controlling reach into every aspect of their daily lives is to be reversed and alternative social arrangements are to be created. In other words, postmodernism denies human agency in the face of powerful social forces that can only be resisted through collective action which draws on solidary impulses created in and through people's behaviour when they recognise that they share experiences of oppression, or what Freire (1974) calls 'critical consciousness' of the unequal social relations that they reproduce by replicating the taken-for-granted views of the world that shape their day-to-day activities.

Postmodernism's failure to deal with structural and collective considerations turn it into a politically conservative paradigm in which existing systems are taken for granted (Haber, 1994), and is for me its most worrying element. That is, the system is perceived as simply being there – a presence that merely is – rather than a social reality that is created in and through social interactions embedded within particular ways of viewing the world and the ensuing power struggles over and about different world-views. In other words, the success of a particular group in becoming ascendant through the various systematic struggles that are waged to establish hegemonic relations provides the framework within which inegalitarian social relations are structured. Or, in the words of Cooper and Burrell (1988, p. 94), postmodernists perceive systems as having 'lives of their own which make them fundamentally independent of human control'. So, postmodernism fails because it cannot see that in concerning itself solely with discursive practises, it cannot rise above the meta-narrative that it has itself created about the lack of meta-narrative within its own analytical framework.

In postmodernism views of the world, power is not only coercive and repressive, but also productive. Drawing on Foucault's (1983, 1984) insights, postmodern theorists perceive power as an insidious and ubiquitous force that subsumes any form of opposition to its dictates in hegemonic discourses. Moreover, hegemonic power does not allow for the creation of alternative knowledges which can challenge the dominant one because knowledge is conceptualised as an institutionalised and controlling system of thought (Foucault, 1983, 1984). Thus, the continued existence of a particular system is guaranteed in perpetuity in a theoretical framework that does not allow for change (Haber, 1994). This understanding of power is profoundly pessimistic and conservative. However, it is one that is consistently challenged in practice because people do resist oppression and do strive to create better conditions for themselves and others, particularly for their children who are taken as representing their continuity in succeeding generations. Social work has a laudable tradition of challenging oppression, even though its resistance to it may have been called something else at different historical epochs. These responses have ranged from the settlement movement to anti-oppressive practice, and the idea of improving people's social circumstances exemplifies a continuity that underpins practitioners' desire to help vulnerable others today.

The limitations of focusing discourses of change primarily on language

From an anti-oppressive perspective, a further problem with post-modern discourses is the emphasis that its theoreticians place on language as a vehicle that individuals can use for understanding, experiencing and changing the world. This means that objects have meaning because they are inscribed in a linguistic network (Lyotard, 1986) in which each term has value ascribed to it because other terms are simultaneously present (Saussure, 1966). For example, this understanding of the world indicates that the signifier 'black' has meaning only in comparison to the signifier 'white' (Haber, 1994). However, I would argue this is so only in racist discourses, where the idea of valuing one signifier more than another ascribes a negative value to the 'difference' between the two, rather than a positive or even neutral one. In other words, there is more to thought than words, although these are conveyed to others in and through language. But in the case considered above, an antagonistic relationship has been established between the terms, and it is this that conveys a meaning or significance that results in 'black' being deemed inferior to 'white', even when scientific evidence disputes this valuation and has convincingly established that all human beings belong to one race.

In postmodern discourses, then, reality is expressed and structured through language which can then become a source of individual empowerment or disempowerment. To put it crudely, in postmodern discourses, we are what we say, even though our experiences, particularly in social work practice, indicate that we should always probe beneath the presenting problem or what people say they are (or not) doing to find that there are other stories that need to be placed alongside the first narrative that is selectively provided in the first encounter. Of course, any story is only ever partial, and what is left out is as important as what has been included. But what has been left out is less easily amenable to discourse analyses that have to focus on a text to then derive what has been omitted as part of a deductive process that is itself inscribed with meanings.

Nonetheless, the postmodern epistemological position roots reality in individual subjectivities which can then provide the basis for centring the self. Lacan (1977) decentres the self by arguing that subjectivity is created in language which results in a fragmented and multiple self rather than a rational or integrated one. In my view, this construction of language can be further problematised because it is predicated on a binary notion of subjectivity, that is, the self is either fragmented or integrated. I would argue that the self involves both. It can be integrated into particular ways of seeing the world and isolated within it at the same time. Also, postmodern conceptualisations of the issue miss the gap between language and feeling. There is more to people's experiences than the language they use to describe them. This is why the integration of content, process and outcome is so important.

The integration of people through language alongside their exclusion by it is particularly relevant in the lives of social work clients. They are integrated into the very discourses that exclude them. For example, a mother on welfare who wants to be a 'good' mother is integrated into, or is part of, the dominant discussions about mothering and what constitutes the appropriate discharge of the duties it entails, whilst being simultaneously created as an excluded part of it by being labelled a 'bad' mother precisely because she is on welfare and under surveillance. Carole makes this clear when she talks about her experience of being a young mother who requires social work assistance:

> I was going to be a *good* mother to Eric [her son], not like mine who let me go into care. I was going to do everything right – look after my baby and keep him with me. Then I met Don [her last partner]...At first everything was great. Then he started to hit me and got very violent. When I told

the social worker about it, she took my child away. She said I was a *bad* mother because I put me and Eric [the baby] in danger, even though Don never hit Eric. She took him [Eric] away and I never got him back until long after I left Don. That was hard. I left him [Don] and found another place to stay, but he found me and just barged in. He kept doing this. Every time I moved, he would find me. Even now, I live in fear that he might barge through the door and I'm miles away from where we lived. When Eric finally came back to me, it took ages for me to feel like a proper mother again. He'd grown up so much you see, and I'll never be able to make up for those missing months. I feel I let him down, just like my mom did [to] me.

Additionally, clients want to be integrated into the dominant society and have the same opportunities and resources that they see others as having (Dominelli, 1982). With regards to this case, Carole subscribes to the dominant view that being a 'good' mother means being able to provide for her children, as white, middle-class parents do and as the dominant ideology demands of her (Strega et al., 2000). Although discursively formed in and through discourses about mothering, these women are, at the same time, constructed outside the dominant ideology and the chances of being successfully integrated as 'good' (that is, white, middle-class) mothers without collective action on their part are slim. The importance of taking collective endeavours to promote their interests as they define them is a lesson that has also been articulated by various social movements – the women's movement, the civil rights movement, the disability movement, to name a few.

The postmodern world becomes one of interpretations which become integrated into descriptions of what existence is like for the person providing a particular narrative or point of view (Howe, 1994). In eschewing prescription on the grounds that any interpretation is equally valid, postmodernism belies the realities of oppression experienced by many people whose particular views of reality are negated for differing from the dominant norm. Thus, postmodern relativism undermines oppressed people's oppositional politics and their attempts to forge collective action, based on a unity that is deliberately created around a particular aspect of identity, to develop cohesion amongst those who would otherwise exist in their own individualised, fragmented isolation. From an oppressed person's point of view, postmodernism can become an oppressive meta-narrative that insists on their coping with their oppression, wherever it emanates from, on their own. This essentially condemns them to living within the status quo.

Ironically, the pessimism of postmodernism arises at the same time as issues of environmental degradation, atmospheric pollution, international crime syndicates and increasing militarised violence are calling out for international, that is, collective action that transcends local borders and draws upon people's capacities to care about each other in ways that affirm their dignity as human beings across the globe – a task for which social workers are eminently qualified.

The interplay between competing meta-narratives

In assuming that people are subjected to only one meta-narrative which they term modernism, postmodernists fail to recognise that a person's life is shaped by a number of interlocking systems and ideologies which have more than one (meta)narrative that applies to them. Each different system promotes views of itself that endorse its particular objectives and world-view at any given historical conjuncture. Each produces its own discourses embedded in meta-narratives that have points of convergence and divergence with others. Three systems that play key roles in shaping what happens at the level of the individual are: the state, civil society and corporate capital. From the individual's point of view, although these are all experienced at the personal and local level, each has a separate domain in which it is the major player. For example, corporate capital has transcended national borders to operate independently of state and individual control in local, national and international arenas. Thus, corporate capital enjoys a fairly unfettered existence as long as the primacy of the marketplace continues to dominate people's understandings of their situation, for it privileges its needs over and above all others.

Nation-states that seek to trammel the activities of corporate capital through legislation do so at their own peril. A multinational corporation will not take long to move its operations elsewhere where the conditions are more amenable to its interests. So, instead of seeking to control their activities in ways that take account of other demands emanating from the discourses provided by different voices or interests within their borders, nation-states fall over each other in a lottery for the highest bidder of public resourcing that can be channelled into private coffers. The subsidies they provide are usually aimed at securing local jobs and take the form of outright grants, tax exemptions, providing resources to build an industrial infrastructure and securing quiescent labour relations (Wichterich, 2000). By responding thus the state engages in a response that takes at least one local voice into account in the decisions it makes.

But in responding to this particular interest group, the state is also ignoring other voices of which it is also aware, for example the one promoted by groups such as Friends of the Earth, who argue for a set of controls over corporate capital that favours environmental sustainability over jobs. In other words, the state mediates between competing discourses on the basis of what is prioritised by the ideological leanings of its ruling politicians and their capacity to respond to certain pressure groups more than others. Moreover, the state operates primarily in the national arena, although it has attempted to enhance its powers by engaging in regional and at times international coalitions for particular purposes. A national remit restricts a state's ability to hold corporate capitalists accountable for the decisions they make even though they may impact substantially upon their national and local terrains.

Any given state is more powerful in controlling individual citizens than multinational corporations whose resources may well dwarf its own. For example, in 1995, approximately 37,000 transnational corporations with sales of $5.5 trillion – equivalent to the gross national product (GNP) of the United States – controlled one-third of all private sector assets in the world (Carlsson and Ramphal, 1995, p. 172). Most of these companies are to be found within the industrialised West and Japan, a group of countries known as the G7, who represent 10 per cent of the world's population. In this context, the least developed countries with a larger percentage of the world's population and located primarily in the poorer parts of the world, particularly Africa, have little opportunity to flex either their political or economic muscles against the dictates of such corporations.

The state, on the other hand, relies on the regulation of people both within and outside its borders to ensure that those who belong to its polity are those entitled to remain within its boundaries whilst others are excluded. In theory, it has the potential to regulate corporate capital but, given that one state competes with others to attract investments and jobs, it is unlikely to exercise controls that might be challenged by corporate capital, unless there is a coalition of states at international level to achieve such an objective. However, this would be difficult for states to do in the current neo-liberal conjuncture. So, controlling people and their movements is an easier option.

These controls are applied internally with regards to its own populations, where poor people find their lives more regulated than their richer compatriots, especially if they come to the notice of the authorities because they are in need of social resources. And it occurs with regards to movements of people who comprise groups of (im)migrants, refugees and asylum seekers from outside its borders, all of whom may require the services of social workers at some point. So, controlling the borderlands at a number of different levels becomes a key concern of the state and shapes the nature of the relationship between the state and the individual whether they are its citizens or not. At the same time, these borders are becoming increasingly permeable, not only to those who arrive from overseas with or without the appropriate documents, but also as a result of state attempts at regionalising to strengthen their political muscle, as say the European nation-states have sought to do, and through the ease with which financial capital flows in and out of national territories.

Social workers are asked to provide services for these people, but under conditions that are not of their making and without adequate resources (Khan, 2000). Given the untenability of their position, social workers, who see the connections between the micro-level practices that they are obliged to engage in and the macro-level forces that influence these, could do more to initiate debates about where resources are being channelled and why. Also, they could raise questions about and demand answers from corporate decision-makers who lay waste to the communities that they work with and within.

The current historical conjuncture, with its emphasis on the importance of civil society, provides an opportunity for social workers to embark upon such dialogues with policymakers and the public. Civil society is constituted by an amorphous set of organisations and networks, including those that deliver social work services, that come together to realise their own potential. In the process of doing so, these may destabilise hegemonic definitions of social problems, redefine these to create new forms of self-empowerment, challenge *power over* relations that perpetuate social injustices, and work towards establishing more harmonious social relations. Those organisations and groups that pool their resources in and through civil society organisations are governed by a moral vision of a better and more just social order, that is, one that is geared to including all peoples within its remit (Shragge and Fontan, 2000). Social workers are often employed in the agencies and networks that make up civil society and have a crucial role to play in promoting this humanitarian view of the world.

Those involved in civil societies do not necessarily have direct access to established political power (Roper Renshaw, 1994) including that which resides in the nation-state. However, civil society itself forms a political entity, in that it is a collective grouping that seeks to challenge existing configurations of power relations and explicitly sets about the task of meeting this objective and others that its participants have set in pursuit of their vision. Additionally, stakeholders in civil society are actively involved in mobilising people to achieve their aims. These mobilisations revolve around the idea that the people, particularly marginalised ones, are protagonists in their own stories. That is, they are active creators of the ensuing narratives and not passive recipients of other people's charitable generosity.

These mobilisations can take place at local, national and international levels. Currently, in the international realm, civil society, as represented through non-governmental organisations (NGOs), including those representing social work, has been mobilising its constituents to influence the decision-making capacities of the UN, international financial institutions such as the World Bank and International Monetary Fund, and governments. Social workers are also represented in discussions with these bodies through the International Association of Schools of Social Work and the International Federation of Social Workers. Although these NGOs continue to overrepresent those living in the West (Carlsson and Ramphal, 1995), they do reflect collective action that aims to call corporate capitalists to account. They also work hard to bridge the divide between peoples living in the (usually richer) North and those in the (usually poorer) South. A number of NGOs have also been crucial in organising anti-globalisation protests as part of their drive to hold capitalism accountable for the misery it is bringing to large numbers of the world's population, whether this is in reducing the biodiversity of the earth, depriving poor people of their own knowledges, or failing to develop local economies in environmentally sustainable ways (Shiva, 2000). Social work academics, practitioners and students need to become more familiar with these debates and consider the implications of these for their work in the local contexts.

Civil society is the most open of the three systems that I have discussed. Moreover, civil society draws on a common humanity that seeks to deal with differences in identity by developing social trust and solidarity through endeavours aimed at securing social justice for all. By caring for others, social trust is enhanced and relationships of reciprocity are strengthened as each individual expects to give and take from the relationships that are developed. However, civil society networks are also the most vulnerable of these systems, as any increase in their scope has to occur through their potential to realise the social capital and material resources accrued amongst its members. And governments and corporations can very easily refuse the organisations representing civil society entry into their meetings and decision-making bodies. Additionally, the state can use legislative interventions to decide which organisations will be recognised as forming part of civil society and be funded or given tax exemptions to stretch their resources further. Civil society can operate to do the state's bidding, even if this is exercised through financial inducements, as well as mount critiques against it. So there is an interdependent relationship that characterises the relations between the two, which may not always work in favour of civil society.

Additionally, not all bodies that form part of civil society are either benign or progressive. Some have become huge organisations with massive resources that may dwarf those of either the communities in which they are located or the professionals engaged to work with them. Activists have to constantly be on guard against the appropriation of their energies and goodwill by organisations that seek to empower themselves at the expense of others rather than contribute to the well-being of those whose quality of life is poor. Furthermore, even well-intentioned organs of civil society have to exercise care to ensure that paternalistic relationships are not fostered by how they work with others, particularly those in marginalised groups who have been accustomed to having others speak on their behalf (Deacon et al., 1997). And they must be aware of the danger of using their greater resources to impose their particular views of what constitutes best practice or *the* way forward, in situations where they have limited links to the local populace and have been unable to engage them fully in their decision-making processes (Mohanty et al., 1991). Unfortunately, a number of NGOs have left a legacy of exclusionary interventions in many parts of the developing world (Basu, 1997). However, some have been exemplary in their endeavours to include local people in their decision-making.

Civil society also operates primarily at the level of community, although it often has links to national and international networks. Corporate capital, on the other hand, acts across national borders, more or less at the will of those who run corporate enterprises. For corporate decision-makers, community is little more than a site for their operations. And they tend to define communities in fixed, usually geographical terms. They also see communities as *dependent* upon them for their survival through the opportunities for economic development that they allegedly bring. This development is always cast as being good for the community. So, at the level of community, their discourses ignore the price that women and children living in the locality pay by working in unhealthy conditions and low-paid jobs (Wichterich, 2000). Also, corporate capitalists have contributed towards the loss of better-paid jobs for men, but their responsibility for it remains invisible, while the damage that they have done to the environment remains unacknowledged. These by-products of corporate activities can be highlighted by social workers who support local communities.

In the current constellation of social relations within these three systems, the one dominated by corporate capitalists operates largely as a closed club, in which membership is for the privileged and dependent on wealth and the sharing of an ideology that places profit-making at the centre of the universe of social relationships. Multinational corporations are engaged in the critical control of social and private resources and creating meanings of ownership that endorse their view of the situation. Thus, they are often involved in massaging figures, politicians' understandings and the media in ways that favour their particular points of view. Social workers can counter their images by using the data they collect from their involvement with individuals in their localities.

Civil society and collective action

Through collective action at the level of community, social workers and their organisations in civil society can begin to engage with the boundaries established by corporate managers and challenge their current configuration. In the course of its mobilisations, civil society can also demonstrate the permeability of various borders – whether of civil society, the state or corporate capital. For example, many of those currently involved in civil society have taken action against globalisation in Seattle, Washington and Prague. Their behaviour has demonstrated that organisations that began as part of civil society in one locality can extend their scope beyond their particular community borders to encompass others within their own national territory and those residing overseas. Even though this action has been based on realising social capital through networks of information exchanges and limited direct interventions in particular locations, those involved in this particular configuration of civil society have been able to challenge the agenda for action that had been proposed by multinational corporations, governments and international financial institutions. In doing so, they have emphasised the importance of looking at issues of 'race' (Mohanty, 1991), gender (Dominelli, 1997a), age (Help Age, 2002), disability (Disability World, 2001) and debt (Jubilee 2000).

Jubilee 2000, for example, has a network of people and organisations, including those involved in social work, aimed at intervening in the debt crisis of low-income countries in the Third World and aims to get governments and corporations to 'forgive' these debt payments. Its activities illustrate the potential of civil society groupings to organise internationally to challenge hegemonic discourses established by powerful global institutions around Third World debt (Wolfensohn, 2000). Jubilee 2000 also illustrates the capacities of people to organise around issues of social justice without demanding that people become like them to ensure that they receive their fair share of resources, without having to have direct personal connections with those whom they are trying to assist, and without insisting that people do as they say in order to receive help. In other words, Jubilee 2000 represents a collective way of organising around injustice that leaves those who benefit from this action to decide themselves how they want to proceed in future initiatives aimed at self-empowerment. Jubilee 2000 also exemplifies the power of moral action, that is, one that is rooted in solidaristic altruism, or caring for and about others (Knijri and Ungerson, 1997). However, the danger of acting in a paternalistic manner remains a concern that those involved in Jubilee 2000 have to constantly address.

Organising within civil society has meant embarking on processes that seek to mobilise human capacities on a voluntary or self-help basis. This is both a strength and weakness of civil society, which has to ensure that its potential to activate people is not exploited to make good the gaps in welfare provisions that have been left by the state and corporate capital so that these two can be absolved of the responsibility for meeting them. Thus, these three systems are engaged in struggles over meaning – the mystification, demystification and remystification of symbols – to achieve particular purposes. Neither the outcome of the struggle, nor its democratic impulse can be taken for granted. Civil society organisations that are not held to account and constantly scrutinised for their potential to assume *power over* relations that delegitimate different voices can become sites in which tyranny can develop, as the Nazis proved in Germany (Lorenz, 1994).

Conclusions

Collective action has been important in alleviating past injustices. It remains a crucial vehicle of resistance available for developing strategies that aim to reduce current forms of oppression. For these reasons, it is important that the pessimism of postmodern perspectives is transcended and that people's willingness to improve their world and that of others be kept afloat.

Issues of identity, agency and power remain integral parts of the struggle to improve social relations in an unequal world. However, they are not determined a priori. They are contested matters that have to be discussed and struggled over and for. Social workers can participate in these struggles over meaning. Through these contestations, more egalitarian social configurations can be developed and new alliances can be formed to cross different social divides without demanding that these be obliterated in a sameness that forces an unstable unity upon reluctant participants.

Corporate capital, the state and civil society are key systems that have been organised to engage in negotiated realities around everyday life at the local, national and international levels. Action aimed at mobilising community groups, so that corporate capital, and the havoc it wreaks on individual lives and local communities, is stemmed, remains an important concern for practice. Civil society organisations, particularly NGOs with both a local and broader reach, have played a key role in raising questions about a social order predicated on reproducing social injustice and exploitative relations on a global plane. And social workers, through their international organisations, have played an important part in highlighting injustice throughout the world.

Developing organisations at the level of civil society and promoting the social economy are two means whereby corporate capital and ruling politicians can be held to account by ordinary people with limited means. Social workers have significant roles to play in advocating for a more just world and mobilising people to innovate and act in ways that will bring this about. Rejecting collective action that attempts to improve both individual and group well-being, as postmodernists would have us do, is tantamount to lending support to a vision of societies that privileges some at the expense of others. This usually means that those who have traditionally been marginalised are tossed aside in the contest for the private appropriation of public resources. Social workers need to stand against such interventions and argue for a broader sharing of the earth's resources in ways that safeguard the richness and diversity of human beings and the planet we live in.

Conclusions

Anti-oppressive practice, with its commitment to egalitarian relations, is an important way of thinking about social work interventions in an inegalitarian world. Its aims of improving social relations for marginalised and excluded peoples and securing social justice within an egalitarian and democratic framework remain important, despite postmodern attempts to destabilise the relevance of these objectives for practice. Although their realisation is fraught with difficulties, their continued endorsement is crucial to social well-being at both individual and collective levels. Thus, continuing to pursue the objectives of anti-oppressive practice has to remain on the social work agenda for the foreseeable future.

A holistic approach of responding to the person in his or her environment is an integral part of anti-oppressive practice, as it enables both client and practitioner to situate themselves within the broader social contexts in which they both negotiate the environments within which they locate their daily lives and the minutiae of their routines for living. The power relations within which they are embedded are those they both influence and are affected by, through the course of their interactions with one another. Reconfiguring the power relations within which they are situated constitutes an important part of the negotiations that their engagement entails. As a result of their negotiated interactions, the personal, institutional and material components of their relationship are in dynamic flux.

Negotiated realities are enacted at both the individual and collective levels. With regards to their work with individuals, practitioners use a set of values that are rooted in recognising the agency of the person(s) involved within a framework of power-sharing and equality. This requires social workers to focus on their clients' dignity as human beings with the capacity to exercise power. Whilst these ways of responding to individuals in need aim to reduce professional distance and encourage client autonomy, these are circumscribed by practitioners' responsibility to the bureaucratic organisation that employs them and the broader public that endorses their remit to intervene in difficult situations. Thus, social workers are constantly negotiating within a context of ambiguity and uncertainty, involving the rationing of resources in the face of need, not being available when vulnerable clients require their services most, and having to adhere to policies that may be at odds with their own personal beliefs. Many of these negotiated realities apply to work undertaken with groups as well as individuals.

Social workers use a range of personal and professional values, knowledges and skills to guide their behaviour in an ethical, accountable and responsible manner. These enable them to work with clients to assess their situations and devise strategies of empowering interventions and action that will enable them to meet their overall goals. In working towards these objectives, they will invoke methods of affirming client self-esteem and capacities to act effectively in pursuit of agreed agendas for action, strengthening their coping mechanisms, extending personal networks and support systems, and, where necessary, securing changes in their lifestyles to produce competent, active citizens.

Practitioners also have to be able to overcome unwarranted bureaucratic obstacles that come their way, particularly in the aftermath of neo-liberal welfare regimes and the constraints that the 'new managerialism' imposes on practice. Crucial to being able to react effectively will be knowledge that facilitates the creative use of the resources at their disposal and the development of a critical awareness of themselves as people in their own right. Social workers will have to be conscious of the impact of their own identity on their capacity to work with those who are different from them. They will have to ensure that they are able to respect and celebrate difference, such as 'race', gender, class, age, sexual orientation, physical abilities, religious affiliation and culture.

In these respects, anti-oppressive practice goes beyond forms of social work that focus on a specific social division, for example anti-racist social work and feminist social work, to address all dimensions of oppression that impact on a person, and consider the complexities of the social relationships in which both clients and workers are embedded and within which they exercise agency, or their power to achieve their particular objectives. Thus, practice becomes constituted in terms that acknowledge that any solution or arrangement that is reached is constantly being (re)negotiated to take account of changing conditions or reproduce previous ones. Its refusal to divide people from each other also endorses a citizenship that moves social work away from the dustbin of residualism that provides services relevant only to poor people and towards universal public services underpinned by a civic ethic to deliver better goods than those mired in making a profit. And it draws upon personal, institutional and cultural capacities to build strong communities and individuals who are able to fulfil their potential and realise their well-being.

The environment within which social workers operate consists of personal, social and physical elements embedded within a set of power relations, values and spiritual (or not) views of the world which interact and mesh with each other to compose the specific contexts that involve them in a constantly moving scenario. The relationship between social worker and client is an evolving one which achieves stability through the reproduction of certain of its aspects over time. Change occurs when its constituent parts are reconfigured in different ways. Both parties are, therefore, active in forming, reforming and transforming their relationship. Thus, the power relations between them have no predetermined outcome. The practitioner can become disempowered and the client can be empowered through their inter-actions together. The outcome will depend on how the negotiations between them are conducted and the 'allocative and authoritative resources' each can call upon during the course of their interaction. Additionally, social workers will have to be able to hold the many levels that impact upon and shape client realities as well as their own. This is a skill that has to be developed and cultivated. Learning how to obtain the information that he or she needs at the time he or she needs it, instead of trying to work on the basis of stereotypical assumptions about people's behaviour, will be crucial to empowering practice in difficult and complex situations.

Working in anti-oppressive ways encompasses working within values that espouse interdependence, reciprocity, equality, democracy, and a sophisticated understanding of the complexities of the social relations that shape an intervention and the dialogical interactions which in turn (re)shape these. Their aim is to promote social justice and individual and collective empowerment. Practitioners mobilise social and physical resources for the purposes of engaging in actions that endorse the change effort for both the individuals and groups that they

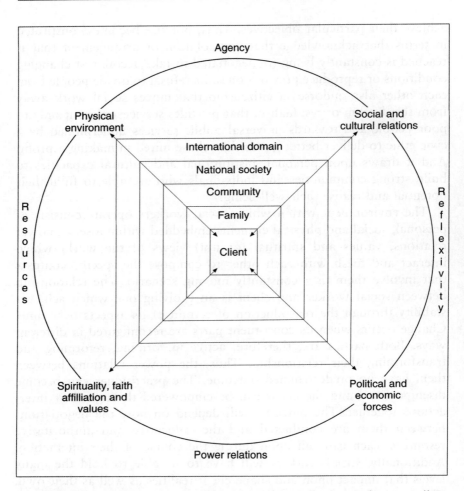

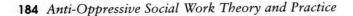

Diagram 8.1 Holistic intervention chart for anti-oppressive practice

work with. They also need to be prepared to interrogate their own and their agencies' practices to determine whether or not they are conducive to change.

Anti-oppressive practice also involves social workers as whole beings integrating their feelings, thinking, actions and a process of reflexivity in their evaluation of their work in practice. Reflexivity is an ongoing process through which social workers constantly (re)consider and (re)evaluate their endeavours. To indicate the different areas encompassed in the realisation of anti-oppressive practice, I have incorporated the key features of a holistic approach to client–worker relationships in Diagram 8.1.

In seeking to actualise client empowerment, anti-oppressive practice differs from that promulgated through traditional social work relationships, with their emphasis on professional expertise to acknowledge power differentials, and recognises client agency, knowledge and skills. These become validated as important ingredients in the client–worker relationship rather than being deemed insignificant. Additionally, and most crucially, anti-oppressive practitioners appreciate that society's expectations and norms, and customs for apportioning resources and doing things, play a key role in facilitating and endorsing particular ways of being, and making available opportunities that have a significant impact on what is or is not possible for a client to achieve. Thus, an individual's potential for change or taking control of his or her life is never simply a matter of what he or she does or does not want to do.

Holding an individual *totally* responsible for the position that she or he is in represents a somewhat irresponsible way of getting the person concerned to assume responsibility for his or her behaviour and is eschewed by anti-oppressive practitioners. An approach that takes account of *both* individual inputs and social ones provides a more adequate way forward because it requires both the individual and others in society to shoulder responsibility for the predicament of any given human being. It also enables those involved to acknowledge their interdependency and show an awareness of how one person's behaviour impacts on others as well as oneself.

Facilitating joint (individual and social) responsibility for what happens to people in need also indicates that those representing 'society', namely politicians and social workers, cannot absolve themselves of what is going on, nor can they shunt responsibility for personal well-being onto a marginalised person while maintaining that they support the formation of an inclusive social order. Social workers, as those signifying society's commitment to vulnerable people, are entitled to critique the inadequacy of existing social arrangements and mobilise themselves, clients and others to bring about egalitarian social relations that foster social justice. Without such action, they would not be doing their job, but would be exacerbating the very problems that they have been asked to solve by clients, employers and the general public.

Bibliography

Adamson, N, Briskin, L and McPhail, M (1988) *Organising for Change: The Contemporary Women's Movement in Canada*. Oxford: Oxford University Press.

Adelson, N (2000) *'Being Alive Well': Health and the Politics of Cree Well-Being*. Toronto: University of Toronto Press.

Ahmad, W (ed.) (1993) *'Race' and Health in Contemporary Britain*. Buckingham: Open University Press.

Ahmed, B (1990) *Black Perspective in Social Work*. Birmingham: Venture Press.

Appleyard, B (1993) 'Why Paint so Black a Picture?' *Independent*, 4 August.

Armitage, A (1996) *Aboriginal People in Australia, Canada and New Zealand*. Toronto: McClelland and Stewart.

Arnup, K (ed.) (1995) *Lesbian Parents: Living with Pride and Prejudice*. Charlottetown: Gynergy Books.

Asante, M (1987) *The Africentric Idea*. Philadelphia: Temple University Press.

Badran, M and Cooke, M (eds) (1990) *Opening the Gates: A Century of Arab Feminist Writing*. Bloomington, IN: Indiana University Press.

Balbo, L (1987) 'Crazy Quilts: Rethinking the Welfare State Debate from a Woman's Point of View', in Showstack Sassoon, A (ed.) *Women and the State: The Shifting Boundaries of Public and Private*. London: Hutchinson.

Banks, S (1994) *Social Work Ethics*. London: Macmillan – now Palgrave Macmillan.

Banks, S (2001) *Social Work Values and Ethics*. London: Palgrave – now Palgrave Macmillan.

Barker, H (1986) 'Recapturing Sisterhood: A Critical Look at "Process" in Feminist Organisations and Community Action', *Critical Social Policy*, 16, Summer, pp. 80–90.

Barker, M (1981) *New Racism. Conservatives and the Ideology of the Tribe*. London: Junction Books.

Barlett, D L and Steele, J B (1998) 'Corporate Welfare: Special Report', *Time*, p. 4.

Barn, R (1993) *Black Children in the Public Care System*. London: Batsford.

Barnes, C and Oliver, M (1998) 'Discrimination, Disability and Welfare: From Needs to Rights', in Swain, J, Finkelstein, V, French, S and Oliver, M (eds) *Disabling Barriers – Enabling Environments*. London: Sage and Open University Press.

Barnes, M and Maple, N (1992) *Women and Mental Health: Challenging the Stereotypes*. Birmingham: Venture Press.

Barrett, M and McIntosh, M (1981) *The Anti-Social Family*. London: Verso.

Barrett, M and McIntosh, M (1985) Ethnocentrism and Socialist Feminist Theory, *Feminist Review*, **20**, pp. 23–47.

Basu, M (1997) *The Challenge of Local Feminisms: Women's Movements in Global Perspective*. Boulder: Westview Press.

BASW (British Association of Social Workers) (1996) *A Code of Ethics for Social Work*. Birmingham: BASW.

Bauman, Z (1992) *Intimations of Postmodernity*. London: Routledge.

Bayes, M and Howell, E (eds) (1981) *Women and Mental Health*. New York: Basic Books.

Begum, N (1992) 'Disabled Women and the Feminist Agenda', in *Feminist Review*, **40**, Spring, pp. 71–84.

Begum, N, Hill, M and Stevens, A (1993) *Reflections: The Views of Black Disabled People on their Lives and on Community Care*. London: CCETSW.

Belenky, M F, Clinchy, M B, Goldberger, N R and Tarule, M J (1997) *Women's Ways of Knowing: The Development of Self, Voice and Mind*. New York: Basic Books.

Benhabib, S (1992) *Situating the Self: Gender, Community and Postmodernism in Contemporary Ethics*. Cambridge: Polity Press.

Bhatti-Sinclair, K (1994) 'Asian Women and Domestic Violence from Male Partners' in Lupton, C and Gillespie, T (eds) *Working with Violence*. London: BASW/Macmillan – now Palgrave Macmillan.

Bhavani, K K (1993) 'Taking Racism and the Editing of Women's Studies' in Richardson, D and Robinson, V (eds) *Introduction to Women's Studies*. London: Macmillan – now Palgrave Macmillan.

Biesteck, F P (1961) *The Casework Relationship*. London: Allen & Unwin.

Biggs, S with Phillipson, C and Kingston, P (1995) *Elder Abuse in Perspective*. Buckingham: Open University Press.

Bishop, A (1994) *Becoming an Ally: Breaking the Cycle of Oppression*. Halifax: Fernwood Publishing.

Blair, T (1999) 'PM's 20 Year Target to End Poverty', *Guardian*, 19 March.

Blom-Cooper, L (1986) *A Child in Trust: The Report of the Panel of Inquiry into the Circumstances Surrounding the Death of Jasmine Beckford*. London Borough of Kent: Kingwood Press.

Bolger, S, Corrigan, P, Dorking, J and Frost, N (1981) *Towards a Socialist Welfare Practice*. London: Macmillan – now Palgrave Macmillan.

Bourdieu, P and Wacquant, L (1992) *An Invitation to Reflexive Sociology*. Cambridge: Polity Press.

Boxer, J (1998) *Mental Health and Equal Opportunities*. London: UCL Press.

Brandwein, R (1986) 'A Feminist Approach to Social Policy', in Van Den Berg, N and Cooper, L (eds) *Feminist Visions for Social Work*. Silver Spring, MD: NASW.

Brandwein, R (1991) 'Women's Studies' in Mehta, V and Yasas, F (eds) *Exploring Feminist Visions*. Pune: Streevani.

Brinton, C (1966) *The Anatomy of Revolution*. New York: Random House.

Broadbent, J and Laughlin, R (1990) *Recent Financial and Administrative Changes in the NHS: A Critical Theory*. Sheffield: Sheffield University Management School Series.

Brooks, D (ed.) (1996) *Backward and Upward: The New Conservative Writing*. New York: Random House.

Brown, A (1992) *Groupwork*, 3rd edn. Aldershot: Ashgate.

Bruyere, G (2001) 'First Nations Approaches to Social Work', in Dominelli, L, Lorenz, W and Soydan, H (eds) *Beyond Racial Divides: Ethnicities in Social Work*. Aldershot: Ashgate.

Bryant, B, Dadzie, S and Scafe, S (1985) *The Heart of the Race: Black Women's Lives in Britain*. London: Virago.

Bulmer, M and Rees, M A (eds) (1996) *Citizenship Today: The Contemporary Relevance of T H Marshall*. London: University College London Press.

Callahan, M (2000) 'Best Practice in Child Welfare: Lessons from the Field' in Callahan, M, Hessle, S and Strega, S (eds), *Valuing the Field: Child Welfare in International Context*. Aldershot: Ashgate.

Canadian Business (CB) (1997) 'The Social Economy', 70(7): 150–5.

Carlsson, I and Ramphal, S (1995) *Our Global Neighbourhood: The Report of the Commission on Global Governance*. Oxford: Oxford University Press.

Castles, F, Gerritsen, R and Vowles, J (1996) *The Great Experiment*. London: Allen & Unwin.

CCETSW (Central Council for Education and Training in Social Work) (1989) *Requirements and Regulations for the Diploma in Social Work. Paper 30*. London: CCETSW. Revised in 1991 and 1995.

Chaplin, J (1988) *Feminist Counselling in Action*. London: Sage.

Chesney-Lind, M (1973) 'Judicial Enforcement of the Female Sex Role: The Family Court and the Female Delinquent', *Issues in Criminology*, 8: 51–69.

Ciatu, N A, Dileo, D and Micallef, G (1998) *Curaggia: Writing by Women of Italian Descent*. Toronto: Women's Press.

Clarke, J and Newman, J (1997) *The Managerialist State*. London: Sage.

Cleaver, E (1971) *Soul on Ice*. New York: Pan Books.

Clegg, S R (1989) *Frameworks of Power*. London: Sage.

Cochrane, A (1993) 'The Problem of Poverty', in Dallos, R and McLaughlin, E (eds) *Social Problems and the Family*. London: Sage.

Coleman, J S (1988) 'Social Capital in the Creation of Human Capital', *American Journal of Sociology*, 94, supplement, pp. 95–120.

Coll, C, Suney, J, Weingarden, K (eds) (1998) *Mothering Against the Odds: Diverse Voices of Contemporary Mothers*. New York: Guilford Press.

Collins, P H (1991) *Black Feminist Thought: Knowledge, Consciousness and the Politics of Empowerment*. London: Routledge.

Compton, B and Galaway, B (1975) *Social Work Processes*. Homewood, IL: The Dorsey Press.

Connell, R W (1995) *Masculinities*. Cambridge: Polity Press.

Cook, A and Kirk, G (1993) *Greenham Women Everywhere: Dreams, Ideas and Action from the Women's Peace Movement*. London: Pluto Press.

Cooper, R and Burrell, G (1988) 'Modernism, Posmodernism and Organisational Analysis: An Introduction', *Organisational Studies*, 9(1): 91–112.

Corrigan, P and Leonard, P (1978) *Social Work Under Capitalism*. London: Macmillan – now Palgrave Macmillan.

Cowburn, M and Dominelli, L (2001) 'Masking Hegemonic Masculinity: Reconstructing the Paedophile as the Dangerous Stranger', *British Journal of Social Work*, **31**: 399–415.

Craig, G and Mayo, M (1995) *Community Empowerment: A Reader in Participation and Development*. London: Zed Books.

Cross, W E (1978) 'The Thomas and Cross Models of Psychological Nigrescence', *The Journal of Black Psychology*, **5**(1): 13–27.

Culpitt, I (1992) *Welfare and Citizenship: Beyond the Crisis of the Welfare State*. London: Sage.

Cunningham, F, Findlay, S, Kadar, M, Lennon, A and Silva, E (1988) *Social Movements/Social Change: The Politics and Practice of Organizing*. Toronto: Between the Lines.

Daenzer, P (1993) *Regulating Class Privilege: Immigrant Servants in Canada, 1940s–1950s*. Toronto: Canadian Scholars Press.

Dale, J and Foster, P (1986) *Feminists and State Welfare*. London: Routledge & Kegan Paul.

Dalrymple, J and Burke, B (1995) *Anti-Oppressive Practice: Social Care and the Law*. Buckingham: Open University Press.

Davies, M (1985) *The Essential Social Worker*. Aldershot: Gower.

Deacon, B, Hulse, M and Stubbs, P (1997) *Global Social Policy: International Organisations and the Future of Welfare*. London: Sage.

Disability World (2001) 'Disability Buzz' in *Disability World*, **10**, Sept–October, at http://www.disabilityworld.org

DoH (Department of Health) (1995) *Child Protection: Messages from Research*. London: HMSO.

Dominelli, L (1982) 'A Wasted Future? Employment for Young Offenders' in *The Probation Journal*, **29**(1): 6–9.

Dominelli, L (1986) 'The Power of the Powerless: Prostitution and the Reinforcement of Submissive Femininity', *Sociological Review*, Spring, pp. 65–92.

Dominelli, L (1987) 'Women Organising: The Implications of the Women's Peace Movement for Community Action – The Women of Greenham Common', *Continuum*, **VI**(2): 3–10.

Dominelli, L (1988) *Anti-Racist Social Work*, 2nd edn. Basingstoke: Macmillan – now Palgrave Macmillan.

Dominelli, L (1989) 'Betrayal of Trust: A Feminist Analysis of Power Relationships in Incest Abuse and its Relevance for Social Work Practice', *British Journal of Social Work*, **19**: 291–307.

Dominelli, L (1990) *Women and Community Action*. Birmingham: Venture Press.

Dominelli, L (1991) *Gender, Sex Offenders and Probation Practice*. Aldershot: Avebury.

Dominelli, L (1991a) '"Race", Gender and Social Work' in Davies, M (ed.) *The Sociology of Social Work*. London: Routledge.

Dominelli, L (1991b) *Women Across Continents: Feminist Comparative Social Policy*. Hemel Hempstead: Harvester Wheatsheaf.

Dominelli, L (1992) 'More than a Method: Feminist Social Work' in Campbell, K (ed.) *Critical Feminisms*. Milton Keynes: Open University.

Dominelli, L (1992a) 'Sex Offenders and Probation Practice' in Senior, P and Woodhill, D (eds) *Gender, Crime and Probation Practice*. Sheffield: PAVIC Publications.

Dominelli, L (1994) 'Anti-Racist Models of Social Work Education' in Dominelli, L, Patel, N and Thomas Bernard, W (eds) *Anti-Racist Social Work Education*. Sheffield: Sociological Studies.

Dominelli, L (1996) 'Deprofessionalising Social Work: Equal Opportunities, Competence and Postmodernism', *British Journal of Social Work*, 26 (April) pp. 153–75.

Dominelli, L (1997) 'Feminist Theory' in Davies, M (ed.) *The Blackwell Companion to Social Work*. Oxford: Blackwell.

Dominelli, L (1997a) 'International Social Development and Social Work: A Feminist Perspective', in Hokenstad, M C and Midgley, J (eds) *Issues in International Social Work: Global Challenges for a New Century*. Washington, DC: NASW Press.

Dominelli, L (1997b) 'Social Work and Social Development: A Partnership in Social Change' *Journal of Social Development in Africa*, 12(1): 29–39.

Dominelli, L (1997c) *Sociology for Social Work*. London: Macmillan – now Palgrave Macmillan.

Dominelli, L (1997d) 'The Changing Face of Social Work: Globalisation, Privatisation and the Technocratisation of Professional Practice' in Lesnick, B (ed.) *Change in Social Work: International Perspectives in Social Work*. Aldershot: Arena.

Dominelli, L (1998) 'Globalisation and Gender Relations in Social Work' in Lesnik, B (ed.) *Countering Discrimination in Social Work*. Aldershot: Ashgate.

Dominelli, L (1998a) 'Women, Social Work and Academia' in Malin-Prothero, S and Malina, D (eds) *Speaking Our Places*. London: Taylor Francis.

Dominelli, L (ed.) (1999) *Community Approaches to Child Welfare. International Perspectives*. Aldershot: Avebury.

Dominelli, L (2000) 'Empowerment: Help or Hindrance in Professional Relationships' in Ford, D and Stepney, P (eds) *Social Work Models, Methods and Theories: A Framework for Practice*. Lyme Regis: Russell House Publishing.

Dominelli, L (2002) *Feminist Social Work Theory and Practice*. London: Palgrave Macmillan.

Dominelli, L and Gollins, T (1997) 'Men, Power and Caring Relationships', *The Sociological Review*, 45(3): 396–415.

Dominelli, L and Hoogvelt, A (1996) 'Globalisation, Contract Government and the Talyorisation of Intellectual Labour' *Studies in Political Economy*, 49, pp. 71–100.

Dominelli, L and Hoogvelt, A (1996a) 'Globalisation and the Technocratisation of Social Work', *Critical Social Policy*, 16(2): 45–62.

Dominelli, L and McLeod, E (1982) 'The Personal and the Apolitical: Feminism and Moving Beyond the Integrated Methods Approach' in Bailey, R and Lee, P (eds) *Theory and Practice in Social Work*. Oxford: Basil Blackwell.

Dominelli, L and McLeod, E (1989) *Feminist Social Work*. Basingstoke: Macmillan – now Palgrave Macmillan.

Dominelli, L, Jeffers, L, Jones, G, Sibanda, S and Williams, B (1995) *Anti-Racist Probation Practice*. Aldershot: Avebury.

Donati, P (1996) *Sociologia del terzo settore*. Roma: La Nouva Italia Scientifica.

Durrant, J (1989) 'Continuous Agitation', *Community Care*, 13 July, pp. 23–5.

Dworkin, A (1981) *Pornography: Men Possessing Women*. New York: Perigee.

Egan, G (1998) *The Skilled Helper: A Problem Management Approach to Helping*. Pacific Grove, CA: Brooks/Cole Publishing Company.

Essed, P (1991) *Understanding Everyday Racism: An Interdisciplinary Theory*. London: Sage.

Fernando, S (1991) *Health, Race and Culture*. Basingstoke: Macmillan – now Palgrave Macmillan.

Finch, J and Groves, D (1983) *A Labour of Love: Women, Work and Caring*. London: Routledge & Kegan Paul.

Flax, J (1990) 'Postmodernism and Gender Relations in Feminist Theory', in Nicholson, L (ed.) *Feminism/Postmodernism*. New York: Routledge, Chapman & Hall.

Fook, J (1993) *Radical Casework: A Theory of Practice*. London: Allen & Unwin.

Fook, J (2001) 'Hybrid Identities' in Dominelli, L, Lorenz, W and Soydan, H (eds) *Beyond Racial Divides: Ethnicities in Social Work*. Aldershot: Ashgate.

Foucault, M (1980) *Power/Knowledge: Selected Interviews and Other Writings, 1972–77*. New York: Pantheon Books.

Foucault, M (1983) 'The Subject and Power'. Afterword to Dreyfus, H and Rabinow, P (eds) *Michel Foucault: Beyond Structuralism and Hermeneutics*. Chicago: Chicago University Press.

Foucault, M (1984) *The Foucault Reader*. Rabinow, P (ed.). New York: Pantheon.

Foucault, M (1988) 'Technologies of the Self' in Luther, H M, Gutman, H and Hutton, P H (eds) *Technologies of the Self: A Seminar with Michel Foucault*. Amherst: University of Massachusetts Press.

Frankenburg, R (1997) *Displacing Whiteness: Essays in Social and Cultural Criticism*. London: Duke University Press.

Frankfort, I (1972) *Vaginal Politics*. New York: Quadrangle Books.

Franklin, A and Franklin, B (1996) 'Growing Pains: The Developing Children's Rights Movement in the United Kingdom' in Pilcher, J and Wagg, S (eds) *Thatcher's Children? Politics, Childhood and Society in the 1980s and 1990s*. London: Falmer Press.

Freire, P (1972) *The Pedagogy of the Oppressed*. Harmondsworth: Penguin.

Freire, P (1974) *Education for Critical Consciousness*. New York: Seabury.

French, M (1985) *The Power of Women*. Harmondsworth: Penguin.

Fryer, P (1984) *Staying Power: The History of Black People in Britain*. London: Pluto.

Furniss, E (1995) *Victims of Benevolence: The Dark Legacy of the Williams Lake Residential School*. Vancouver: Arsenal Pulp Press.

George, J (1997) 'Global Greying: What Role for Social Work' in Hokenstad, M C and Midgley, J (eds) *Issues in International Social Work: Global Challenges for a New Century*. Washington, DC: NASW Press.

Gilder, G (1981) *Wealth and Poverty*. New York: Bell Books.

Giddens, A (1990) *The Consequences of Modernity*. Cambridge: Polity.

Giddens, A (1994) *Beyond Left and Right: The Future of Radical Politics*. Stanford, CA: Stanford University Press.

Gilroy, P (1995) *The Black Atlantic: Modernity and Double Consciousness*. Cambridge, MA: Harvard University Press.

Gordon, P and Newnham, A (1985) *Passport to Benefits: Racism in Social Security*. London: Child Poverty Action Group and Runnymede Trust.

Gorz, A (1988) *Métamorphose du travail. Quête de sens*. Paris: Galilée.

Graef, R (1992) *Living Dangerously: Young Offenders in Their Own Words*. London: HarperCollins.

Graham, H (1983) 'Caring: Labour of Love', in Finch, J and Groves, D (eds) *A Labour of Love: Women, Work and Caring*. London: Routledge & Kegan Paul.

Grimwood, C and Popplestone, R (1993) *Women in Management*. London: BASW/Macmillan – now Palgrave Macmillan.

Haber, H F (1994) *Beyond Postmodern Politics: Lyotard, Rorty, Foucault*. London: Routledge.

Haig-Brown, C (1988) *Resistance and Renewal: Surviving the Indian Residential School*. Vancouver: Tillicum Librarby/Arsenal Pulp Press.

Hallett, C (1991) *Women and Social Services*. London: Sage.

Hanmer, J and Statham, D (1988) *Women and Social Work: Towards a Woman-Centred Practice*. Basingstoke: Macmillan – now Palgrave Macmillan.

Hanscombe, G and Forster, J (1982) *Rocking the Cradle: Lesbian Mothers*. London: Sheba Feminist Publishing.

Harding, S (1993) 'Rethinking Standpoint Epistemology: What is "Strong Objectivity"' in Alcoff, L and Potter, E (eds) *Feminist Epistemology*. New York: Routledge.

Hartsock, N (1987) 'The Feminist Standpoint: Developing the Ground for a Specifically Feminist Historical Materialism' in Harding, S (ed.) *Feminism and Methodology*. Bloomington, IN: Indiana University Press.

Hartsock, N (1990) 'Foucault on Power: A Theory for Women?' in Nicholson, L (ed.) *Feminism/Postmodernism*. New York: Routledge.

Healy, K (2000) *Social Work Practices: Contemporary Perspectives on Change*. London: Sage.

Hearn, J (1987) *The Gender of Oppression: Men, Masculinity and the Critique of Marxism*. Brighton: Wheatsheaf.

Help Age (2002) *State of World's Older People*. London: Help Age International.

Hester, M, Kelly, L and Radford, J (eds) (1996) *Women, Violence and Male Power*. Buckingham: Open University Press.

Hester, M, Pearson, C and Harwin, N (2000) *Making an Impact: Children and Domestic Violence – A Reader*. London: Department of Health.

Horley, S (1990) 'A Shame and A Disgrace', *Social Work Today*, 21 June, pp. 16–17.

Howe, D (1994) 'Modernity, Postmodernity and Social Work', *British Journal of Social Work*, **24**(5): 513–32.

Humphries, B (ed.) (1996) *Critical Perspectives on Empowerment*. Birmingham: Venture Press.

Jenkins, R (1996) *Social Identity: Key Ideas*. London: Routledge.

John-Baptiste, A (2001) 'Africentric Social Work' in Dominelli, L, Lorenz, W and Soydan, H (eds) *Beyond Racial Divides: Ethnicities in Social Work*. Aldershot: Ashgate.

Jones, C (1993) 'Distortion and Demonisation: The Right and Anti-Racist Social Work Education', *Journal of Social Work Eduction*, **12**(3): 9–16.

Jordan, B (2000): *Social Work and the Third Way: Tough Love as Social Policy*. London: Sage.

Jubilee 2000. From the website http://www.jubilee2000uk.org

Kadushin, A (1972) 'The Racial Factor in the Interview', *Social Work*, pp. 173–89.

Kassindja, K (1998) *Do They Hear You When You Cry*. New York: Delta Books.

Kelly, L (1988) *Surviving Sexual Violence*. Cambridge: Polity.

Kelsey, J (1997) *The New Zealand Experience*. Aukland: Aukland University Press.

Kemp, A, Madlala, N, Moodley, A and Salo, E (1995) 'The Dawn of a New Day: Redefining South African Feminism', in Basu, A (ed.) *The Challenge of Local Feminisms: Women's Movements in Global Perspective*. Boulder: Westview Press.

Khan, P (2000) 'Asylum Seekers in the UK: Implications for Social Service Involvement' *Social Work and Social Sciences Review*, 8(2): 116–29.

Khan, P and Dominelli, L (2000) 'The Impact of Globalisation and Social Work Practice in the UK', *European Journal of Social Work*, 3(2): 95–108.

Khan, P and Dominelli, L (2000a) Social Work Practice and Globalisation: A Research Report. Paper Presented at the Dubrovnick Summer School, Dubrovnick, Croatia, 18–23 June.

Kilkey, M (2000) *Lone Mothers between Paid Work and Care: The Policy Regime in Twenty Countries*. Aldershot: Ashgate.

Knijn, T and Ungerson, C (1997) 'Introduction: Care Work and Gender in Welfare Regimes', *Social Politics*, Fall, pp. 323–7.

Kuyek, J N (1990) *Fighting for Hope: Organizing to Realise our Dreams*. Montreal: Black Rose Books.

Kyle, D and Koslowski, B (2001) The Sex Trade in Women: The Polish Example. Paper presented at the Sex Trade in Women Conference, Vienna, 21 June.

Lacan, J (1977) *Ecrits: A Selection*. Translated by A Sheridan. New York: W W Norton.

Laird, J (1994) 'Lesbian Couples and Families: A Cultural Perspective' in Mirkin, M P (ed.) *Treating Women in their Social Contexts: A Feminist Reconstruction*. New York: Guildford Press.

Langan, M and Day, L (eds) (1989) *Women, Oppression and Social Work*. London: Routledge.

La Rossa, R (1995) 'Fatherhood and Social Change', in Nelson, E and Robinson, B (eds) *Gender in the 1990s: Images, Realities and Issues*. Toronto: Nelson Canada.

Leonard, P (1997) *Postmodern Welfare: Reconstructing an Emancipatory Project*. London: Sage.

Levitas, R (ed.) (1986) *The Ideology of the New Right*. Cambridge: Polity.

Lister, R (1997) *Citizenship: Feminist Perspectives*. Basingstoke: Macmillan – now Palgrave Macmillan.

London-Edinburgh Weekend Return Group (1979) *In and Against the State*. London: Conference of Socialist Economists.

Lorenz, W (1994) *Social Work in a Changing Europe*. London: Routledge.

Lunghini, G (1995) *L'età dello spreco. Disoccupazione e bisogni sociale*. Torino: Bollati Boringhieri.

Lum, D (2000) *Culturally Competent Practice: A Framework for Growth and Action*. San Francisco: Wadworth Publishing Company.

Lyotard, J (1986) *The Postmodern Condition: A Report on Knowledge*. Manchester: Manchester University Press.

MacPherson, C B (1962) *The Political Theory of Possessive Individualism: Hobbes to Locke*. Oxford: Oxford University Press.

Mama, A (1989) *Hidden Struggle: Statutory and Voluntary Responses to Violence Against Black Women in the Home*. London: Race and Housing Unit.

Maslow, A (1970) *Motivation and Personality*. New York: Harper & Row.

Maxime, J (1986) 'Some Psychological Models of Black Self-Concept' in Ahmed, S, Cheetham, J and Small, J (eds) *Social Work with Black Children and Their Families*. London: Batsford.

McAdam, D and Snow, D (1997) *Social Movements: Readings on Their Emergence, Mobilization and Dynamics*. Los Angeles: Roxbury.

McLeod, E and Dominelli, L (1982) 'The Personal and the Apolitical: Feminism and Moving Beyond the Integrated Methods Approach', in Bailey, R and Lee, P (eds) *Theory and Practice in Social Work*. Oxford: Basil Blackwell.

Melucci, N (1989) *Nomads of the Present: Social Movements and Individual Needs in Contemporary Society*. London: Hutchinson Radius.

Memmi, A (1965) *The Colonizer and the Colonized*. Translated by H Greenfield. Boston: Beacon Press.

Memmi, A (1984) *Dependence: A Sketch for a Portrait of the Dependent*. Boston: Beacon Press.

Merton, R (1957) *Social Theory and Social Structures*. New York: Free Press.

Millar, J (1999) Lone Mothers and the New Deal. Paper presented at the Social Policy Seminar Series, Southampton University, Southampton, October.

Mills, C W (1970) *The Sociological Imagination*. London: Pelican Books.

Mishra, R (1990) *The Welfare State in Capitalist Societies*. London: Routledge.

Mishra, R (1995) *Globalisation and the Welfare State*. Cheltenham: Edward Elgar.

Modood, T (1988) '"Black" Racial Equality and Asian Identity', *New Community*, 14(3): 397–404.

Modood, T and Werbner, P (1997) *The Politics of Multiculturalism: Racism, Identity and Community in the New Europe*. London: Zed Books.

Modood, T, Beishon, S and Virdee, S (1994) *Changing Ethnic Identities*. London: Policy Studies Institute.

Mohanty, C (1991) 'Cartographies of Struggle' in Mohanty, C, Russo, A and Torres, L (eds) *Third World Women and the Politics of Feminism*. Bloomington, IN: Indiana University Press.

Mohanty, C, Russo, A and Torres, L (eds) (1991) *Third World Women and the Politics of Feminism*. Bloomington, IN: Indiana University Press.

Morris, J (1991) *Pride Against Prejudice: Transforming Attitudes to Disability*. London: Women's Press.

Morris, L (1995) *Dangerous Classes: The Underclass and Social Citizenship*. London: Routledge.

Mullaly, R (1993) *Structural Social Work*. Toronto: McClelland & Stewart.

Mullender, A (1997) *Rethinking Domestic Violence: The Social Work and Probation Responses*. London: Routledge.

Mullender, A and Morley, R (eds) (1994) *Children Living with Domestic Violence: Putting Men's Abuse of Women on the Childcare Agenda*. London: Whiting & Birch.

Mullender, A and Ward, D (1991) *The Practice Principles of Self-Directed Groupwork: Establishing a Value Base for Empowerment*. Nottingham: University of Nottingham, Centre for Social Action.

Murray, C (1984) *Losing Ground: American Social Policy*. New York: Basic Books.

Murray, C (1990) *The Emerging British Underclass*. London: Institute of Economic Affairs.

Murray, C (1994) *Underclass: The Crisis Deepens*. London: Institute of Economic Affairs.

Naples, N A (ed.) (1997) *Community Activism and Feminist Politics: Organizing Across Race, Class and Gender*. London: Routledge.

Narayan, D, Patel, R, Schafft, K, Rademacher, A and Koch-Schulte, S (2000) *Can Anyone Hear Us?* Vol. 1: *Voices of the Poor*. New York: Oxford University Press.

NASW (National Association of Social Workers) (1996) *The Code of Ethics*. Washington, DC: NASW.

Ng, R (1988) *The Politics of Community Services: Immigrant Women, Class and the State*. Toronto: Garamond Press.

Nicholson, L (ed.) (1990) *Feminism/Postmodernism*. New York: Routledge, Chapman & Hall.

O'Connor, J (1973) *The Fiscal Crisis of the State*. New York: St Martin's Press.

Oliver, M (1990) *The Politics of Disablement*. Basingstoke: Macmillan – now Palgrave Macmillan.

Orme, J, Dominelli, L and Mullender, A (2000) 'Working with Violent Men from a Feminist Social Work Perspective', *International Social Work*, 43(1): 9–106.

Pahl, J (1985) *Private Violence and Public Policy*. London: Routledge & Kegan Paul.

Parsons, T (1951) *The Social System*. New York: Free Press.

Parsons, T (1957) *Essays in Sociological Theory*. New York: Free Press.

Parton, N (1994) 'The Nature of Social Work Under Conditions of (Post)Modernity', *Social Work and Social Sciences Review*, 5(2): 93–112.

Parton, N (1998) 'Risk, Advanced Liberalism and Child Welfare: The Need to Rediscover Uncertainty and Ambiguity', *British Journal of Social Work*, 28, pp. 5–27.

Pascall, G (1986) *Social Policy: A Feminist Analysis*. London: Tavistock.

Patel, N (1990) *Race Against Time: Ethnic Elders*. London: Runnymede Trust.

Pease, B and Fook, J (eds) (1999) *Transforming Social Work Practice: Postmodern Critical Perspectives*. London: Routledge.

Phillips, M (1993) 'An Oppressive Urge to End Oppression', *Observer*, 1 August.

Phillips, M (1994) 'Illiberal Liberalism', in Dunant, S (ed.) *The War of the Word: The Political Correctness Debate*. London: Virgo.

Phillipson, C (1998) *Reconstructuring Old Age: New Agendas in Social Theory and Practice*. London: Sage.

Pierson, C (1998) *Beyond the Welfare State: The New Political Economy of Welfare*. Cambridge: Polity Press. First Published in 1991.

Pinker, R (1993) 'A Lethal Kind of Looniness', *Times Higher Educational Supplement*, 10 September.

Pringle, K (1995) *Men, Masculinities and Social Welfare*. London: University College London.

Pritchard, J (1992) *The Abuse of Elderly People: A Handbook for Professionals*. London: Jessica Kingsley.

Radcliffe-Brown, R A (1952) *Structure and Function in Primitive Society*. New York: Free Press.

Ralph, D, Regimbald, A and St-Amand, N (1997) *Open for Business: Closed to People*. Halifax: Fernwood Publishing.

Rank, H R (1994) *Living on the Edge: The Realities of Welfare in America*. New York: Columbia University Press.

Rawls, J (1973) *A Theory of Justice*. Oxford: Oxford University Press.

Remfry, P (1979) 'North Tyneside Community Development Project', *Journal of Community Development*, 14(3): 186–9.

Rifkin, J (1995) *The End of Work*. New York: Archer/Putnam.

Ristock, J L and Pennell, J (1996) *Community Research as Empowerment: Feminist Links, Postmodern Interruptions*. Oxford: Oxford University Press.

Ritzer, G (2000) *The McDonaldization of Society*. London: Pine Forge Press.

Robinson, L (1995) *Psychology for Social Workers: Black Perspectives*. London: Routledge.

Robinson, L (1998) *'Race': Communication and the Caring Professions*. Buckingham: Open University Press.

Roediger, D (1990) *The Wages of Whiteness: Race and the Making of the American Working Class*. New York: Verso.

Rojek, C, Peacock, G and Collins, S (1988) *Social Work and Received Ideas*. London: Routledge.

Roper Renshaw, I (1994) 'Strengthening Civil Society: The Role of NGOs', *Development*, 4, pp. 46–9.

Ruffolo, G (1985) *La qualità sociale*. Bari: Laterza.

Rutherford, J (1992) *Men's Silences: Predicaments in Masculinity*. London: Routledge.

Sales, T (2001) 'Threat to 250 Jobs if Benford Moves Out', *Leamington Spa Courier*, 5 October, p. 4.

Saussure, F (1966) *Course in General Linguistics*. Translated by W Baskin. New York: McGraw-Hill.

Shah, Z (2001) British Pakistanis in Luton. PhD thesis. Southampton: University of Southampton.

Shiva, V (2000) *The Reith Lectures*. BBC, Radio 4.

Showstack Sassoon, A (ed.) (1987) *Women and the State: The Shifting Boundaries of the Private and Public*. London: Hutchinson.

Shragge, E and Fontan, J (eds) (2000) *Social Economy: International Debates and Perspectives*. Montreal: Black Rose Books.

Small, S (1994) *Racialised Barriers: The Black Experience in the United States and England in the 1980s*. London: Routledge.

Smith, D E (1987) *The Everyday World as Problematic: A Feminist Sociology*. Toronto: University of Toronto Press.

Smith, D E (1990) *The Conceptual Practices of Power: A Feminist Sociology of Knowledge*. Boston: North Eastern University Press.

Stack, C (1975) *All our Kin: Strategies for Survival in a Black Community*. New York: Harper & Row.

Staples, R (1988) *Black Masculinity: The Black Male's Role in American Society*. San Francisco: Black Scholar Press.

Status of Women (2001) *Women's Economic Independence and Security: A Federal/Provincial/Territorial Strategic Framework from the Ministers Responsible for the Status of Women*. Ottawa: Status of Women.

Strega, S, Callahan, M, Dominelli, L and Ruttman, D (2000) The Experiences of Mothers in Government Care. Paper given at the 29th Congress of the International Association of Schools of Social Work, Montreal, 30 July–2 August.

Swann, L (1985) *Education for All: The Report of the Committee of Enquiry into the Education of Children of Ethnic Minorities*. London: HMSO.

Tait-Rolleston, W and Pehi-Barlow (2001) 'A Maori Social Work Construct' in Dominelli, L, Lorenz, W and Soydon, H (eds) *Beyond Racial Divides: Ethnicities in Social Work*. Aldershot: Ashgate.

Teeple, G (1995) *Globalisation and the Decline of Social Reform*. Toronto: Garamond.

Thane, P (1996) *Foundations of the Welfare State*, 2nd edn. London: Longman.

Thompson, N (1993) *Anti-Discriminatory Practice*, 2nd edn. Basingstoke: Macmillan – now Palgrave Macmillan.

Thorpe, R and Irwin, J (1996) *Women and Violence: Working for Change*. Sydney: Hale and Iremonger.

Titmuss, R (1963) *Essays on the Welfare State*. London: George Allen & Unwin.

Tizard, B and Phoenix, A (1993) *Black, White or Mixed Race? Race and Racism in the Lives of Young People of Mixed Parentage*. London: Routledge.

Trew, W (1999) Anti-Oppressive Practice. Paper delivered at the Anti-Oppressive Practice Conference, Leeds University, 10 June.

Twigg, J and Atkin, K (1994) *Carers Perceived: Policy and Practice in Informal Care*. Buckingham: Open University Press.

Tronto, J (1993) *Moral Boundaries: A Political Argument for an Ethics of Care*. London: Routledge.

UNDP (United Nations Development Programme) (1996) *Human Development Report, 1996. Economic Growth and Human Development*. New York: UNDP.

UNDP (United Nations Development Programme) (1998) *The 1998 Report on Human Social Development: Consumption for Human Development*. New York: UNDP.

UNDP (United Nations Development Programme) (2000) *Overcoming Human Poverty, 2000*. New York: UNDP.

UNDP (United Nations Development Programme) (2000a) *Human Development Report, 2000: Human Rights and Human Development*. New York: UNDP.

Ungerson, C (1990) *Gender and Caring Work and Welfare in Britain and Scandinavia*. Hemel Hempstead: Harvester Wheatsheaf.

Walby, S (1990) *Theorising Patriarchy*. Oxford: Basil Blackwell.

Walton, R (1975) *Women in Social Work*. Routledge & Kegan Paul.

Ware, V (1992) *Beyond the Pale: White Women, Racism and History*. London: Verso.

Weber, M (1978) *Selections from Max Weber*. Translated by W C Runciman. Berkeley: University of California Press.

Wendell, S (1996) *The Rejected Body: Feminist Philosophical Reflections on Disability*. London: Routledge.

Wetzel, J W (1997) Human Rights and Social Work Practice. Paper delivered at the CSWE Annual Programme Meeting, New York City, 8 March.

White, M (1993) 'Deconstruction and Therapy', in Gilligan, S and Price, R (eds) *Therapeutic Conversations*. New York: Norton.

White, M and Epston, D (1990) *Narrative Means to Therapeutic Ends*. New York: Norton.

Wichterich, C (2000) *The Globalized Woman: Reports from a Future of Inequality*. London: Zed Press.

Wilensky, H and Lebeaux, C (1965) *Industrial Society and Social Welfare*. New York: Macmillan – now Palgrave Macmillan.

Williams, F (1989) *Social Policy: A Critical Introduction – Race, Gender and Class*. Cambridge: Polity.

Wilson, M (1993) *Crossing the Boundary: Black Women Survive Incest*. London: Virago.

Wilson, T J (1996) 'Feminism and Institutionalised Racism: Inclusion and Exclusion at an Australian Women's Refuge', *Feminist Review*, 52, Spring, pp. 1–26.

Wolfensohn, J D (2000) 'Forward' in Edstrom, J (ed.) *New Paths to Social Development: Community and Global Networks in Action*. Washington, DC: International Bank for Reconstruction and Development/World Bank.

Young, R (1990) *White Mythologies: Writing History and the West*. London: Routledge.

Younghusband, E (1978) *Social Work in Britain, 1950–1975*. London: Allen & Unwin.

Zucchino, D (1997) *Myth of the Welfare Queen*. New York: Touchstone Books.

Author Index

A
Adelson, N, 19
Ahmed, B, 2, 27, 60
Appleyard, B, 60, 62
Armitage, A, 54
Arnup, K, 60
Asante, M, 63

B
Badran, M, 63
Balbo, L, 9
Banks, S, 62, 64
Barker, H, 66
Barker, M, 78
Barn, R, 54
Barnes, C, 32,
Barnes, M, 99
Barrett, M, 73
Basu, M, 63, 111, 177
BASW, 64
Bauman, Z, 28
Begum, N, 100
Belenky, M F, 1
Benhabib, S, 40
Bhatti-Sinclair, K, 52
Bhavani, K K, 79
Biesteck, F P, 64, 100
Biggs, S, 28
Bishop, A, 32, 151
Blair, T, 3, 29, 134
Bolger, S, 83, 148
Bourdieu, P, 95
Boxer, S, 60
Brandwein, R, 50
Brinton, C, 162

Broadbent, J, 148
Brooks, D, 77
Brown, A, 50, 111
Bruyere, G, 19
Bryant, B, 16, 73
Bulmer, M, 135
Burke, B, 32, 33
Burrell, G, 169

C
Callahan, M, 167
Campbell, A, 136
Carlsson, I, 70, 174, 176
Castles, S, 25
CCETSW, 77
Chaplin, J, 89
Chesney-Lind, M, 56
Clarke, J, 27, 32, 120, 132
Cleaver, E, 18, 47, 49, 112
Clegg, S R, 16
Clinton, H R, 3
Cochrane, A, 3
Coleman, J S, 133
Coll, C, 42
Collins, P H, 63, 73, 110, 147
Connell, R W, 49, 63, 105
Cook, A, 114
Cooper, R, 94, 169
Corrigan, P, 60, 61, 89, 147
Cowburn, M, 128
Craig, G, 2
Cross, M, 13, 15
Culpitt, I, 27, 59
Cunningham, F, 61

D

Daenzer, P, 124
Dale, J, 29
Dalrymple, J, 32
Davies, M, 59, 60
Day, P, 60
Deacon, B, 177
DoH, 168
Dominelli, L, 1–2, 16–18, 23, 25–6,
    30–3, 51, 53, 59–61, 66, 74,
    88–90, 95, 100, 114, 118–19,
    124–5, 127–8, 130–1, 141, 144–6,
    167, 172, 178
Donati, P, 131–2
Dworkin, A, 90

E

Egan, G, 100
Epston, L, 86
Essed, P, 13, 63

F

Fernando, S, 60, 70
Finch, J, 33
Flax, J, 40
Fontan, J, 132, 157, 175
Fook, J, 50, 89
Forster, J, 60
Foster, J, 29
Foucault, M, 16–18, 22, 169–70
Frankfort, E, 75, 89, 147
Franklin, B, 31
Freire, P, 74, 147
French, M, 16–17, 54
Fryer, P, 80
Furniss, E, 54

G

Giddens, A, 12, 129, 152
Gilder, G, 42
Gilroy, P, 80
Gordon, P, 30, 136
Gorz, A, 135
Graef, R, 106
Graham, H, 33

H

Haber, H F, 169–70
Haig-Brown, C, 54
Hanmer, J, 60
Hanscombe, G, 60

Harding, S, 39
Hartsock, N, 39, 87
Hester, M, 52
Horley, S, 90
Howe, D, 172
Hughes, 30
Humphries, B, 3

J

Jenkins, R, 40
Jones, C, 3
Jordan, B, 21, 29, 124, 135

K

Kadushin, A, 92
Kelsey, J, 72, 132
Kemp, A, 118
Khan, P, 124, 141, 144–5, 175
Kilkey, M, 3, 44
Kirk, G, 114
Knijn, T, 179
Kuyek, J N, 118, 131–2

L

La Rossa, R, 105
Lacan, J, 171
Laird, J, 38
Langan, M, 60
Laughlin, R, 148
Lebeaux, C, 2
Leonard, P, 56, 60–1, 89, 147
Lister, R, 51
Lorenz, W, 28, 54–5, 122, 163, 179
Lum, D, 53
Lunghini, G, 133
Lyotard, J, 170

M

Mama, A, 75
Maslow, A, 21
Maxime, J, 155
Mayo, M, 2
McAdam, D, 127, 128, 131
McIntosh, M, 73
McLeod, E, 60, 89–90
Melucci, N, 113
Memmi, A, 45, 99
Merton, R, 44
Millar, J, 42
Mills, C W, 74
Mishra, R, 2

Modood, T, 48, 49
Mohanty, C, 63, 177–8
Morris, J, 20, 60
Morris, L, 100, 135
Mullaly, R, 61
Mullender, A, 74–5, 90, 127
Murray, C, 73

N
Naples, N A, 127–8
Narayan, D, 130
NASW, 64–5
Ng, R, 130
Nicholson, L, 163

O
Oliver, M, 20, 25, 48, 60, 99, 147
Orme, J, 74

P
Parton, N, 28
Pascall, G, 29, 51
Patel, N, 27
Pennell, J, 126
Phillips, M, 60, 62, 74, 77
Phillipson, C, 60
Pinker, R, 60, 62, 72, 77

R
Radcliffe-Brown, R A, 50, 78
Ralph, D, 72, 119, 132, 134
Ramphal, S, 70, 174, 176
Rank, H R, 119, 123–4, 126
Rawls, J, 76
Remfry, P, 26
Rifkin, J, 133–4
Ristock, J L, 126
Ritzer, G, 21
Robinson, L, 15
Roediger, D, 49
Roper Renshaw, I, 175
Ruffolo, G, 136
Rutherford, J, 40

S
Sales, T, 134
Saussure, F, 170

Shah, Z, 16, 56
Shiva, V, 176
Shragge, E, 132, 157, 175
Small, S, 80
Smith, D E, 63
Snow, D, 127–8, 131
Stack, C, 44
Statham, D, 60
Strega, S, 44, 168, 172
Swann, L, 60

T
Teeple, G, 2, 125, 132
Tew, W, 19
Thompson, N, 4
Titmuss, R, 135

U
UN, 70, 83, 125, 176
UNDP, 21, 70, 82, 83
Ungerson, C, 179

W
Wacquant, L, 95
Ward, D, 127
Ware, V, 16
Washington, J, 178
Wendell, S, 19, 48, 55, 63, 100
Werbner, P, 49
Wetzel, J W, 70
White, M, 86
Wichterich, C, 3, 21, 82, 123, 125,
   134, 173, 178
Wilensky, H, 2
Williams, F, 26, 29, 30
Wilson, M, 75
Wolfensohn, J D, 179

Y
Young, R, 168
Younghusband, E, 23

Z
Zucchino, D, 3, 119, 132, 134–5

Subject Index

A

abuse, 27–8, 35, 80, 168
abusers of welfare, 30, 42
acceptance, 11, 39, 48, 56, 79, 94, 101, 104, 106, 163
accommodate, 32, 41
accommodation, 8, 11, 39, 47, 79
accommodationist, 11–13, 47, 79
accountability, 2, 25–6, 125, 136, 142, 144
acquisition of information, 52, 53
active citizen, 99, 124, 182
acts of subversion, 12
adoption, 76
adultist power relation, 56
affirmation, 78, 104–5, 112, 119
Africa, 70, 174
ageist, 28
agency, 8–9, 16–17, 25, 33, 53–4, 65–9, 72, 87, 91, 96–9, 115–16, 129, 149–50, 153, 156, 160, 167–9, 181–2
aid, 83
alliance, 53, 120, 152
altruism, 121, 179
altruistic ideals, 29
ambiguity, 88, 182
Anglo-Saxon culture, 54
Anglo-Saxon origins, 54
antagonistic relations, 170
anti-oppression, 8, 13
anti-oppressive practice, 2–8, 33–9, 46–7, 53, 61, 69–71, 75–7, 82–5, 88–9, 96, 100, 110–11, 146, 163, 170, 181–5

anti-racism, 77, 92
apartheid, 80
assessment, 28, 51–3, 77, 87, 99, 133, 145
assimilation, 14, 29, 48
assistance, 6, 71, 97–8, 126, 134, 139, 167, 171
assumptions, 1, 29, 54, 97, 113, 151, 163
attitudes, 52, 66, 68, 95, 98, 99, 148, 154
Australia, 19, 54, 64

B

backlash, 62, 74, 77
bad mother, 172
benefits, 3, 30–1, 42, 44, 48, 123–4
best interests of the child, 56
Beveridge's five giants, 146
binary divide, 37
binary dyad, 80, 92
binary opposites, 78
binary opposition, 37–8
black feminist, 73, 79
black middle-class woman, 16, 46
black people, 1, 13, 16, 27, 30, 38, 51, 55, 57, 63, 68, 70, 81–2, 92, 95, 98, 100, 122, 151, 155
black women, 16, 51, 100
Blair's administration, 3, 29, 134
body, 19, 20, 29, 48, 55–7, 62
Britain, 2–3, 26, 30, 42, 50, 77–8, 93, 101, 103, 114, 121, 123, 125, 132, 135–6
British Columbia, 136

bureaucracy, 33, 144
bureaucratic rationality, 72
bureaucratism, 135
bureau-professionalism, 62

C

Canada, 30, 54, 132, 134, 136
Canadian Business, 132
capacity, 3, 15–19, 23, 25, 29, 36,
    43, 46, 50, 53, 58, 66, 74, 76–8,
    82, 93, 96–100, 103–7, 113–20,
    129, 131–8, 143–5, 148, 152–4,
    158–9, 162–7, 173–6, 179, 182–3
capitalism, 3, 21, 28, 35, 48, 130–3,
    135–8, 139, 142, 146, 169, 176
capitalist development, 131–3, 138
capitalist economic relations, 131–5,
    169
caring, 1–3, 23, 27–33, 52, 105,
    121, 128, 150, 163, 176, 179
caring professionals, 1, 3, 150
caseload, 95
casework, 73–4, 89
change, 8, 10–16, 32–5, 60, 69–71,
    74, 78–9, 83–6, 89, 91, 96, 101,
    109–11, 115–18, 128–9, 143–52,
    158–70, 183–5
child care, 42
child welfare, 42, 149
children, 3, 21, 28, 31, 35, 42–4,
    51–5, 65, 74, 80–3, 90–4, 98,
    102, 105, 121, 124, 149, 165–8,
    170–2, 177
choice, 6, 27, 41–4, 71, 97–8,
    119–20, 162
citizenship, 1, 5, 6, 26–30, 48–51,
    58, 67, 76, 99, 107, 113, 120–6,
    134–6, 162, 183
citizenship rights, 29, 99, 107, 126
civic ethic, 139, 183
civil rights movement, 12, 49, 172
civil society, 1, 43–4, 125, 173–80
claimant, 26
class, 4, 9, 16, 44, 46, 60–1, 82, 89,
    98–100, 144, 147, 164, 172, 182
classism, 28
Clause 28, 103
client agency, 65, 84, 95–8, 164,
    167, 185
client discourses, 143

client–worker relationships, 100,
    166–7, 185
code of ethics, 64–7, 142, 149
collaboration, 14, 18
collective action, 18, 109, 112–14,
    119–21, 126–7, 131, 139, 146,
    162, 169, 172–80
collective responsibility, 121, 126
commissioner, 120
commodification, 21, 142, 145
commodification of clients, 142, 145
commodification of need, 21
commodity, 130, 145
commonalities, 19–21, 45, 100, 110,
    115
communication, 34, 137
communities, 6, 22, 26, 30–4, 43, 50,
    58, 81–4, 97, 108–11, 126–40, 146,
    153, 157, 159, 175–8, 180, 183–4
community care, 30
community development, 138
community work, 127
competence-based social work, 88,
    144
complaint, 66–7, 95, 102
confidentiality, 64
conscientisation, 13
consciousness-raising, 34, 71, 74,
    125, 146–7
constraints, 25, 29, 36, 43, 47, 87,
    149, 157, 182
contested discourses, 6, 12–13, 16,
    20, 53, 63–4, 73, 79, 83, 91, 117,
    121, 142, 150, 180
context, 9–10, 20–7, 32–3, 36–41,
    49, 51, 54, 61–9, 71–4, 88–9,
    97–8, 107, 111, 122–6, 130, 142,
    150, 152, 174, 182
continuities, 48, 50, 90, 91
contract culture, 82
contractual power, 120
controlling poor people, 137
Copenhagen, 126
corporate accountability, 26
corporate activities, 178
corporate decision-makers, 136, 175,
    177
corporate elite, 169
counselling, 55
crime, 34, 71, 133, 173

criminal justice system, 90
cultural capital, 91
cultural difference, 78
cultural relativism, 146
cultural wars, 77

D
daily practices, 17
decision-making, 68–9, 84, 88, 95, 97, 117, 143, 156–7, 176–7
dehumanise, 78
dependency, 30–1, 56, 98–9, 119
dependent, 30–3, 42, 51, 55, 95, 98, 156, 177–8
deserving, 27–9, 66, 121–3, 141
dialogical, 183
dialogue, 62, 118, 132, 148, 155
diaspora, 51
diasporic groups, 50
dichotomous terms, 7, 38, 40, 56, 148
difference, 8, 14–17, 20, 37–9, 41, 44, 49, 51–3, 56–7, 61–2, 92, 96, 100, 110, 113–17, 123, 129, 132, 139, 146, 153–9, 163–4, 170, 176, 182
differential power relation, 73
dignity, 26, 35, 64, 66–7, 143, 173, 182
dilemma, 68
Diploma in Social Work, 77
disability, 4, 9, 44, 46–8, 60–4, 98–100, 164, 172, 178
disability movement, 100, 172
disabled people, 1, 20, 25, 32, 48, 57, 99–100, 110, 122, 147
disablism, 55
disadvantaged, 8, 28–9, 35, 45, 130, 153
discontinuities, 79, 90–1
discourses, 17, 49, 88, 93, 112, 171
discourses, dominant, 27, 31, 49, 86, 88, 93, 98, 102, 105, 112, 122
discourses of the everyday, 17
discretion, 88, 145
discretionary power, 28
discrimination, 4, 12–13, 78–80
disempower, 39, 57, 75, 102
diversity, 20, 39, 122, 161, 180
domestic violence, 52, 74, 111

dominant group, 8, 11–17, 38–41, 47–50, 54–7, 78, 92, 112, 157
dominant norm, 11–12, 51, 55, 172
drug-taking, 104, 106
dualism, 45, 47, 62–3
dualism of inequalities, 45
dualistic concept, 62–3
dyad, 44–5

E
education, 29, 34, 60, 70, 104, 124
egalitarian, 1, 8, 13–15, 33–6, 39, 49, 57, 60, 84, 88, 98, 129, 146, 151–5, 160–4, 181, 185
egalitarian social relations, 1, 49, 185
egalitarian society, 33, 155
egalitarianism, 35
elder care, 27
elders, 1
emancipation, 26, 32, 74, 77
emancipation of women, 74
emotional abuse, 80
emotions, 100, 105, 115, 155
empathy, 46, 93
empirical evidence, 116
employer, 25, 68, 72, 143, 158, 167
employment, 42, 68, 82, 124, 131, 136, 143, 149, 165
empowerment, 1–4, 18, 23–6, 31, 43, 61–2, 86–9, 95, 99, 103, 108, 116–19, 126–7, 139, 143, 146, 168–71, 175–9, 183
enabling processes, 61, 70, 122, 142
ends, 10, 17, 71, 116, 147–52, 168
entitlement, 86, 146
environmental, 127, 131, 173–4
epistemology, 63
equal opportunities policies, 2, 150, 153
equality, 8, 13, 20–1, 29–31, 38, 65, 76, 84, 92, 108, 113, 118, 121, 136, 146, 182–3
ethical code, 66
ethical principle, 63–4, 67
ethics, 62–70, 134
ethnic monitoring, 151
Eurocentric approaches, 70
evaluation, 184

everyday life, 9, 12, 68, 164, 166, 180
everyday practice, 9, 68
everyday routine, 164
exchange relation, 134
exclusion, 3–4, 8, 14–18, 28, 34, 41–8, 63, 66, 78, 99–100, 111–17, 120, 124–6, 137, 171, 177
exclusionary processes, 14, 18, 28, 47, 66, 99, 114, 117, 177
expert knowledge, 34, 84
expertise, 1, 26, 54, 72, 96, 115, 141, 143
extended family, 27, 51

F
faith affiliation, 16, 22, 24, 26, 184
false equality trap, 66, 84, 113
familialist relations, 31
family, 25, 27, 30–1, 38, 51, 55, 67, 72–3, 94, 97, 104–6, 111, 128, 165–7, 184
family relationships, 73, 94
family support, 167
father, 55, 104–7
Father Biesteck, 64
fatherhood, 105
fear, 4, 15, 79, 93–4, 144, 156–8, 172
femininity, 27, 75
feminism, 42, 62, 75, 77
feminist principles, 75
feminist social work, 182
feminists, 16, 31, 42, 63, 90
fields of contestation, 39
fiscal rationality, 143
flattened hierarchies, 156
fragmentation, 20, 66, 74–5, 109, 129, 139, 146
Freud, 73
Freudian analysis, 73

G
G7, 174
gender, 4, 9, 13, 16, 21, 27, 30, 35, 44–6, 54, 60, 63, 90, 98, 100, 110, 123, 134, 155, 164, 178, 182
globalisation, 1, 32, 88, 137, 146, 176, 178

government, 3, 62, 82, 93, 124–6, 130, 134–6, 176–9
Greenham Common Women's Peace Movement, 114
group, 6, 8, 11–20, 23–4, 30, 36–8, 41, 44–7, 50, 56–7, 75, 78, 80, 84, 90–4, 97, 100, 103, 109–19, 122, 126–7, 130, 139, 150, 153–4, 162, 169, 174, 180
Group of 77, 70
Gujerati Muslim, 50

H
hegemonic discourse, 20, 31, 170, 179
helping relations, 76, 98, 150
heritage, 50, 55, 118
heterosexual, 19, 30–1, 48, 51, 52, 63, 103
hierarchical organisation, 157
hierarchy of body worth, 20
holistic approaches, 5, 47, 84–7, 136, 143–5, 148, 151, 155, 159, 181, 184
holistic intervention, 184
homogeneity, 28, 122
homophobia, 103
homosexual, 103
honorary, 14, 15
household sector, 33
housework, 51
housing, 20, 30, 42, 75
human relations, 64
human rights, 35, 62, 67, 70–1, 83–4, 146
human rights violation, 71
hybridity, 49, 50

I
identity formation, 10, 38, 40–2, 47, 50, 90–1, 105
identity of social work, 54
ideological supremacy, 78
ideology, 2–3, 29, 51–2, 78, 122–6, 166, 172, 178
inalienable rights, 56
inclusion, 14–15, 28, 33, 44–8, 113–17, 122–3
inclusionary processes, 15, 28, 117

income, 3, 5, 70, 124, 131, 135,
137, 179
incorporation, 14, 152
incorporationist approaches, 13–15
independence, 30, 42, 82
independent, 30, 32, 42, 145, 169
individualises people, 109
individualism, 121, 128–9, 133
individuals, 2, 6–20, 25–9, 33–6, 40,
43, 46–51, 57–8, 61, 67, 70–93,
99–100, 107–22, 125–9, 132–9,
145–7, 165–6, 170, 178, 181–3
inegalitarian relation, 9, 45, 77, 154
informal, 33, 110, 138
information exchange, 178
injustice, 20, 64, 101, 142, 179–80
insider–outsider, 46
institution, 30, 160
institutional practice, 22, 33
institutional racism, 98, 157
integration of theory and practice,
75
intentionality, 60
interaction, 2, 7, 10, 16–17, 20,
24–5, 36, 40–3, 46, 50, 65, 87–8,
91, 95–7, 102–4, 118, 121, 126,
147–9, 167, 183
interactive processes, 36, 91
interconnected relations, 86
interdependency, 5, 30, 81, 99, 117,
120–1, 132, 146, 156, 161–2,
177, 183–5
interdependent relations, 5, 117,
121, 132, 156, 161, 177
international organisations, 35, 180
international social work, 83
interpretation, 172
intersecting universes, 40, 115
Irish Catholic, 78
Islamophobia, 78
isolation, 80, 116, 120, 129, 146,
157, 172

J
Jewish, 50
Jubilee 2000, 71, 178, 179
justice, 4, 8, 60–1, 64, 69, 76–7,
83–4, 101, 108, 116, 121,
129–31, 139, 142, 176, 179,
181–5

K
knowledge, 10, 24–6, 36, 53, 63, 88,
96–8, 100–1, 108, 116–17, 124–6,
143, 157, 170, 182–5

L
labour, 30, 33, 144–5, 151, 173
language, 49, 50, 92, 95, 135, 170–1
law, 29, 90
legitimacy, 31, 43
lesbian, 1, 20, 38, 46–8, 51, 101–2,
110
lesbian women, 1, 20, 38, 48, 110
liberal feminist, 127
liberalism, 27, 134
liberation, 3, 15, 38–9, 57, 61–2,
111
liberationist school of social work,
61–2, 68–9, 74–6
life-cycle, 82
lifestyles, 27, 182
linguistic network, 170
lobbying, 110, 127
lone mother, 42
long-term, 82, 135, 152, 159
low-income countries, 70

M
macro-level interventions, 61, 81–2,
86, 161–6, 175
macro-level changes, 61, 162, 165–6
mainstream services, 62
mainstream social work, 60
maintenance approaches, 59, 61,
68–9, 72, 76–7, 85, 165
maintenance school of social work,
59, 68, 72, 76–7, 85
malestream theory, 63
man in the house, 52
management, 69, 137, 143, 149–51,
159
managers, 72, 122, 137, 142,
147–52, 156 159, 160, 178
managing others, 72, 122, 137
manhood, 105, 106
manufactured need, 21
marginalised profession, 29, 144
marginality, 31, 80

market, 2–3, 6, 21, 72, 82, 89, 119–20, 128, 132–6, 141, 144–6, 161
market culture, 72
market-driven approaches to welfare, 6
market-led regimes, 144
Martin Luther King, 12
masculinity, 49, 52, 63, 74, 90, 104–7, 165–6
Maslow's hierarchy of needs, 21
means, 3, 9–10, 15, 19, 20, 29, 34–5, 41, 45, 52, 66, 70–1, 81–6, 100, 111–16, 123, 132, 137, 142, 150, 158–9, 170–2, 180
men, 1, 19–20, 27, 35, 38, 42, 45, 48, 52, 56, 62–3, 74, 82, 89–90, 98, 103, 105–110, 127, 128, 134, 144, 166, 178
mental health, 1, 44, 149
meso-level, 81, 86
messy realities, 77, 139
micro-level, 61, 81, 85, 116, 164–6, 175
middle-class, 16, 29, 51, 54, 147, 172
minimum wage, 75, 134
misogynist rationale, 63
mixed parentage, 55
mobilising people, 58, 110, 128–30, 139, 146, 176, 180
mobilising women, 147
modernising agenda, 123
modernism, 173
modernity, 28
moral and ethical dilemmas, 61
moral position, 76
mother, 42, 51, 55, 67, 167–8, 171–2
multinational, 26, 134, 173–4, 178
mutuality, 5–6, 121, 126

N
national borders, 173, 177
nation-state, 1, 25, 28–9, 48, 50–1, 71, 122–3, 173–5
Nazis, 111, 179

needs, 1, 3, 20–2, 25–31, 34–5, 45–8, 50–1, 54, 57, 61–4, 69–76, 82, 84, 87, 90, 93–9, 102–8, 110, 113, 116–19, 121–4, 127–39, 142–5, 149, 155–9, 162–8, 171–6, 182–5
neglect, 52
negotiated realities, 24, 180, 182–3
negotiation, 20–1, 25, 85, 148, 150, 159
neo-liberalism, 26, 125, 133, 138, 161
network, 132–3, 153, 179
neutrality, 71–2
New Deal, 29
New Labour, 3, 29, 123–4
new managerialism, 141–4, 182
new racism, 78–9
New Right, 2, 42
new social movement, 38–9
New Zealand, 19, 54, 64, 132
normal, 17–18, 34–8, 56, 86, 110, 114
normative yardstick, 18, 52, 135
norms, 17, 19, 33, 47, 66, 78, 85, 90, 102, 123, 146, 149, 185
Northern Ireland, 78
nuclear family, 72
nurturer, 51

O
objectification of the body, 20
offender, 128
old age, 27, 56, 82
older people, 27, 30, 38, 55, 98, 110, 121
ontology, 63
oppressed people, 4, 7–17, 35, 41, 45–8, 56–7, 99, 110–13, 162, 166, 172
oppression, 1, 3–13, 17–20, 23, 33, 35, 38–41, 45–7, 52, 57–60, 76, 77, 83–5, 88, 92, 110–12, 147–51, 166, 169–72, 180, 182
oppressive relations, 4, 8–16, 33–7, 41, 46, 57, 59, 92, 112–13, 118, 122, 162
oppressors, 15, 46, 50

organisation, 14, 33–4, 65–9, 100,
111, 115, 137, 139, 142, 144,
149, 150–9, 166, 182
organisational change, 6, 35, 69,
146–8, 157–60
othering, 17–18, 39, 44–7

P
parallel universes, 39, 115
parenthood, 42
parenting, 43, 44
parents, 3, 42, 55
partnership, 115
passive victims, 17–8, 53–4
passivity, 8, 57, 96, 120, 163
paternalistic relationships, 115, 177
patriarchal relations, 73
pensions, 31, 82, 137
people, 1–64, 68–72, 77–8, 80, 83,
86, 92, 95, 98–100, 106–15, 157,
159, 161–2, 166, 169–85
people smugglers, 124
performance indicators, 143
permeable boundaries, 48
personal advisors, 29
personal relationships, 61, 167
personal social services, 29, 108,
141–2, 146–8
perspectives, 25, 68, 159, 170
physical abuse, 80
physical environment, 21–4, 107,
131, 184
PIE component, 100
Poland, 124
policies, 3, 22, 35, 42–3, 61, 68–9,
89, 130, 144, 149–50, 156, 182
policymaking, 83
political correctness, 62
politicisation, 38, 80
poor people, 3–4, 71, 83, 107, 120,
130, 133–7, 141, 147, 169, 174,
176, 183
poor women, 42–3
postmodern, 49, 161–4, 168–72,
180–1
postmodern insights, 164
postmodern theory, 168
postmodern welfare, 161
postmodernism, 163, 168–9, 172–3
postmodernity, 168

poverty, 3, 21, 29, 42, 71, 82–3, 86,
106, 123–6, 129, 133, 137, 165
poverty eradication, 126
poverty impact, 82
power, 6–9, 11, 14, 16–18, 21,
24–5, 31, 34–8, 41, 45–9, 52–4,
60–3, 66, 72–3, 77–80, 84, 86–9,
91–9, 102, 109–13, 117–21,
125–6, 129–30, 134–5, 138,
143–4, 147–8, 150, 153, 156–7,
162, 164, 167–70, 175–6, 179–84
power differentials, 92, 96, 157, 184
power of relations, 17–18, 47, 52,
77, 98, 109–10, 113, 118–20,
162, 179
power over dynamics, 77, 98, 113,
120, 162
power over relations, 9, 11, 17–18,
62, 77, 79, 91, 95, 98–9, 102,
113, 118–20, 148, 162, 175, 179
power relations, 6, 16–24, 35, 38,
41, 45, 52–3, 72, 79, 86–9, 93,
96–8, 121, 129–30, 164, 168,
176, 181–5
power relations of normalisation, 86
power to dynamics, 18
power to relations, 16–18, 45, 63,
117–18, 150, 167, 182
practice, 1–6, 9, 24, 26–9, 32–6, 39,
46–7, 54, 56–7, 60–2, 66–70,
72–7, 83–6, 89–93, 96–7, 100–03,
108, 120–2, 130, 136, 139,
144–8, 152, 154, 163–5, 168–71,
177, 181–3
practitioners, 22–5, 35–6, 53–4,
65–6, 75, 86–8, 90–7, 100–03,
120, 143–5, 163, 181–4
private appropriation, 180
private divide, 9, 12, 33, 43–4, 74,
82, 89, 116, 130–1, 135–7, 142,
173–4, 178, 180
private sector, 82, 137, 174
private sphere, 9, 74
private trouble, 74, 89, 116
privatisation, 82, 131, 137
privilege, 14–7, 31, 34, 38, 53, 61,
63, 78, 80–2, 110, 162–4, 168
privileged status, 46
probation, 90, 111, 128
probation officers, 90, 111

probation service, 128
process, 9, 13, 17, 27, 32–4, 39–41,
   45, 52–4, 57, 66–8, 71, 76,
   88–90, 96, 99–100, 103, 105,
   110–20, 131–2, 137, 143–8,
   151–6, 162–4, 167, 171, 175, 184
profession, 2, 5, 26–9, 31–5, 51, 54,
   60–4, 70–3, 83, 101, 107–8, 122,
   141, 147
professional activity, 33
professional behaviour, 61
professional discourses, 147, 167,
   168
professional expertise, 62, 66, 73,
   95, 116, 143, 163, 184
professional social work, 6, 32, 83,
   90, 144
professionalism, 59, 71
profits, 3, 21, 82, 131
progress, 13, 34, 81, 152
promotion, 2
prostitution, 124
public domain, 12, 44, 74, 112, 132,
   137
public gaze, 116
publicly-funded welfare, 26
punishment, 91

Q
Quebec, 132

R
racial consciousness, 13
racial oppression, 13, 78
racialised identities, 13
racialised power relation, 79, 80, 81
racialised relation, 80
racism, 49, 55, 78, 95–8, 110, 151,
   154–9
radical social work, 60–1, 89, 148,
   150, 164
ration, 27
rational beings, 62
rationality, 10, 62–3
rationing dynamic, 123
Reagan, 136
recipients of aid, 83
reciprocated caring, 139
reciprocity, 5–6, 65, 121, 126, 132,
   162, 176, 183

regulated framework, 108
regulation, 43–4, 174
regulatory regime, 67, 141
rejectionist relations, 11–12, 39, 47,
   56, 79, 138
relations of domination, 8, 57, 92,
   99
relationships, 13, 27, 32, 36, 40–1,
   53–6, 60, 64–6, 82, 86–8, 91–3,
   96, 99–107, 120–1, 134, 143–51,
   164, 175–7, 181–5
renewal, 78
reproduction of oppressive relations,
   13
research, 65, 126, 130
residualism, 2, 26, 29, 107, 108,
   141, 146, 183
resistance, 8–12, 39, 46, 86, 127,
   152, 170, 179
resource, 70, 84, 130, 143–4
respect, 4, 15, 26–7, 56, 64, 67, 94,
   130, 137, 155, 182
responsibility, 4, 25, 28, 31, 51, 60,
   63–4, 98, 121–5, 128, 141–4, 156,
   158, 162, 165–6, 178–9, 182, 185
rights, 31–2, 35–6, 44, 56, 70, 78,
   117, 119, 121, 146
risk, 26, 51, 82, 137, 145
Rogerian counselling, 86
role conflict, 44
roles, 4, 22, 44, 52, 56–60, 97, 129,
   156–9, 173, 180
rootedness, 164

S
sanctions, 28
self-definition, 38, 49–50, 112
self-determination, 64
self-sufficiency, 27, 30, 121, 125,
   132–9
sex offender, 128
sexist relations, 45
sexual abuse, 73, 74, 80
sexual orientation, 4, 9, 44–8, 54,
   60, 63–4, 98, 100, 103, 164, 182
sexuality, 43, 48, 103
short-termism, 151–2
signifier, 19, 170
single parent, 42, 51
single parent mother, 42

site of struggle, 39
slavery, 80
social action, 74
social agenda, 112
social care, 88
social change, 61, 82, 148, 151, 162–8
social construction of disability, 48
social control, 8, 27–8, 54, 71
social democracy, 3
social development, 126, 130–2, 139
Social Development Summit, 70
social divisions, 4–5, 8–9, 13–16, 19–20, 38–9, 44–6, 57, 61–3, 75, 98–100, 108, 130, 162–4, 182
social economy, 131–3, 139, 180
social environment, 72, 107, 129, 131
social ills, 72–4, 82
social interactions, 13, 18–19, 35, 40, 56, 63, 91, 99, 130, 147–8, 169
social order, 11–15, 18, 20, 27–8, 33–5, 41, 57, 61, 67, 71, 101, 112, 122, 163, 175, 180, 185
social policy, 31, 42
social relations, 4, 9–11, 14–17, 20–1, 24, 34, 36, 39–41, 45, 48, 57, 61–3, 74, 77, 85, 89, 99, 122–7, 133–9, 145–9, 151–2, 158, 162, 169, 175, 178, 181–4
social rights, 70
social services, 33, 55, 68, 90, 106, 119, 150
social work, 1, 4–5, 8, 23–9, 31–6, 51–77, 83–9, 91–4, 97, 100–2, 106–12, 115, 119, 121–3, 126, 129–32, 137, 139, 141–50, 159, 163–9, 171–5, 178–85
social work agenda, 181
social work as a profession, 29, 33
social worker, 4, 8, 23–9, 32–6, 51–8, 60–1, 64–7, 73–5, 83–9, 93–4, 97, 100–2, 106–8, 110, 112, 121–3, 126, 129–30, 132, 137, 139, 143–5, 149, 159, 164–8, 172–5, 178, 181–5
socialisation, 26, 66, 90–1, 129
solidaristic, 133, 169, 179

solidarity, 5–6, 31, 39, 44, 71, 101, 121, 125–8, 132–6, 139, 162, 176
spaces, 44, 56, 86, 116, 127, 148, 168
spirituality, 19, 24, 184
static construction, 52
statism, 135
status, 5, 8–11, 14–15, 19, 22, 27–8, 32, 38–9, 41–2, 45–7, 51, 54, 56–7, 61, 64–5, 68, 73–4, 86, 95, 112, 123, 155, 166, 172
stereotypes, 23, 53, 75, 91, 93
stories, 86, 111, 168, 171, 176
strategic essentialism, 39
strategic responses, 11
strong objectivity, 39
structural, 4, 9–11, 27, 33, 39, 55, 58, 61, 71, 74, 77, 82–3, 85, 89, 95, 101, 104, 112, 117, 119, 124–9, 137, 147–9, 151, 166–9
structural causes of poverty, 124
structural inequalities, 58, 61, 71, 77, 95, 119
struggles, 31, 38, 48–9, 77–8, 110, 112, 169, 179–80
students, 3, 52, 176
subjectivity, 115, 171
subordinate group, 8, 11, 41, 45, 50
sustainability, 174
symbols, 179

T

tactical fixedness, 39
target, 9, 71, 81, 85, 141, 146
technological surveillance, 143
Thatcher, 103, 136
theorising oppression, 7
theory, 27–9, 40, 86, 165, 174
therapeutic relation, 85–8
therapeutic relationships, 85–6
therapy, 86
Third Way, 2, 135–6
Third World, 70, 179
Third World debt repayment, 70
Third World poverty, 70
totalising, 49, 52, 86, 93, 97, 163
traditionalists, 53
transformative relations, 12, 17, 33, 69, 87, 152
transforming their relationships, 183

U

uncertainty, 15, 182
undeserving clients, 27–8, 30, 44, 123
unequal power relations, 97
unifying force, 28
unintended consequences, 20
United Kingdom, 6, 54, 62
United Nations, 70, 83, 123, 126, 176
United States, 2–3, 30, 50, 77, 132–6, 174
unity, 29, 49, 100, 113, 129, 162–3, 172, 180
universal public services, 183
universal truth, 73
universalising discourse, 70
universalism, 26–9, 122
user-centred approaches, 116
utilitarianism, 135
utopian realism, 129

V

values, 8, 10–11, 14, 21, 24, 35, 38, 41, 56–7, 63–4, 78, 89–90, 103, 108, 118–21, 149, 152, 161, 182–5
valuing difference, 157
victim, 126, 165–6
violence, 12, 41, 45, 74, 80, 89, 106, 130, 165–6, 173
Virginia Bottomley, 62
voluntary sector, 142
vulnerability, 15, 27
vulnerable group, 27–8, 57, 126

W

wages, 123, 131
ways of being, 52, 185
ways of knowing, 63, 92
welfare, 1–6, 22, 26–33, 42, 54, 70, 119–28, 131, 135–46, 159–64, 167, 171, 179, 182

welfare bureaucracy, 164
welfare recipients, 126
welfare state, 2–3, 6, 22, 26–33, 42, 54, 121, 136, 141, 161, 163
well-being, 19, 27, 31, 60, 71, 77, 104, 110, 121–6, 129–31, 134–6, 139, 142, 160, 163, 177, 181–5
white feminist, 63, 79
white men, 26, 49, 63, 77, 82
white supremacy, 54, 80
white women, 52, 82, 100, 110
women, 1, 16–21, 27, 30–5, 38, 42–5, 48, 51–2, 55–7, 62–3, 67–8, 74–5, 82–3, 87, 89–90, 98, 100, 103–4, 110, 114–15, 122–4, 127, 134, 150, 165–8, 172, 177
work, 2–6, 15–16, 22–4, 27–9, 31–6, 42, 52–7, 59–66, 69, 72–7, 83–9, 92–8, 103, 107–13, 117, 119, 121–30, 133–5, 139, 144, 147–9, 153–7, 162, 165–7, 170–1, 175–7, 181–3
workfare, 3, 29, 134–5
working poor, 123–4
working relations, 22, 33, 65, 92, 107, 130, 141, 156, 164
working routine, 144
working-class, 16, 46, 51, 147, 153
working-class communities, 153
workplace, 4, 144, 158
World Bank, 70, 176
worldview, 138

Y

yardstick, 17, 48, 63
young offenders, 106
young people, 30, 102
young women, 101–4
youths, 56

Z

zero-sum, 16, 17, 53, 118, 147